MODERN INDIAN ENGLISH NOVEL

A CRITICAL STUDY OF THE POLITICAL MOTIF

MODERN INDIAN ENGLISH NOVEL

A CRITICAL STUDY OF THE POLITICAL MOTIF

M.K. BHATNAGAR

Published by
ATLANTIC PUBLISHERS AND DISTRIBUTORS
B-2, Vishal Enclave, Opp. Rajouri Garden, New Delhi-110027
Phones : 5413460, 5429987, 5466842

Sales Office
4215/1, Ansari Road, Darya Ganj, New Delhi-02
Phones : 3273880, 3285873, 3280451
Fax : 91-11-3285873
web : www.atlanticbooks.com
e-mail : info@atlanticbooks.com

ISBN 81-269-0225-6

Typeset at
APD Computer Graphics, Delhi
Printed in India at
Nice Printing Press, Delhi

PREFACE

Modern Indian English Novel is a study in the structure of the consciousness of the institutional parameters in all their sociological, cultural, psychological and philosophic nuances, as rendered in the novel in English in India in the three-four decades after Independence. Consciousness, as conceived fundamentally, whether in the formulations of Hegel, Nietzsche or Aurobindo, is essentially moral and philosophical. Any authentic chronicle — in a mode artistic or otherwise — necessarily presupposes a direct confrontation with the moral and philosophical incongruities and unresolvabilities of history. A litterateur's confrontation with and a possible synthesis of the socio-historical and socio-psychological processes inevitably reins in the newly formulated aspirations of the emerging civil societies and the characteristic representations of the decolonized imagination. The attempt here is not merely to gauge the centrifugal nuances of such artistic preoccupations but also to focus on the kaleidoscopic patterns which the artistic rendering generates.

The study confronts the stereotyped preliminary posers by seeking to explain how literature cannot remain unaffected by the social and political developments for they are but inseparable components of the artist's consciousness as a human being. What follows is a close scrutiny of the varied ways wherein the sundry stages of the litterateurs' involvement with the here and now has been mirrored in Indian English fiction. One key configuration of this is chronicling the political web in all its labyrinthine intricacies, moulded in a human idiom. Moving beyond mere externals, the texts, when explored in depth, yield disquieting insights into the psychological make-up of a whole nation through a tracing of the contours of the crippling creed, diagnosed as the malady. Gandhi was a whiff of fresh air in the claustrophobic environs of the collective psyche but the aimless drift and ossification of the Gandhian panacea post-Gandhi forms another unpalatable but inevitable perception, as rendered in the novels included in this study. What distinguishes modern Indian English fiction is the manner wherein it goes beyond mere chronicling the diverse dimensions of the social, political, psychological and philosophic rot. It goes beyond and the study isolates for critical analysis the values highlighted in modern novel in English in India which would reveal the way out of the labyrinth. Last but not the least the artistic alchemy, which metamorphoses such ideological matter to a slice of life of perennial significance, also forms part of the presentation in this study.

It is a pleasure to acknowledge the invaluable help rendered by eminent writers, distinguished critics and insightful researchers and students in facilitating the ordering of inchoate perceptions. Naming them all would just not be possible because of the sheer numbers involved. I am grateful, in particular, to Mulk Raj Anand, Manohar Malgonkar, Khushwant Singh, Nayantara Sahgal and Chaman Nahal for patiently hearing my tentative impressions and for offering fruitful comments. The University here in general and the Department of English in particular helped in its own distinctive way by creating conditions conducive to my seeking expression, communication and thereby justification through such academic pursuits exclusively.

There are a number of people — friends and members of my family — who, with their quiet encouragement and patience, have contributed immensely to the successful completion of the study. I am sure they would not mistake my silence for ingratitude. I shall be failing in my duty if I do not acknowledge with thanks the gentle persistence with which Dr. K.R. Gupta helped me pursue the work and enabled this study to see the light of the day.

M.K. BHATNAGAR

NOTE

The list of the novels taken up here along with the cue-titles which stand for them in this study, is as follows :

BHABANI BHATTACHARYA

So Many Hungers! (Bombay : Jaico, 1964)	as *Hungers*
Music for Mohini (New Delhi : Orient Paperbacks, 1984)	as *Music*
He Who Rides a Tiger (New Delhi : Arnold-Heinemann, 1977)	as *Tiger*
A Goddess Named Gold (Delhi : Orient Paperbacks, 1960)	as *Gold*
Shadow from Ladakh (London : W.H. Allen, 1967)	as *Ladakh*
A Dream in Hawaii (Delhi : Vision Books, 1983)	as *Hawaii*

MANOHAR MALGONKAR

Distant Drum (Delhi : Orient Paperbacks, 1960)	as *Drum*
Combat of Shadows (London : Hamish Hamilton, 1962)	as *Combat*
The Princes (London : Hamish Hamilton, 1963)	as *Princes*
A Bend in the Ganges (Delhi : Orient Paperbacks, 1964)	as *Ganges*
Bandicoot Run (Delhi : Orient Paperbacks, 1982)	as *Bandicoot*

NAYANTARA SAHGAL

A Time to be Happy as *Happy*
(New Delhi : Sterling Paperbacks, 1975)

This Time of Morning as *Morning*
(New York : W.W. Norton & Co. Inc., 1965)

Storm in Chandigarh as *Storm*
(London : Chatto and Windus, 1969)

The Day in Shadow as *Shadow*
(Delhi : Vikas Publishing House, 1971)

A Situation in New Delhi as *Situation*
(New Delhi : Himalaya Books, 1977)

Rich Like Us as *Rich*
(London : Heinemann, 1985)

CONTENTS

1
Introduction

THE INEXTRICABLE link between art and the environment wherein it is created can never be over-emphasized. Art is, and always has been, a social activity in reality. It is one aspect of the cultural superstructure which has its foundations in the economic, political, social, philosophic and religious patterns of the time. It throws into bold relief those multi-dimensional conscious and unconscious urges of a society which are seeking gratification and realization in the world of actual reality.

> The soil which nurtures artistic talent is the culture of the people, the tastes, spiritual demands and life of the artist's contemporaries. In other words, the artist is only the co-author of a magnificent creation known as the culture of the people.[1]

Durkheimian sociology visualizes not only the existence of man in society but also of society in man. In the social psychology of G.M. Meed also, the idea of self is a social creation. "Art has never been on the side of the purists."[2] Moreover, in the works of a genuine artist, there is no conflict between the individual and the social; the dialectics of their interrelation is such that "the more the individuality of the artist stands out, the more actively he expresses the mood of his contemporaries — in short, the more partisan his approach. For those who are not disturbed by paradoxes, one might say that the more individual the artist, the less he belongs to himself, for the more individual he is, the more people need him."[3]

Art, thus, is an organic part of the total cultural-complex in which it takes its origin. The organic nature of art makes it draw nourishment from diverse sources including politics, taken in its wider, elemental sense, as embracing the multiplicity of the contemporary scene with its economic, social, cultural and governmental aspects. It was long ago that Hippolyte-Adolphe Taine had realized that a literary work is "a transcript of contemporary manners"[4] and, from such 'monuments of literature,' we might recover "a knowledge of the manner in which men thought and felt."[5] Thomas Mann's growth from *Reflections of an Apolitical Man to Kultur and Politik* depended on the realization that

> What is political and social is an indivisible part of what is human and enters into one problem of humanism, into which our intellect must include it and...in this problem a dangerous hiatus destructive for culture may manifest itself if we ignore the political, social element inherent in it.[6]

There could be isolated a number of factors which 'politicize' literature and lend to the relationship between literature and politics a sharp possessive character. Boris Suchkov cites some of these : "the intensification of the class struggle and national liberation movements, the crystallization of political and social urges, born as much out of the changing patterns in the mode of production, distribution and possession as the widely spread consciousness of the encircling environment...."[7] While the modern writer — for example, Jean Paul Sartre in his celebrated manifesto — has had to address himself to the question, "What is Literature?," he has found it increasingly difficult to separate himself from the historical and the political events of his time. As political situations have changed and polarized, as national interests have given way to international problems, as the emphasis on theological and ontological issues has been transferred to ethical and political formulations — in short as socio-political dialectic has replaced metaphysical concepts, and the unpolitical and even the anti-political attitude towards culture definitely has been on the decline and, in some ways, has even become extinct — modern literature has witnessed the invasion of its aesthetic sanctuary by themes of immediate human interest.

Coming to the Indian context, we discover that politics as a discipline and political consciousness as a component of the mental make-up of the people is of quite recent origin. The political system and social structure, so far from having grown up together, have only recently been introduced to each other. Historically, the Indian has lived in a state of political indifference for thousands of years. Right since the earliest times a vast majority of the people — not merely the peasantry but also the traders and professionals — lived and moved within their set grooves thoroughly immunized from politics. The affairs of state were entrusted exclusively to the *kshtriyas* under the *varnashram* dispensation, and they (the *kshtriyas*), in tacit alliance with the Brahmins, kept the other strata in a virtual state of depoliticization.

The common Indians' alienation from the political process can be perceived as the direct outcome of the priority accorded to *dharma* and *moksha,* in ancient thought, over *artha* and *kama.* Man's interest in the actual world of living, his status *vis-a-vis* the organization of people bound by common rules did not directly engage the Indian philosophers. What was lacking obviously was an interest in and a full consciousness of matters concerning the organizational aspect of society. Unlike in China and Greece, politics was never a major concern in India until recent times. Rather there was a positively a political orientation inherent in the traditional ethos of Indian society, an obvious proof of which would be the traditional indifference of Indians to recorded history. Unlike the Chinese and the Arabs, Indians have had no comparable account of recorded history until comparatively recent times. Before this recent growth of political consciousness is traced, the term 'political consciousness' itself, perhaps, needs some elaboration.

'Political consciousness,' for the purpose of this study, is deemed to be a worldly interest in the organizational and institutional aspects of society and in the manner in which they condition the parameters within which the individual feels free to realize himself. A good illustration of such a consciousness emerges from the following rationale given by a prominent Telugu short story writer for his thematic concerns :

> In these days of acute political awareness the love theme has lost its popularity. Readers tend to think that all love stories are deceptive and that their authors are enemies of the society. These are days for critics of institutions who condemn the feudal values in our society. God and Karma are no more the causes of injustice and unfairness to man. People have found out that it is the economic system that is at the root of all evil and that it can be corrected by collective action.[8]

In the specific context of a country like India, subjugated for thousands of years, either by aliens or by indigenous overbearing potentates, political consciousness primarily becomes an acute concern with people. It borders on the individual's intellectual involvement with political questions like who governs, what the governance is like and how it affects the individual in his day-to-day living. In the pre-Independence times, this consciousness manifested itself as national consciousness. Even after the attainment of freedom, discerning observers of contemporary reality did not cease probing the political process to determine the role of the individual therein, even though with the obvious change in rulers, the thrust of such questions had undergone a corresponding change.

As has already been suggested above, in the present times the individual mode of living and the collective context of socio-political organization have become so interfused that no dividing line can be drawn between the two. Socio-economic interest as well as political consciousness has now assumed the character of a dominant emotion. "The elemental urges of freedom and food and security," as Jawaharlal Nehru terms them in his speech included in *So Many Hungers!,*[9] move vast masses of people. The novelist obviously cannot remain an idle spectator. There are also conscious endeavours on the part of novelists to espouse general aspirations — socio-political in nature. This way the intellectuals — alienated from both the rulers and the ruled — can relate themselves to the political mainstream. Their artistic preoccupation gives them the halo of a visionary. Lenin puts it well. Gorky has to "meddle in politics" for the people look up to him for guidance in crucial matters of immediate concern.[10] It is this sense of responsibility and commitment to the people which makes Nayantara Sahgal record "the mounting feelings of impending disaster"[11] in novels like *The Day in Shadow* and *A Situation in New Delhi.*

The present study aims at tracing the growth of such political consciousness which functions as a dominant emotion and examining how Indo-Anglian fiction has been fully responsive to the different phases of this awareness. Later would be attempted a somewhat detailed examen of the manner in which the novels of Bhabani Bhattacharya, Manohar Malgonkar and Nayantara Sahgal reflect some significant components of this political consciousness.

Before we go on to the novels for a study of political consciousness therein, we are faced with the poser : Do the novelists form a sociological group which is significant enough for a study of the political consciousness of the age they write in? It would be readily conceded that writers constitute an important segment of the intellectuals of a society. Karl Mannheim discerned in such 'socially non-homogeneous intelligentsia' a relatively classless stratum, comprising an increasingly inclusive area of social life, bound together by education and subsuming in itself all those interests with which social life is permeated. Because of these characteristics such intellectuals are capable of acquiring a relatively complete and objective view of their society, and especially of the different interest groups within it, and of acting independently to promote better consciousness of social interests.[12] Forming an articulate group within the intelligentsia, the novelists give shape to the hitherto inchoate political consciousness of their 'literate' clientele. This is obviously not the political consciousness of the professional politician. It is political consciousness as it forms part, an organic part, of human consciousness in the environmental context. It is, in fact, part of the total consciousness. Not merely, that. By virtue of the immense force they exert as creators of a fictional universe, they also seek to influence political opinion. Their presentation of the lives of their protagonists against the organizational aspect of a society inevitably incorporates the joys and frustrations of the protagonists as much as an examen of the society itself. Indeed it is only the latter which, on the one hand, defines and delimits the former, and on the other hand, provides an expansive context for creative vision and action. It is in crises — political, economic and social — that a novelist, casting his net wide, comes to acquire crucial political importance. His sensitive human antennae help him highlight and clarify the human and the political dimensions of the issues involved. A novelist may not only bring to the surface the not-so-obvious — as the examen of Indo-Anglian fiction later here would illustrate — but also anticipate possible crises as well as forewarn. In this sense, the novelist reflects not only a political consciousness but also a political message.

REFERENCES

1. N. Shamota, *On Artistic Freedom* (Moscow : Progress Publishers, 1966), 106-7.
2. Jean Paul Sartre, *What is Literature*? (New York : Washington Square Press, 1966), 14.
3. N. Shamota, 107.
4. Hippolyte-Adolphe Taine, "From the Introduction to the History of English Literature," in *Twentieth Century Criticism — The Major Statements,* eds., William J. Handy and Max Westbrook (New Delhi : Light and Life Publishers, 1976), 309.
5. *Ibid.*
6. Quoted by Yuri Barbash in *Aesthetics and Politics* (Moscow : Progress Publishers, 1977), 46.
7. *Ibid.*
8. Buchibabu, "Nirantara-trayam" *Kalalo Jarina Kanniru* (Vijaywada : Adarsa Grantha Mandali, 1969), translated from original Telugu by Velcheru Narayana Rao and quoted in his article, "The Political Novel in Telugu," *Politics and the Novel in India,* ed., Yogendra K. Malik (New Delhi : Orient Longman, 1978), 94.
9. Bhabani Bhattacharya, *So Many Hungers!* (Bombay : Jaico Publishing House, 1964), 42.

10. V.I. Lenin, *Collected Works* (Moscow : Progress Publishers, 1967), XXIII, 334-35.
11. Nayantara Sahgal, *Voice For Freedom* (Delhi : Hind Pocket Books, 1979), 151.
12. Vide Karl Mannheim, *Ideology and Utopia* (London : Kegan Paul, 1936), Chapter III, Section 4, "The Sociological Problem of the Intelligentsia," 136-45.

□□□

2

Political Underpinnings in the Early Phase

FICTION IS the expression of the most intimate social awareness of the society in which it is born and evolves. It can well be perceived as society ruminating aloud and bringing into focus its very sinews. As a creative process, fiction records the creative evolution of the society itself. Thus the evolution of fiction and the evolution of the consciousness of the societal apparatus are simultaneous and interlocked. Indo-Anglian novel, right since its beginning, has had inextricable bonds with the socio-political milieu wherein it took birth and has been written since.

The nascent national political consciousness in India which was slowly percolating to the grass-roots has been faithfully mirrored in Indian English fiction. Indeed this sense of commitment to national awareness was an important factor which made the early novelists chisel the genre. The very earliest attempts — novels like *A Journal of Forty Eight Hours* (1835) by K.C. Dutt and *The Republic of Orissa* (1845) by S.C. Dutt, discovered and discussed in Bengali and English respectively by Dr. Pallab Sen Gupta and Prof. Amalendu Basu[1] reveal that they articulate the political message most palpably. Not merely was the birth of the genre accompanied with the articulation of political concerns, its blossoming and coming of age is also seen to be the direct outcome of the growing up of the national political movement for freedom.

M.K. Naik, in his study of the evolution and growth of Indian English fiction, notices the umbilical link between political consciousness and the Indian novel in English. "Up to the 1930's," he says, "there was no Indian novelist who could claim sustained and considerable achievement in fiction originally written in English. Then came a sudden flowering, and it is significant that it came in the 1930's — a period during which the glory that was Gandhi's attained perhaps its brightest splendour. The Indian freedom struggle was already more than a generation old, yet with the advent of Mahatma Gandhi it was so thoroughly democratized that freedom consciousness percolated for the first time to the very grass-roots of the Indian society and revitalized it. It is possible to see a connection between this development and the rise of the Indian novel in English; for fiction, of all literary forms is most vitally concerned with social conditions and values."[2]

Political consciousness flows in the very life-blood of Indian English fiction. In fact, in countries with a long history of subjugation by foreign powers, "nationalism becomes a preoccupation of the writers. They are important not just for their art but also as teachers, helping the nation to an awareness of itself, its aspirations, its troubles."[3] We may usefully refer to Lenin and his reference to Gorky in this context. Lenin poses the question : "Why should Gorky meddle in politics?" and he himself answers the question. Because "the workers have grown accustomed to regard Gorky as their own" and "it is this trust on the part of the class-conscious workers that imposes on Gorky a certain duty to cherish his good name."[4] In India, too, political consciousness as the very staple of fiction, points to the fact of the writers' and the readers' mutual participation in a common situation in the life of the community.

Political consciousness, with which the novels of the early practitioners of Indian English fiction are imbued, can also be viewed as part of the novelists' endeavour to relate themselves to the mainstream. The intelligentsia in the pre-Independence phase found itself in an unenviable position of being the privileged unprivileged — privileged for they possessed western education, social clout, and often wealth, to boot; unprivileged for they were acutely aware of their subject-status in a subjugated state, their education and other distinction only serving to heighten the unsavoury reality. They could relate themselves neither to the English rulers nor to the masses. Their espousal of the cause of those exploited politically, economically or sociologically, far from integrating them with the masses, consolidated their elitism, containing as it did overtones of *noblesse oblige*. In that crucial phase of Indian history, occupying an uncomfortable and undefined space, the intellectual instinctively did what in the words of Stephen Spender, he was expected to do : "if he is not to be destroyed, he must somehow connect himself...with...political life and influence it...."[5]

Political consciousness, as national consciousness in particular, was conspicuous by its absence up to the nineteenth century, as was also the case with the other states in Asia and Africa. To quote Benjamin Disraeli's general observation, in India too, such consciousness was "a work of art and a work of time," gradually shaped by "a variety of influence — the influence of original organisation, of climate, soil, religion, laws, customs, manners, extraordinary accidents and incidents in their history and the individual character of their illustrious citizens."[6] Let us attempt here a quick recapitulation of the major phases of the Indian national mood.

Rabindra Nath Tagore asserts that political consciousness in India precipitated and got moulded as nationalism under the direct impact of and as a reaction to the English rule.[7] The spread of political concern, however, was the consequence rather than the cause of the political struggle for freedom. The Indian freedom movement must be thought of less as expressing the aspirations and mobilising the energies of an already existing entity and more as a force of ideas and organization, attempting to create that identity. In a country of India's geographical dimensions and social and religious heterogeneity, it would seem as if national political consciousness had only one strong base — British rule, the one common consolidated enemy.

The English contributed in another way too. Western education through the medium of the English language exposed the Indians to English constitution, the British institutions, the idea of freedom and other liberal political ideologies. This gave them new ambitions against the colonial experience by defining their vague aspirations into a shape and direction. This aggrieved elite, made politically conscious but also left high and dry economically on account of the discriminatory policies of the government in matters of employment and commerce, threw up leaders like Bal Gangadhar Tilak, Lajpat Rai and Bipin Chandra Pal who were to function as disseminators of this consciousness.

It is pertinent to take stock of the all-round national regeneration encompassing the spiritual and the temporal parameters which swept the country at this stage. While the perceptions of the temporal state directly affected the social and the political aspirations of the people, the spiritual renaissance vitalized the socio-political realm of values. Religious culture was increasingly evoked to legitimize national aspirations, political in character. Swami Dayananda, for example, in the sixth chapter of his famous work, *Satyartha Prakash,* vehemently advocates *Swarajya* as part of *swadharma* and prefers freedom to the most benevolent foreign rule.

Despite the frequent usage of the Hindu idiom in the political campaigns of leaders like Tilak, the need for wide ranging reforms in the ritual-and-superstition ridden Hinduism was felt as an essential pre-condition for all-round development of the country and for the growth of national political consciousness. In the later half of the nineteenth century crusades like Brahmo Samaj, Prarthana Samaj and Arya Samaj sought to revitalize Hinduism by glorifying the individual as well as the social order. The school of *Vedanta* propagated by Ramakrishna Paramhansa, with Vivekananda as its most powerful exponent, sought to highlight the primacy of action over love of mere knowledge. Vivekananda went to the extent of calling the playing of football a more important activity for the young than even the study of Gita.[8] This helped in demolishing the in-built philosophic prejudices against the this-worldly attitudes and values and facilitated greater involvement of the people with their immediate environment.

The second half of the 19th century witnessed "the flowering of national political consciousness and the foundation and growth of an organized national movement."[9] During this period the modern Indian intelligentsia created political associations to spread political education and initiate political work in the country. A suitable starting point is the 1880's for, by that time, "the political, economic and intellectual forces of both British power and traditional Indian society had interacted to produce a climate fit for the function of national political consciousness."[10] With the formation of the Indian National Congress in 1885, the Indian struggle for freedom was formally launched. Simultaneously, the programme of the political awakening of the masses was taken in hand in an organized way.

For the creation of public interest in political questions and the organization of such political awareness, the Congress formulated its political and economic programme with a view to unifying the Indian people on the basis of a common political and economic programme. Historians like R.C. Dutt propounded 'the drain theory' whereby India's poverty was presented as the result of colonial exploitation by the English. The new message became a powerful strategy to arouse the Indians politically. In this phase the idea of *Swadeshi* was used by leaders like Tilak as an economic pressure on Manchester, a weapon of political agitation against imperialism and as a means to arouse and involve the people politically for the attainment of *Swaraj*. *Swadeshi* brought into politics new classes of people without distinction of caste and creed. It infused a new sense of competence, confidence, independence, fearlessness and sacrifice. The *Swadeshi* movement inspired a new type of nationalistic poetry, prose and journalism. The message of *Swadeshi,* because of its direct relevance to the welfare of the masses made powerful sense in a way wherein theoretical and abstract political concepts couldn't.

The early nationalists believed in constitutional reforms and slow orderly progress within the British dominion. The tangible gain of this phase of political consciousness was the education of the people in modern politics, the awakening of nationalist ideas and the creation of unified public opinion on political questions.

However, the early political leaders failed to win worth-while concessions from the rulers. This threw up a large number of new leaders who were more radical in their demands. They believed in a militant form of nationalism. Leaders like Bipin Chandra Pal, Aurobindo Ghosh, Tilak and Lajpat Rai sought to inculcate in the people virtues like courage, self-confidence and a spirit of sacrifice which would enable them to wrest freedom from the rulers rather than having to beg for it. They had an abiding faith in the strength of the masses and they planned and prepared to win freedom through mass action. The ill-advised plan of partitioning Bengal (1905) gave the leaders an issue to rally the people together.

The failure of the campaign to have the partition of Bengal repealed saw the rise and growth of revolutionary terrorism. Many secret societies were set up, especially in Bengal, Maharashtra and Punjab under the guise of clubs or associations for physical culture. The Lucknow Pact (1916) brought the Hindus and the Muslims together to present a common front against the imperialists. But it predictably failed for it didn't involve the masses. Rather, by giving respectability to separate electorates, it diverted the political consciousness of the people to communal channels in the long run. The same was to be the aftermath of the Khilafat Movement (1919-20) later.

While the news of the Russian Revolution (November 1917) put heart into the nationalists, the Montagu-Chelmsford Reforms failed to enthuse them. The advent of Gandhi into the political arena provided a new light of hope. Gandhi brought a sea-change in the Indian scenario by making the people not only politically conscious but also politically active. The brushes with authority he had at Champaran in Bihar and Kaira and Ahmedabad in

Gujarat (1917-18) led to his emergence as a victorious leader in the cause of the oppressed rural and urban sections of the community. This created a halo round his personality which would make the masses do anything at his bidding. He fashioned his personal life along ways familiar to the villagers. He spoke a language they readily understood. He took recourse to a deeply religious idiom which invariably touched a sympathetic chord in the hearts of millions. All these factors accounted for the immense hold Gandhi had over the people.

It is desirable here to take stock of the fissiparous forces splitting the national political consciousness vertically. As Jawaharlal Nehru put it in *The Discovery of India,* there had been "a difference of a generation or more in the development of the Hindu and the Muslim middle classes."[11] And this lag accounted for the unequal growth of political leadership among Muslims. The educational and economic backwardness of the Muslim masses was conveniently exploited by the feudal elements who wielded a great influence in their community. They presented Muslims as a minority threatened by the dominant Hindus. The Hindu tinge in the political work and ideas of the militant nationalists as well as of leaders like Tilak was enough to stir these apprehensions.[12] The All India Muslim League was set up in 1906 to safeguard the rights of the Muslims. The Minto-Morley reforms encouraged claims for separate constituencies, a classic case of *divide et imper* in all its naked crudity. Henceforth the Muslim masses were to be fed increasingly on a political diet of separatism by the League.

Gandhi sought to forge unity by focussing attention on the passing of the oppressive Rowlatt Bill. In Punjab this led to the massacre at Jallianwala Bagh on 13 April, 1919, in which hundreds of innocent people were killed in cold blood. This tragedy shook the whole nation. Gandhi now proposed a course of decisive action. At its Nagpur session the Congress was revolutionized and given a pyramidical structure with close links with the grass-roots. The reduction of the age of membership to eighteen and the active campaign of educating the masses politically took the party's struggle for freedom to the very door of India's millions. Gandhi made the Congress an instrument of political socialization by incorporating in its programme constructive tasks like khadi, removal of untouchability, prohibition and national education. Bringing the whole nation under one umbrella, Gandhi launched the fight against the imperialists : complete boycott of courts, government-run schools and colleges, picketing of liquor shops, bonfires of imported cloth and the establishment of national schools, colleges and arbitration courts. However the outbreak of violence at Chauri-Chaura (U.P.) led to the termination of the movement.

Political inactivity, the irrelevance of the Khilafat cause after the abolition of the Caliphate in Turkey, and frustration led to the outbreak of communal violence in different parts of the country in 1924, '25 and '26, engulfing even small townships. Another ominous development was the emergence of sectional political groups, particularly among the so-called 'untouchables' and other depressed classes. These groups ventured to have direct negotiations with the government for their sectarian interests, a practice encouraged by the rulers themselves. The major national parties, *viz.*, the Congress, the Liberal Foundation, the Muslim League and others, did come together in August 1928 to form a draft constitution, yet it skirted around the question of communalism. Soon both Mohammed Ali Jinnah and the Sikh communalists walked out of the common forum.

The thirties marked the re-emergence of revolutionary terrorist activities. The exploits of Ramprasad Bismil, Ashfaqulla, Chandra Shekhar Azad, Bhagat Singh, Sukhdev and Rajguru captured the popular imagination, especially of the underprivileged lower-middle class, which hero-worshipped the terrorists since the days of the 1905 movement. The Gandhian non-violence hadn't appealed to their imagination so much. The Congress itself was nevertheless an umbrella organization, comprising of elements ranging in the political spectrum from militants to Gandhian votaries of non-violence. The *Purna-swarajya* declaration by the Congress and the pledge of

Independence taken publicly by people all over India on 26 January 1930 gave the people a direction again. In March 1930, Gandhi began the Civil Disobedience Movement at Dandi. A strong current of national political consciousness reactivated the people. More than any other movement, this campaign brought forth women in large numbers into the political mainstream. Sensing the national mood, the Karachi Congress (1931) placed on record its admiration of the bravery and sacrifice of Bhagat Singh, Rajguru and Sukhdev — the names were "as widely known all over India and...as popular as Gandhiji's."[13]

The recrudescence of communal differences brought forth yet another distortion in the political perspective of the people. The Communal Award (1932), providing for separate Hindu, 'Untouchable' and Muslim electorates for the new federal Legislatures, sought to tear the national fabric asunder. Mahatma Gandhi's active interest in the welfare of 'Harijans' — the name he gave to the 'Untouchables' — brought forth the 'Poona Pact,' by which the Harijans were persuaded to stay within the Hindu fold. It also helped spread ideas of nationalism and democracy among people hitherto relatively untouched by Indian nationalism.

The Government of India Act (1935) brought the princely states into the national mainstream, for the Federal Union was to comprise of them as well as of the provinces of British India. The people in these states had generally been isolated from the national political mainstream. They were living in abominable economic and political backwardness. However, the political upsurge engulfing the whole of British India didn't leave them untouched, and soon Praja Mandals came into being in most of the princely states. The Congress had left political activity in each state to be organized by the local Praja Mandal. However the indirect help and participation of the Congress was all too evident. Jawaharlal Nehru was elected the President of the All India States' Peoples' Conference in 1939.

The Congress came to power in all provinces except Bengal

and Punjab in July 1937 on the basis of the Government of India Act (1935). That was the dawn of a new era in the country. The sudden access to power and patronage bred the usual evils of opportunistic place-hunting and factional squabbles.[14] Another crucial development was the Congress rejection of a coalition in the United Provinces with the Muslim League. The Congress insisted in July 1937 on a total absorption of the League assembly party — an insistence which is seen as total repudiation of the pre-election understanding between the two parties. The great post-1937 League revival, centred in U.P. in particular, has been interpreted in some quarters as an outgrowth of the Congress posture.[15] The League launched an intense propaganda barrage making out that the Muslims were an endangered minority. The Pakistan Resolution of March 1940 passed by the League was in keeping with this scenario.

The Second World War broke out in September 1939. India was dragged in without any consultations whatsoever. The general political opinion was to support the Allies if they were to change their ways and fight the fascists really and truly to save the world for democracy. Subhash Bose, however, was for utilizing this opportunity to uproot the alien rule once for all. When the Congress took a different line, he fled the country. He joined hands with the Axis powers and formed the INA with the Indian POW's captured by the Japanese. The Japanese forces ran through South-East Asia and as they drew nearer, Bose's rallying cry 'Jai Hind' seemed to electrify the whole nation. However the Japanese and the INA could have at best only a brief toe hold of India before the tide turned against them. They were for a while in occupation of the islands off the Indian mainland, even though their stay there was not something for the natives to enthuse over.

Meanwhile the Quit India Movement got underway in 1942. But, with the arrest of Gandhi and other top leaders on the very first day, the leaderless masses instinctively but desperately reacted with sporadic outbursts of violence. There was a widely prevalent mood of despair and disillusionment. Organized violence as well as non-violence seemed to have belied the high expectations their proponents had reposed in them. The Bengal famine of 1943 proved all over again how an alien government could never be looked forward to redress the economic and political problems of the masses. The national political movement suffered perhaps the most decisive jolt as the Muslim League walked out of the Interim Government formed by the Congress after the acceptance of the Cabinet Mission Plan. Communal riots during and after August 1946 sealed all hopes of the divergent political aspiration of people being realized in a unified homeland. The painful pathway to the partition was paved by now. The actual process of near mass-migration of Hindus and Muslims from areas apportioned to Pakistan and India respectively was littered with corpses. The integration of the princely states with the Indian union confronted the erstwhile rulers with a stark political reality even if it had been almost a foregone conclusion.

The immediate post-Independence phase saw a soaring of hopes despite the pricks of prohibition, obscurantism and socialism felt in some quarters. The era of planned development was heralded and the first two plans were quite successful. However, as realpolitik replaced abstract, airy utopias, there grew a general disenchantment with politics and politicians. Fissiparous forces, a legacy of the colonial rule, soon appeared to mar whatever enthusiasm remained in the air. Demands for linguistic states led to riots in different areas. The failure of the Government to contain Chinese expansionism in 1962 made the whole nation pause and ponder over matters of national policy and security. With the death of Jawaharlal Nehru, the affairs of the Congress became turbulent. The Congress split in 1969, ostensibly on account of differences over the choice of the party candidate for the Presidential election, assumed a character of ideology and struggle for power. The party government at the Centre was reduced to a minority and had to rely on support from any quarter. Radical rhetoric was inevitable in such circumstances. Such populism, even though it brought forth an unprecedented electoral triumph in 1971, had a streak of authoritarianism, ill-sheathed under the masquerade. The fast deteriorating economic position after a protracted war with Pakistan (December 1971) and the burden of the upkeep of hundreds of thousands of refugees from Bangladesh made the people wake up. To counter uprisings, the government's reaction was to proclaim a national emergency and incarcerate all the leaders of the opposition (June 1975). However far from being suppressed, the activated political consciousness of the people made them continue their struggle for the shaping of a system wherein they could realize themselves and it was this spirit which saw them through the interregnum.

It would be appropriate to quote here, at some length, Mohan Rakesh, a very perceptive short-story writer and novelist in Hindi. This is how he sums up the post-Independence reality insofar as it affected the sensitive artists :

> When we started writing, the problem of partition was not a major problem facing the country... [it] had been covered over by the slow-dust of the emerging reality of this country. You were more concerned, for example, with what was happening around you than with partition, for what was happening around you seemed more devastating than partition itself. My contention is that partition killed perhaps a few hundred thousand while the post-partition developments in this country have killed millions and in one sense killed many more of us somewhere within ourselves.[16]

Mohan Rakesh unambiguously suggests here one aspect of the political consciousness of the post-Independence scene. The simplistic and sentimental glorification of nationalism is over insofar as the national government is divested of its halo. Issues are judged by the concern shown for the people. From *Bharat Mata*, symbolized by an abstraction or concretized by a national government, the focus seems to have moved to her children.

To recapitulate in brief the growth of political consciousness in India, there were discerned three stages, neatly marked out. These stages didn't materialize in sequential order, for, given the geographic and socio-economic complexity of the country, the simultaneous existence of two or more stages would be easily possible. Perceiving the British Raj as their *mai bap*, early Indians sought to attain political adulthood under the benign guidance of their colonial masters. This was the first phase. Then, as the awareness of the wide gulf between expectation and reality sank in, widespread disenchantment followed. Therefore, the second phase was a reaction to the first and heralded a revival of traditional values to counterbalance the shame of subjugation. The awareness of subjugation and faith in regenerated tradition was followed by a demand for greater political participation. This was the third phase. All these phases are well-mirrored in Indo-Anglian fiction as the following examen would illustrate.

Early novels like *A Journal of Forty Eight Hours of the Year 1945* (1835) by K.C. Dutt, *The Republic of Orissa : Annals From the Pages of the 20th Century* (1845) by S.C. Dutt and *Govinda Samant* (1874) by Lal Behari Day depict a stage when national political consciousness had not yet developed and the perspective was necessarily blinkered. Consequently primacy was accorded to localized resentment and rebellions. *A Journal* limits itself to the rebellion in Calcutta alone and that too organized by the educated elite only. It is, however, conceded that the uprising is depicted to be the direct result of the repressive colonial rule rather than of some personal or communal grouse. *The Republic of Orissa* casts its net a bit wider, depicting the rebellion in Orissa, Bengal and Bihar even though the *pièce de-résistance* is the revolution of an Orissa tribe. Equally noteworthy is the portrayal by the novelist, of Oriyas, Bengalis and Biharis as separate nations, though living amicably in India, a land of many nations. *A Journal* and *The Republic of Orissa* set their stories ahead in future, one by a hundred and ten and the other by seventy-five years. This setting and appearance of a harmless fantasy given to the story — obviously to escape official censure — lead to the bringing in of imaginary developments. The British Governor-General is set on massacring the natives in *A*

Journal. The legalization of slavery is presented as the immediate cause of anger in *The Republic of Orissa.* Such flights of fancy obviously lessen the appeal of these novels. However one redeeming feature of the two works is the solid substratum of topicality. *A Journal* refers critically to the misdeeds of Clive, Wellesley and Warren Hastings, whereas *The Republic of Orissa* is reminiscent of the contemporary resentment and unrest in the peasants and the tribals which had led to frequent armed uprisings.

Govinda Samant (1874) by Lal Behari Day shares with *A Journal* and *The Republic of Orissa* their limiting as well as redeeming features. Even though set exclusively in the rural Hindu section of Bengal, it contains the topical issue of the repression let loose by the colonial indigo-planters and it succeeds eminently in exposing the evil nexus between the feudal Zamindars, the apathetic police and the law enforcement authorities and the alien rulers.

The Prince of Destiny (1909) by S.K. Ghose and *Hindupore* (1909) by S.M. Mitra, both exhibit the state of political consciousness of the time when the foreign rule was deemed a divine dispensation and the endeavour was to groom the people for self-governance. Both the novels abound in idealized Englishmen and women. *The Prince* pits die-hard conservatives in a course of confrontation with liberal Englishmen and enlightened Indians in which it is liberality and enlightenment which emerge victorious. *Hindupore* presents idealized Indians and Englishmen communicating with perfect cordiality, even bonhomie, despite the arrogance and cruelty of a few Englishmen and the petulant impatience, bordering on ingratitude, of a few Indians. The Indians look up to the Englishmen to bring back the pristine glory that was India's. The Englishmen too are shown highly appreciative of India's hoary tradition. However the two novels do highlight the pinpricks which confound such a perfect relationship. *The Prince* isolates the interference in the powers and privileges of the native princes, the insolence and arrogance of individual Englishmen and the aspirations for self-governance in Indians as the causes souring the relationship between the English and the Indians. *Hindupore* offers a limited perspective in only highlighting the misbehaviour and disrespectful attitude of Englishmen as the factors precipitating unrest and discontentment among the Indians.

The Young Zamindar (1885) by S.C. Dutt belongs to a different phase of political consciousness altogether. Here too the natives are shown greatly provoked by the insolent interference of the British in the affairs of the princely states and the tribal areas. However instead of seeking to attain political adulthood under the benevolent guidance of the English, the commonly perceived *mai bap,* the attempt by the novelist, here, is to enunciate the great Indian heritage which includes the Muslims in their distinctiveness, but as part of the Indian nation. A later depiction of the same stage of political consciousness is discernible in Ahamed Ali's *Twilight in Delhi* (1940) which seeks to achieve the same effect; it seems to glorify the indigenous Muslim culture, even though at the same time it bemoans its fading away. The post-1857 anti-British stance of the Muslims is rendered authentically in this novel.

Shunkur — A Tale of the Indian Mutiny of 1857 (1885) is remarkable for its objective and authentic handling of the 1857 uprising. To facilitate the unfolding of the fictional narrative, it creates the milieu in all its essential political details in the background. It pinpoints the causes leading to the great stir — discontent and desperation in dethroned princes, disgruntled zamindars and the overbearing attitude of the English to the sentiments of the natives. What is noteworthy about the novel is the objective rendering of the unspeakable brutalities of the two sides — Nana Saheb and the English. Here the novelist displays a broadened consciousness of human value which goes beyond the narrow confines of nationalism.

Murugan the Tiller (1927) and *Kandan the Patriot* (1932) by S.K. Venkataramani are "novels full of Gandhian politics, exploring and applauding the ideals of Satyagraha and overtly calling on the Indians to work for freedom and regeneration as a nation."[17] This obviously marks a further maturing of political consciousness in that here is discernible an endeavour to reshape the present and bring forth a desired future. Murugan, the protagonist is "an exponent of Gandhian economics,"[18] for he is an advocate of the Gandhian call for going 'back to the village.' The novel graphically highlights the aimlessness of 'western' education and the pernicious impact of unrestrained living. However, its political appeal is hampered by its portrayal of the same idealized types in bureaucracy and administration as in *The Prince of Destiny* and *Hindupore.* Kandan, the exponent of *Kandan the Patriot,* is an exponent of Gandhian politics.[19] In Kandan and Rangan, we have Gandhian protagonists embodying virtues such as self-abnegation, sacrifice and genuine concern for the poor and the oppressed. They air authentically the Gandhian belief in rural reconstruction, prohibition and *Swaraj* in all its political and economic implications. But what is conspicuous by its absence is a well-thought-out plan of action for the attainment of these goals. *Kandan,* despite its avowed Gandhism, captures only an incomplete version of it.

Raja Rao's *Kanthapura* (1938) stands in a peculiarly advanced position with regard to its success in capturing the whole gamut of the complex phenomenon that Gandhi was. Moorthy, "our Gandhi"[20] in the novel, captures, as C.D. Narsimhaiah very precipitatively points out, the three matrices of Gandhism — the sociological, the political and the religious.[21] The novel captures artistically all the major movements launched by Gandhi in the 1930's and thus it presents the very spirit of the age. No historical chronicle can rival Raja Rao's authenticity and power of presentation of the new national political consciousness roused by Gandhi.

Mulk Raj Anand's *Morning Face* (1968) is set in the early years of the 20th century with Gandhi having just entered the Indian stage, and cast a spell with his political utopia, *Hind Swaraj.* However, Anand seeks to capture the political scenario in its entirety. Casting his net wide, he brings in other significant political developments of the period such as the Jallianwala Bagh massacre, the Simon Commission and the Indians' resentment, the Kama-Gata-Maru saga and the exploits of other revolutionaries abroad. However, despite its range, this mélange is devoid of the intensity which marked the age wherein the novel is set. Anand's *The Sword and the Sickle* (1942) does capture the pull of the communist ideology in 1920's under the repressive political and economic conditions of the time. But here too an insistent ironic perspective in relation to the political scenario including Gandhi shows the novelist's ambivalent attitude. The novelist captures the communist movement in its vortex and in its dissipation. With detachment the novelist brings to the fore, through communists like the 'Count,' the follies of the leaders, their lack of discernment, their inability to relate themselves to the situation and their utter ignorance of what precisely they strive to attain. The Congress, too, is painted in the same colour, Gandhi appears as a man obsessed with issues like '*Sanatan dharm*' and the ennobling nature of suffering. The result is that the protagonist is allowed to drift aimlessly.[22] Here "irony and deadly seriousness are mingled in such confusion" that "the reader cannot be sure if the fantastic 'Count,' his comic aspirations, and Lalu's absurd undertakings are at all to be taken seriously."[23] *Untouchable* (1935) by Anand is more forthright in its setting in the 1930's which is marked by the Communal Award, Gandhi's fast to seek the integration of Harijans into the Hindu-fold and the Poona Pact by which it was accomplished. The novel succeeds eminently in capturing the popular image of Gandhi — an *avatar* capable of performing all sorts of miracles and expelling the *Lat Sahibs.*

Tomorrow is Ours (1942) and *Inquilab* (1955) by K.A. Abbas deal with the same political period — the 1920's and the 30's. *Tomorrow is Ours* captures the current that ran through the whole nation at the launching of the non-cooperation movement by Gandhi and also the Communist struggle in China and Russia, which fired the imagination of the people. *Inquilab,* however, reduces the whole exercise of chronicling a phase to dry reportage, Abbas's *Defeat for Death* (1944) limits his canvas to a single momentous incident. It presents in graphic detail the impact created by the 21-day fast undertaken by an old man of 70, obviously Gandhi who had undertaken a fast in 1942 to atone for his followers' recourse to violence. In a manner reminiscent of Browning's *Pippa Passes,* the fast is shown reinvigorating and reawakening a whole community. One won't perhaps come across a more authentic portrayal of the subtle manner of the operation of Gandhian non-violence.

Waiting for the Mahatma (1955) by R.K. Narayan captures to some extent the charisma of Gandhi and also his essential humanity. The Quit India movement is projected as the only political strategy which could wield the nation together. It captures convincingly the latent savagery of quite a few people masquerading as Gandhians. Such violence, with dubious nationalistic motivations, is projected as the factor behind Gandhi's assassination.

Aamir Ali's *Conflict* (1947) depicts another dimension of the Independence movement : the youth — Hindus or Muslims — as the harbingers of the escalating national political consciousness, spreading the eddies to the remotest village in the tumultuous 1940's. Attia Hosain's *Sunlight on a Broken Column* (1961) delineates the vertical schism in the political movement for freedom along communal lines in the same period. Both the components of the national mood would be vouched for in any historical account of the period. Attia Hosain brings her narrative to post-Independence times and records credibly the disillusionment and bewilderment of the Muslims at the turn of events.

Train to Pakistan (1956) by Khuswant Singh, *The Rape* (1974) by Raj Gill and *Ashes and Petals* (1978) by H.S. Gill — all convey a consciousness of the human waste in the wake of Partition. People living in perfect amity for generations together in sleeping villages are fired with communal nationalism with horrendous repercussions in human terms. All these novels convey the impression — and any objective appraisal of events would bear it out — that the partition of Punjab was effected abruptly and arbitrarily, that it was the politicians' hunger for power[24] combined with the indecent haste of the British which exacerbated the tragedy. *The Rape* doesn't even spare Gandhi whom the protagonist dreams of assassinating. The novel is strewn with newspaper reports and political speeches of different leaders, reproduced verbatism, to expose the complicity of all in bringing forth the holocaust. Another noteworthy aspect of the novel is its capturing of the hostile attitude of the Sikhs — at least the generation that was affected by the partition — towards Muslims even after Independence.

Attia Hosain's *Sunlight on a Broken Column* (1961) depicts the effects of the Partition on the Muslims. They are faced with baffling questions : How could one become an alien in one's own birth place? What has a greater pull for the individual — family ties or the country? Chaman Nahal's *Azadi* (1975) focuses on the causes and consequences of the partition from the perspective of a Hindu family.

Mulk Raj Anand's *Death of a Hero — Epitaph for Maqbool Sherwani* (1963) presents one significant aspect of the post-Independence reality — the confrontation between democracy and secularism on the one hand and religious bigotry and obscurantism on the other. Set in Kashmir, the novel presents the general reaction to the attempt of Pakistan in 1948 to grab the Indian state by arranging armed invasion from the Pakistan-occupied part of the state and also by launching an anti-India tirade to incite the people in the name of religion. *The Private Life of an Indian Prince* (1953) by the same novelist again presents the official line, this time with respect to the accession of the erstwhile princely states to the Indian Union after Independence. The princes are presented in their proverbial extravagance, debauchery and whimsicalities, thoroughly incapable of comprehending the new reality. The people, reeling under despotic rule are shown rallying together under the banner of the Praja Mandal, the nationalist political organization of the people of their states. They eventually compel the princes to sign the instrument of Accession to join the national mainstream.

However the novel becomes suspect because of its being too much one-sided and predictable. Abounding in proverbially extravagant, debauched and voluptuous princes, and their arbitrary, imperialist ways, the novelist only seems to be presenting the case of the Government of India for the accession of princely states. Objectivity has been the obvious casualty for Anand over-simplifies the whole thing, totally ignoring the human aspect of his dramatis personae.

Another novel, set in post-Independence India is *Dusk Before Dawn : A Novel of Post-Freedom India* (1978) by Anant Gopal Sheoray. In a painstaking portrayal of hopes gone awry, Sheoray leaves out no section of society : time-serving educationists, apathetic bureaucrats in evil nexus with unscrupulous contractors, opportunistic mediamen, sadistic policemen in cahoots with petty politicians, wily power-brokers, running the state as their fiefdom, haughty upstarts catapulted to ministerial chairs (thanks to minority reservations), servile, spineless judiciary. It is a scathing indictment delivered in forceful terms through the human agents. The only redeeming aspect is the faint hope which comes out in the course of a discussion by a discerning foreign observer of the Indian scene. With the passage of time, the people may mature and rebuild the whole edifice of democracy from its rubble. Although it displays a methodical application of the power of observation and analysis, *Dusk Before Dawn* leaves one cold, for the actors therein exist merely as 'political animals,' conspicuous by their lack of a human interior.

Indian English fiction has thus been imbued with political consciousness. It reflects the chequered political history of the nation's coming to an awareness of its own evolution. It is proposed to study here the whole gamut of modern, post-Independent Indian English fiction, not by way of a sketchy macro appraisal-cum-birds' eye view which would barely touch the complexity of the subject without going into critical depths. What is proposed instead is to focus on key writers who represent the specified context in diverse inclusive ways and through a painstaking perusal of their novels from a micro-perspective, discern the underlying patterns in the subtle portrayal of the political motif in the texts taken up. This exercise targets the trees but not in utter obliviousness of the wood they form part of. The specific has been highlighted only with a view to making the general have greater substance and authenticity.

The novels of Bhabani Bhattacharya (1906 - 1989), Manohar Malgonkar (1913 -) and Nayantara Sahgal (1927 -) — written all of them after Independence — cover a wide spectrum of the nation's concern with politics from the thirties to the late seventies. With a remarkable consistency, these novels tell the nation's story while presenting that of their protagonists. In the process they go well beyond the phases of political consciousness marked by the work of their predecessors. Bhattacharya, Malgonkar and Sahgal hail from different and distant geographic regions and have their differences of perspective and temperament. Yet they belong to the same group insofar as the political consciousness with which their novels are imbued is concerned. Their novels function as a pretty authentic 'national calendar,' chronicling the birth of Independent India and the traumatic soul-searching experiences the country has passed through. What is much more significant is the consistency with which these novels relate the political conduct of the masses with their personal predilections, bred by their faith.

The novels taken up for the purposes of this study are *So Many Hungers*! (1947), *Music For Mohini* (1952), *He Who Rides A Tiger* (1955), *A Goddess Named Gold* (1960), *Shadow From Ladakh* (1966) and *A Dream in Hawaii* (1983) — all the ones written by the novelist to-date. The ones by Malgonkar are *Distant Drum* (1961), *Combat of Shadows* (1962), *The Princes* (1963), *A Bend in the Ganges* (1964) and *Bandicoot Run* (1982). Among the works excluded are *Kanhoji Angrey* (1959) and *The Devil's Wind* (1972) — the former, for it is a historical biography[25] and the latter for it is a history of the so-called Sepoy mutiny of 1857, though from a human angle.[26] Also excluded are *Shalimar* (1968) and *Spy in Amber* (1971) for the former is a fictionalized screenplay,[27] while the latter is the form given to Malgonkar's screenplay by his daughter, Sunita Malgonkar.[28]

Also excluded is *Open Season* (1978) for, to quote Malgonkar, "*Open Season* was not written as a novel, and it is being offered in that garb only because the film was never made."[29] The novels by Sahgal taken up here are *A Time to Be Happy* (1958), *This Time of Morning* (1965), *Storm in Chandigarh* (1969), *The Day in Shadow* (1972), *A Situation in New Delhi* (1977) and *Rich Like Us* (1985), the only one excluded being, *Plans for Departure* (1986). In Sahgal's own words, "with *Rich Like Us* I have reached the end of the road. It exorcised that whole shame-making national experience [*i.e.*, Emergency] from my system.[30] Consequently *Plans for Departure* concentrates on the quest for self-discovery of the protagonist as an individual.[31] Unlike her earlier novels, the canvas here is minuscule. By setting the story in a remote Himalayan hill-station and by focussing on the life of a unidimensional protagonist — in her existence as an individual alone — the author breaks out of the political-feminist straitjacket. Obviously *Plans for Departure* would have contributed little to this study.

There are macro-studies of Indian English fiction wherein the corpus of Bhattacharya and Malgonkar has been taken up in some detail.[32] However Nayantara Sahgal gets just cursory attention.[33] Such wide-range studies obviously cannot be expected to give specific attention to particular texts and discern the pattern that emerges. There are also full length individual studies of Bhattacharya, Malgonkar and Sahgal.[34] Jasbir Jain does study Sahgal as a political novelist — something which hasn't been done for Bhattacharya and Malgonkar. However the study is not uptodate. It is devoid of thrust and is in the nature of insights interspersed. The mode of projection of the novelist's political consciousness has also not been taken up in a systematic and exhaustive manner by the critic. Individual studies have been, as a rule, tied down with explaining all the themes and concerns of the particular novelists. The obvious result has been that specific concerns couldn't be subjected to a probing, comparative perspective.

There are studies of nationalism, as reflected in fiction —

G.P. Sarma's *Nationalism in Indo-Anglian Fiction*[35] and Suresht Ranjen Bald's *Novelists and Political Consciousness — Literary Expression of Indian Nationalism 1919-1947*.[36] However, while Bald's study doesn't take into account the post-independence scenario, Sarma's effort, encompassing almost the whole range of Indo-Anglian fiction from a national perspective, depends largely on detailed treatment of the texts and has, consequently lesser scope for subjecting the nationalism discussed therein to a probing analysis. M.K. Naik's essay "The Political Novel in Indian Writing in English"[37] leaves the same impression on account of its brevity. What is attempted here is not merely an account of the political consciousness reflected in the specified novels of Bhattacharya, Malgonkar and Sahgal, but also a close examination of the larger scenario in this respect along the lines here delineated. The basic preoccupation of these novelists with the organizational aspect of society and the modalities of the distribution of power makes them chronicle the political changes in the country during the last fifty years or so. Going beyond a mere chronicling of the times, these novelists probe the political predicament of the masses and discover the fetters of faith. In Gandhism — the latest endeavour to revitalize faith — these novelists discover both an idiom of comment on and description of political conduct. However Bhattacharya, Malgonkar and Sahgal not merely diagnose, they also prescribe a way out of the impasse, projecting a set of political values they cherish as desirable. All these dimensions of the rendering of the political motif, as reflected in Indian English fiction have been taken up in the following chapters. Lastly the very mode of the projection of such consciousness is taken up for critical consideration.

REFERENCES

1. "Bengali writing in English in the 19th Century," *Bulletin of the Department of English of the Calcutta University,* NS, 3, No. 2 (1967-1968).
2. M.K. Naik, *Raja Rao* (New York : Twayne, 1972), 16.
3. A. Alvarez, *Hungarian Short Stories* (London : Oxford University Press, 1967), x.

4. V.I. Lenin, *Collected Works* (Moscow : Progress Publishers, 1967), XXIII, 334-35.
5. Stephen Spender, *The Destructive Element* (London : Jonathan Cape, 1935), 19.
6. Quoted by Karl W. Deutsch in *Nationalism and Social Communication* (Cambridge : Massachusetts Institute of Technology Press, 1967), 21.
7. See *Nationalism* (London : Macmillan, 1950), Chapter 1.
8. Vivekanand, *Lectures From Colombo to Almora,* (Almora : Advaita Ashram, 1933), 15.
9. Bipan Chandra *et al.*, *Freedom Struggle* (New Delhi : National Book Trust, 1980), 51.
10. Ainslie T. Embree, *India's Search for National Identity* (Delhi : Chanakya Publications, 1980), 22.
11. Quoted by Bipan Chandra in *Modern India* (New Delhi : NCERT, 1971), 251.
12. See Tara Chand, *Freedom Movement* (New Delhi : Government of India Publication, 1967), II, 374-77, 388. Also Tulsi Ram, *Trading in Language* (Delhi : G.D.K. Publications, 1983), 238.
13. Pattabhi Sitaramayya, the official historian of the Congress quoted in *Freedom Struggle, op. cit.*, 180.
14. See Sumit Sarkar, *Modern India* (New Delhi : Macmillan, 1983), 351.
15. See *Freedom Struggle,* 206-10.
16. Interview with Mohan Rakesh, *Journal of South Asian Literature,* Mohan Rakesh Number, ed. Carlo Coppola, 9, Nos. 2-3 (Fall-Winter 1973), 21-22.
17. H.M. Williams, *Indo-Anglian Literature 1800-1970 : A Survey* (New Delhi : Orient Longman, 1976), 4.
18. K.R. Srinivasa Iyengar, *Indian Writing in English* (Bombay : Asia Publishing House, 1962), 228.
19. Iyengar, 228.
20. Raja Rao, *Kanthapura* (Delhi : Oxford University Press, 1974), 106.
21. *Ibid.,* xi.
22. Cf. "If he [Anand] wants us to take Lalu's quest seriously, why does he make him throw in his lot with a crowd of clowns? ...or is [it]...that the author himself is confused about how to portray the development of his hero, facing new challenges after his return home?" M.K. Naik, *Mulk Raj Anand* (New Delhi : Arnold-Heinemann, 1973), 74-75.
23. Meenakshi Mukherjee, "Beyond the Village," in *Critical Essays on Indian Writing in English,* eds. M.K. Naik *et al.,* Dharwar : Karnataka Univ. Press, 1968), 198.
24. *Train to Pakistan* sardonically refers to Nehru's 'tryst with destiny' for power and the same of others for rape and mayhem.

25. G.S. Amur, *Manohar Malgonkar* (New Delhi : Arnold Heinemann, 1973), 125.
26. See Malgonkar's Interview in *The Ellsworth American,* November 12, 1970.
27. Manohar Malgonkar, "Prologue," *Shalimar* (New Delhi : Vikas Publishing House Pvt. Ltd., 1978), n. pag.
28. K.R.S. Iyengar, *Indian Writing in English* (Bombay : Asia Publishing House, 1973), 434.
29. Manohar Malgonkar, "Author's Note," *Open Season* (New Delhi : Orient Paperbacks, 1978), 3.
30. Quoted in R.P. Chaddah, "A Rich Award," *The Sunday Tribune,* January 4, 1987.
31. See the review of the novel by Zerin Anklesaria, "Unsoured Idealism," *The Sunday Standard,* April 6, 1986.
32. Some prominent ones are : R.S. Singh, *Indian Novel in English — A Critical Study* (New Delhi : Arnold Heinemann, 1977), P.P. Mehta, *Indo Anglian Fiction : An Assessment* (Bareilly : Prakash Book Depot, 1968) and Meenakshi Mukherjee, *The Twice Born Fiction* (New Delhi : Arnold-Heinemann, 1971).
33. R.S. Singh, for example, doesn't deal with Nayantara Sahgal at all.
34. Some such studies are K.R. Chandrashekharan, *Bhabani Bhattacharya* (New Delhi : Arnold Heinemann, 1974), G.S. Amur, *Manohar Malgonkar* (New Delhi : Arnold Heinemann, 1973) and Jasbir Jain, *Nayantara Sahgal* (New Delhi : Arnold-Heinemann, 1978).
35. (New Delhi : Sterling Publishers Pvt. Ltd., 1978).
36. (Delhi : Chanakya Publications, 1982).
37. It is included in Yogendra K. Malik, ed., *Politics and The Novel in India* (New Delhi : Arnold Heinemann, 1978), 6-15.

❑❑❑

3

Chronicling the Political Web

WE HAVE seen that quite a few Indian English novelists have set their narratives in the recent political and historical milieu, weaving significant political happenings therein. Bhabani Bhattacharya, Manohar Malgonkar and Nayantara Sahgal are replete with ready instances of this. A novelist opts for a factual background only with a view to finding an order in the seeming welter of history. The very act of weaving a narrative in such a background is an act imbued with political consciousness. By consciously choosing to set their novels in the present rather than in olden times, these novelists act like political chroniclers.

The term 'political chronicle' needs clarification. Here it means neither a mere chronicling of political facts nor a scrupulous recording of all the events in the political history of a society. Using the terminology coined by Nelson Manfred Blake,[1] it can be said that what one gets from the novels of Bhattacharya, Malgonkar and Sahgal is not the "cold truth" of a political scientist but the "hot truth" of an artist. Sensitive to the human reality, they present the political happenings in a wider human framework. So much are the endeavours of the protagonists to realise themselves intertwined with the chronicle of the nation bestirring itself that at times it seems impossible to say where the political chronicle ends and the fictional narrative begins.

It is here that one understands the true import of what otherwise has been reduced to a mere cliche : 'In history nothing is true but names and dates, in literature everything is true but names and dates.' Even the bare facts of history, the 'names and dates' are rendered into a truthful account in Bhattacharya, Malgonkar and Sahgal. They give their novels a strong empirical basis, and despite the focus on individuals rather than incidents, the historical veracity of these novels stands out. Malgonkar seems perfectly justified[2] in claiming :

> Though some would criticize my style, they don't criticize my historical veracity. I take great pains to be absolutely accurate. If I write that something happened on a Saturday or on a moonless night, you can be sure it was on a Saturday or on a moonless night.[3]

Sahgal and Bhattacharya do not claim that exactitude, but they do subscribe to the broad historical framework taking little liberties therewith.

Another misgiving concerns the suitability of contemporary reality for fictional projection. There is quite a vocal section of critics who consider recent happenings to be still in a flux and hence incapable of objective presentation. Here is a representative view : "...an artist who turns recent events into fiction, however clear and ordered the groupings of events and the gradual uncovering of their causes and origins are, cannot easily succeed; for the unconscious mind requires much time to perform its wonder of transmuting incident into art."[4] Bhattacharya terms such doubts as absurd.[5] A creative writer's sensibility can be trusted to filter out the ephemeral details. The second argument put forth by Bhattacharya, in this context, is more pertinent because it refers to the conversion of a state of political awareness into a dominant emotion of the creative mind :

> ...the true artist writes because he must. If the events of today have moved him so deeply that he must have a creative outlet for his feelings, why should he put those feelings in cold storage, as it were, and leave them there until the present time has slipped into the vista of dim yesterdays?[6]

Bhattacharya holds vehemently that no puritanical presuppositions should block the artist's choice of what appeals to him. We may refer to his paper read at the 5th All-India Writers' Conference at Bhubaneswar in 1959 :

> The creative artist has a compulsion to find an outlet for the living images in him. So I say, a novelist may well be concerned with today, the current hour or moment, *if it is meaningful for him, if it moves him sufficiently into emotional response*[7] (emphasis added).

Thus we find that for Bhattacharya the ethic of 'political art' is : a compulsive experience, a living image, a dominant emotion and a meaningful expression. Anything contemporary is not denied artistic value purely for the reason of its being contemporary. Coming to his own works, Bhattacharya confesses candidly :

> My creative writing had its true genesis in the hunger hit streets of Calcutta where the great famine raged. I had an intense need of release from the agony of traumatic experience.[8]
>
> [A novelist] does not have to write on socio-economic problems. I chose to write on them because they fascinated me.[9]

Malgonkar's dealing with themes and issues of contemporary concern is dictated by the need for authenticity :

> I keep writing of India...because I feel no author should write outside his own living circumstances. If he does, it is phoney.[10]

Even from recent times, Malgonkar picks up for fictional rendering only those facets which hold forth a direct appeal to him, which, as Bhattacharya would put it, move him, involve him. Malgonkar is fully conscious of the fact that straying from what he has a feel for to other subjects would mean writing "as insincere as a white man writing about a Negro riot."[11]

Even though Nayantara Sahgal has not set forth her aesthetics of fiction in the way Bhattacharya has, it is obvious from her journalistic writings that her major concern has been with freedom and other related issues as well as with the responsibility of the middle-class intellectuals towards their society. This is what she has to say about her novels :

> I deal with people and their situations but, looking back, each one seems to reflect the hopes and fears the political scene held out to us at that time.[12]

Her novels present the reality of the contemporary scene and, as would be made out hereafter, they not only analyse the present trends in all their human details, but also foresee in which direction the political wind would blow next. It can be reasonably maintained that it is her responsibility to the society that she chooses to discharge through the writing of politically conscious novels. The same choice had been made by Bhattacharya years ago.[13]

Bhattacharya bemoans the non-acceptance of the challenge that recent happenings pose to the creative artists. Western writers have written copiously about the two World Wars. India has passed through the experience of war and the long drawn struggle for Independence. It also faced a calamitous famine in 1943, wherein millions died slowly of starvation. The partition of the country in 1947 awakens nauseous scenes of genocide. Not merely that, open for fictional projection is "a people's dream to attain a better life and...the strength to fulfil the dream." According to Bhattacharya, it is not often that a novelist is fortunate enough to live at a turning point of national life. The turning point faces us with its challenge. Will not some of India's novelists accept the challenge?[14]

What follows is an endeavour to see how Bhattacharya, Malgonkar and Sahgal feel and reflect in their novels what Bhattacharya would term the "strong creative stirrings" in the face of "big events — events that are not only historic in value but also exquisitely rich with the stuff of human passion."[15]

At this juncture, it is desirable to distinguish between a political and a historical treatment of events and personages. The two terms, 'historical' and 'political,' are distinct but not mutually exclusive. Current political happenings and personalities are obviously part of history. History, after all, is the story of humanity recording a string of events which simultaneously are bound by chronology and the chain of cause and effect, sometimes immediate, sometimes remote. Where then to draw a line of distinction? One way to resolve the problem would be to take a simple stock of the author's own position : what is contemporary is political, what is past is historical. A political interpretation of events during a novelist's life time can be considered interpretative and predictive, though particular projections may or may not come true. On the other hand, a historical interpretation is more likely to be a retrospection, or justification of events that have taken place. That is precisely why treatment of contemporary events or those of recent past removed by not more than a generation from the present is more likely to be 'political' whereas older events invite 'historical' presentation.[16] The treatment given to the events and persons of the 1930s and the later period in Bhattacharya, Malgonkar and Sahgal could therefore justifiably be termed a political chronicle. The events of this span of time can be expected to recur as images and dominate as emotions.

Hungers has a threefold matrix of politics, rendered in essentially human terms : the Second World War, the famine in Bengal in 1943, and the course of the freedom struggle at that time.[17] *Tiger* shares all these with *Hungers* but with one significant distinction. *Hungers* evenly distributes the emphasis between the personal and the political — the former is often a working out of the latter. *Tiger,* on the other hand, focuses primarily on personal predilection of the protagonist within a specific political context.

Hungers begins with Britain's declaration of war against Germany and reports the progress of the war in different sectors. The signing of the Land-Lease Act and the Japanese invasion of Indian territory are also brought in. But what is significant is the presentation of the political fall-out of the war in the Indian context. Indians in general are reported to have had one greatly beneficial result from the war : "They...killed their old foe — the sense of race inferiority." "The soldiers from India...fought and defeated white troops in pitched battles even against very heavy odds. The white man's bubble...exploded in the African air" (107).[18] The war, thus, is presented as an event of proud self-realisation for the subject race.

The second dimension of the novel is Bhattacharya's presentation of the pathetic plight of the people reeling under famine and war. The novel captures vignettes of the hell Bengal had to pass through during this unfortunate period with 'dehydrated sticks of humanity' being forced to the lowest animal level. Chandrashekharan uses the testimony of a personal letter from the novelist to him to suggest that "the story is based on factual reports."[19] But what is most noteworthy is that Bhattacharya's portrayal of this calamity is not merely that of a 'social historian's.' He is alive to the vital political issues involved therein. In Bhattacharya's presentation, this human tragedy comes off less as *vis major* and more as the inevitable outcome of the apathy and lack of concern of a tottering administration which was on its last legs, and was desperately endeavouring to stem the twin tides of war reverses suffered abroad and the nationalist upsurge close at hand.[20] Bhattacharya maintains that it was a man-made scarcity : it was caused by an apathetic and corrupt administration, obsessed with the war effort (51, 108, 109, 110) and indigenous greed. With no prospects of food or employment, the people sold off whatever meagre possessions they had, and moved out of ancestral lands, acquiring "the new status of city destitutes" (171).[21] The authorities connived at the distress sales of land and foodstock by farmers and the black-marketeers had a field-day. "The rich grew vastly richer. The poor grew proportionately poor" (109).[22]

Bhattacharya has captured most authentically the state of the nationalist movement for freedom in all its varying nuances. Through the perspective of Rahoul, the reader has a first-hand account of what every awakened Indian thought at that time. Rahoul is instinctively sympathetic to the British cause, for the Second World War, he feels, is "democracy's war against fascist aggression."[23] The hope was that Britain, fighting for democracy, would not deny India the same. That precisely was the reason why the leaders of the nationalist movement, despite their awareness that "the champions of freedom abroad were the eaters of freedom in this land" (40), offered full co-operation in the war-effort.[24]

> India would not hurt Britain in the grave hour of trial. That would not be *ahimsa,* true non-violence. The national movement had more morality than strategy (50).

That was why the national movement for freedom "stood inactive, uncertain which way to turn" (50).[25]

Owing to the lack of a precise strategy, people's frustration was bound to turn violent. "The students were on the edge of revolt. The danger was that once out of restraint, they would take up terrorist tools" (112). The novel captures picturesquely the nationalistic fervour of the villagers in hoisting the national flag and also the inhuman manner in which the "Red Turbans" attack and fire at them. Chapter 7 of the novel is wholly devoted to a description of the Quit India Movement. It begins with the Quit India Resolution (65) passed on August 8, 1942. The very next morning all the leaders of the movement are arrested in a swoop.[26] However, the indomitable spirit of the people cannot be curbed. The frenzy for freedom reaches an unprecedented dimension with "sixty thousand men and women [in prison].... A thousand killed, twice as many wounded. Many had been hanged after a hurried trial — peasant lads had gone to the rope crying with their last breath, 'Victory, victory to freedom'" (100). The authenticity of such a picture can readily be verified from a perusal of any authoritative volume on the history of the period. Majumdar, Raychaudhary and Datta have this to say about the movement :

> According to official estimates, more than 60,000 people were arrested, 18,000 detained without trial, 940 killed, and 1,630 injured through police or military firing during the last five months of 1942.[27]

The irrepressible will of the people did not bow even in the face of the strictest government action. Exorbitant levies were imposed on the rebel villages to pay for a punitive police force (104). To stifle all dissent, postal censors were instituted to screen all mail (110). Prisoners were mercilessly tortured at the slightest provocation (83). *Tiger* presents prisoners being made to carry a yoke on their shoulders and ground the mustard seed by walking endlessly round and round (33).[28] Both *Hungers* and *Tiger* show "the cells...choked with Quit India men" (*Tiger*, 145). *Tiger* records the percolation of political consciousness to the lowest level to such an extent through Quit India Movement that the famine-stricken people of Bengal organized themselves into hunger marchers to fight for their rights. "The roots of this struggle reached back to the jails where Quit India men were held" (174). There was a noticeable widening of the base of the freedom movement with "men drawn from all social levels, down to the humblest" (174).[29] *Hungers* weaves unobtrusively within its texture the statement of Jawaharlal Nehru at his trial in Gorakhpur prison (42). What Nehru refers to in *Hungers* as "the elemental urges of freedom and food and security...moving vast masses of people" (42) are obviously the propelling pulls forcing the people out of the confines of their homes in *Tiger.* They were :

> imprisoned for no crime save the one of loving their country and asking a better way of life for it, a life free from hunger and indignity (174-75).

This promise of freedom, "the horizon of the east illumined by a new dawn" (*Hungers,* 215) is a most truthful evocation of the euphoria that marked the period just prior to and even some time after the attainment of Independence. *Hungers* rightly deserves the eulogy Bhattacharya bestowed on John Steinbeck's *The Grapes of Wrath* : "That good look, depicting an immediate and acute problem of the time of its writing could easily have become brilliant journalism. Instead, it became a true piece of fiction."[30]

Tiger is essentially the story of a crusade to challenge the very organization of society. Set in the early 1940s when the British policy of reservation of seats in the legislature for different communal and social groups was in the air, the novel records the inter-class struggle within the Hindu community.

Placed in its actual historical context, *Tiger* recreates the nascent consciousness among the poor in general and the 'untouchables' in particular, the result of a number of political developments : Macdonald's Communal Award (1932), its later modification through the Poona Pact, the floating of the Anti-Untouchability League, Gandhi's inspiring articles against the pernicious practices of exploitation of the untouchables in the weekly, *Harijan* (1933 onwards), and his going on a 12,500 mile Harijan tour (1933-34), even suspending temporarily the Civil Disobedience Movement to help bring this issue in sharp focus.[31]

Kalo, a *kamar* is the protagonist in *Tiger*. A leader of his community, his fight is against discriminatory social values. Personal humiliation and misery merely act as a catalyst. "His battle was with...the centuries old tradition from which had come the inner climate of his being" (71). His fight is against social, religious and economic exploitation, inherent in the very foundations of Hindu society. Kalo exposes the illogicality and heartlessness implicit in the immobile social stratification along caste lines. His sad experience makes him aware of the sinister nexus between the upper classes and the well-to-do.[32] Bikash Mukherjee is a Brahmin fired with the same crusading zeal as Kalo. His battle is against the inhuman ethnocentricism of the upper strata and their blind and devastating religiosity (167) which makes even the upper class people vulnerable to suppression and exploitation at the hands of their self-styled conscience-keepers. By opting out of the charmed circle, Bikash makes common cause with Kalo and the two, despite occasional straying away from their aim, do succeed in inculcating a class consciousness in the people pushed to the lowest rung through means social, economic and political. A "clash of interests among the great ones" is also precipitated by "their mutual jealousies and hatreds" (136). This breaking of the evil nexus among the socially and economically privileged would hopefully frustrate their strangle hold on the under-privileged. The alien government, tacitly conniving at such exploitation, is also challenged by people under the leadership of men like Biten — B-10, the name Bikash Mukherjee has assumed after shedding his Brahminical sacred thread. The awakened multitude — for the vast majority constitutes the socially, economically and politically exploited — in this new state of political consciousness can fight fully for its rights.

Gold recreates the political atmosphere of the country when, far from being a dream or a vague possibility, freedom had become a distinct certainty and the whole country was agog with excitement. The novel is set in the hundred days prior to the attainment of Independence on August 15, 1947.[33] The novelist captures the strains of political and economic exploitation. The vast masses of the country looked towards future with dreamy eyes even as unscrupulous businessmen and opportunistic politicians were aiming to step into the shoes of the retreating imperialists. There is discernible in a significant section of the people an awareness of the pernicious aftermath of a very long history of subjugation of the masses, for this subjugation has facilitated the unequal distribution of material resources widening the gulf between the rich and the poor (256). Emulating the infamous example of rice-hoarders, unscrupulous traders have cornered essential commodities like cloth to make a fast buck. The very growers of cotton in plenty are thus forced to sleep naked to prolong the life of the little cloth they have (9). Village artisans like Dhannu are forced to sell off in advance all their produce to make both ends meet. The people in general are well aware how this sorry state of affairs is the direct outcome of an alien government. Thanks to the charismatic leadership of Mahatma Gandhi, the people see the issues in a clear perspective.

Gandhi has aroused the sleeping lion that was the Indian populace so that it "faced lorry-loads of Red Turbans as if they were goats"[34] (8). Thus happened a miracle, "a little clay baffled the massive iron rock" (84). Inextricably woven within the texture of the novel is the famous speech of the Indian Prime Minister, Jawaharlal Nehru, delivered at the time of Indian independence (304). It not only imparts historical veracity to the narrative, it is also suggestive of the political consciousness of the people at that time.

Ladakh (1966) takes the novelist to the next tumultuous phase of recent Indian history, the early 1960s when, in the wake of the Chinese aggression in October 1962, the country was faced with the desperate need to match its policies with the contemporary geopolitical realities of the world.[35] The very beginning of the novel places it in a solid, three-dimensional historical matrix. The dilemma the nation in general and the dramatis personae in particular are faced with is inextricably intertwined with the historical and the political details of the setting. The question is the choice of a proper political ideology in the face of internal and external problems. Flying over Ladakh on her way back to Delhi from Moscow where she had gone with a delegation, Suruchi thinks of "Aksai-Chin Road, a motorway the Chinese had built to link up their frontier province of Sinkiang with the Tibetan tableland...across India's map over a wide sector" (2). In the same vein is Satyajit's attempt to pinpoint the geographic location of Ladakh as it goes up to the Chinese borders in Sinkiang and Tibet (23-24).

Even Tibet is not a mere name, it is much more. A full picture of the history and culture of "that high plateau behind the Himalayas" (75) is provided : the earlier attacks by Chinese Emperors, the tide of the people's revolt, the Manchu attack early in the present century, the Revolution of 1911 led by Sun Yat Sen, the shadow of Mao Tse-tung advancing from Peking, the futile appeals to the U.N., the Indian diplomacy (75-76). Within the texure of the novel is also included the political upheavals in China in recent times — the ruthless Kuomintang, the Long March to Shensi and the rise of Mao Tse-tung (76). It is against this backdrop, specifically delineated in its major political contours, that *Ladakh* invokes the very spirit of the India of early 1960s.

The novel projects a picture of the country in a comprehensive context. Freed from colonial subjugation only recently, India had made rapid strides. The pace of progress had been set : "Ten years more, two other Five Year Plans, fifty million kilowatts of hydropower, new-found oil gushing generously from the desert sands of Gujarat and Rajasthan, reserves of uranium yielding atomic power for peaceful use" (33). The novel reads into the Chinese attack a sinister design. Bhaskar reflects :

> I can see how your mind works, Mr. Mao. India, making economic progress at this rate, will become a road block on your path of imperialist expansion. No expansion of territory — that's an outdated concept. Power, you need power over Asia. Then — onward to the African continent.... Aggression in the Himalayas would force this country to begin a massive build-up of the armed forces lest freedom be imperilled. The limited resources, the potential for economic progress would have to be hugely diverted to non-productive effort (33).

That perhaps explains why discarding "geography, history tradition or usage" (79), the Chinese had "surreptitiously annexed sixteen thousand square miles of territory that had been an integral part of India." Not merely that, "they wanted fifty thousand square miles at the eastern end of the frontiers, south of the so-called McMahon line" (79).

India is faced with perhaps the most critical choice in history in the wake of the Chinese attack : whether India should meet force with physical force or with soul force in the footsteps of Gandhi. The two symbols of the extreme options — the spinning wheel and steel — are pitted against each other, the confrontation having been precipitated by Lakakh, as Bhaskar puts it (27). Along with the treacherous attack by China is mentioned the time-bomb of burgeoning population relentlessly ticking, "each five ticks — or could it be four — signalled the birth of an Indian child. A child to be fed, clothed, reared, educated; given cultural fare, given employment, given his due share of the human heritage" (31). Here, again, the same two symbols present the two extreme options : the spinning wheel or small, self-reliant cottage industries and steel or mechanized, heavy industries. The novel renders in artistic terms, with a rigour of logic without compromise, a historic moment of choice for the policy-makers at the very beginning of Independent India : the simple, self-contained, self-sustained, self-reliant village economy with cottage industries or the highly organized, heavily mechanized, internationally dependent economy of a giant size. The implications are no less human and universal than economic and political.

Unobtrusively woven within the texture of the novel is Gandhi's life and the story of his experiments with non-violence in South Africa, the protest against the tax levied on indentured labour, the streams of "pilgrims" pouring to Charlestown, the march to Tolstoy Farm, the defying of the ban on entering Transvaal without permit, the Natal strike, the spread of the movement down the coast from Durban to Isiping, the Nobel Laureate Tagore's tribute to this "steep ascent of manhood," the withdrawal of the heinous permit law and the conceding of victory to Gandhi by General Smuts (65-66).[36] The novelist proposes to present the desperate soul-searching India had to undergo in the 1960s against the background of similar challenges encountered boldly and innovatively by Gandhi in his own time.

Malgonkar's novels, too, rest on a two-tiered foundation of history : history as bare facts, externally verifiable, woven into the fabric of the narrative and a political and historical milieu evoked in minutiae through imperceptible accretion of detail. *Drum* has a solid three-dimensional background of recent history. The novel traverses the course of the action in the Eastern theatre during the Second World War. It takes the readers farther into the tragedy of recent history as it recreates one of its saddest phases — the communal riots in the wake of the partition of the country in 1947. However, it is after moving to the post-Independence period that the chronicling is invested with pertinent political nuances. The novel graphically depicts the spreading tentacles of bureaucracy which prove to be a principal feature of the egalitarian, welfare state established after the attainment of freedom.[37] Some of the inevitable consequences of this bureaucratization presented in the novel are : excessive documentation detrimental to efficiency (14, 124), undue interference of bureaucrats in operational and specialized fields (114);[38] obdurate insistence on procedural formalities to shirk decision (123), indiscriminate sycophancy within the hallowed circles of bureaucracy for career-advancement (92). The mushrooming of the post-Independence crop of self-seeking and unscrupulous leaders at the grass-root level is another facet of the current scenario which doesn't escape the painstaking chronicler in Malgonkar. Henceforth, it is contended, that "the party and the gournment are the shame" (60).[39] Another unpalatable aspect of the post-Independence reality captured authentically by Malgonkar is the rise of sycophancy of their political bosses in military top brass. This, in a way, represents the politicization of the Army.[40]

Combat recreates in all essential details its backdrop of the easternmost corner of India. Malgonkar himself specifies the period and the locale before the story gets underway :

> The action of this story takes place in North-Eastern Assam, India. The time : September 1938 to March 1940 (n. pag.).

Though the story has an Englishman, Henry Winton, as the protagonist, the political nuances of the Indian scene come off unobtrusively. The Second World War is underway and the Englishmen's concern at the situation is exacerbated with the rising nationalism of the natives.

> In India everything that concerns a sahib is politics.... His very presence is the basis of all their political agitation (86).

Winton is rightly warned by other Englishmen against the Indian Press. "If they get a sahib in their mangle, particularly when it concerns something we ourselves profess to do better than the Indians...the political capital the Gandhis and Nehrus will make [of] this sort of thing..." (86). The novel presents the political situation in Assam after the elections to the provincial assembly there under the Government of India Act (1935). The Congress didn't fare well in this part of the country. "They have not been able to collar more than 35 out of a hundred and eight" (30).[41] However, the nationalist aspirations of the people have been fully aroused. This political awakening of the masses gets conveyed indirectly through the lament of the Englishmen. Even though Indians have been given "the fullest possible measure of self-rule with their own ministers in province, yet politicians clamour for more and more power" (75).

Princes deals with an exclusive phase of recent Indian history not so commonly dealt with in Indian English fiction and nowhere taken up with such a sure touch as in Malgonkar.[42] As is almost a practice with Malgonkar, a declaration of the historicity of the locale and the personages precedes the unfolding of the yarn :

> The characters in this novel are intended to personify the thoughts and ideas of a somewhat tightly-knit social group : the one-time ruling princes of India (9).

Malgonkar relates the narrative in *Princes* to the very beginning, November 1, 1858 when a royal Proclamation transferred India from the jurisdiction of East India Company to the Crown. The later happenings in the novel bring the action much closer to contemporary times. The historical and political framework of the novel rests on a three-tiered foundation. The national movement for freedom in areas directly administered by the English is described in essential details. The politics within the princely states is also analyzed in all its complex nuances. The third component is the presentation of the Second World War in its fiery phase : the Middle East theatre with 'old Rommel' entrenched in Egypt (188); his being checked in his audacious push in late April 1941 (190); and the abandoning of Burma in the wake of the Japanese strides (207).[43]

Coming to national politics, one encounters the period 1940-47 recreated in most of its essential details : the Gandhian movement for self-rule (65), the popular spread of the use of Gandhi-cap as a mark of protest and the harsh deterrent treatment meted out to those who donned the cap (66), the Salt

Satyagraha (69),[44] the wide spread disenchantment at the failure of Cripps Mission to resolve the impasse created by the conflicting stands taken by the Indian National Congress, the Muslim League and others (232),[45] the Naval Mutiny (258),[46] and the communal riots consequent upon the decision to partition India (258, 262). However, the most significant component of the chronicle comprises an authentic account of the conditions in the princely states during that eventful period. As compared with the rest of the country, the current of the struggle for freedom passed only in dribblets in princely states. The protagonist in *Princes* marshals an array of irrefutable facts therefor :

> People's backwardness, their inability to respond to the pressures of the twentieth century. Steeped in literacy and almost medieval ignorance, the population of the princely states had not acquired the political consciousness of their brethren in the rest of the country (66).

Abhay also presents an objective appraisal of the princely order *vis-a-vis* the modern world :

> It was pathetic to see how desperately they clung to their illusions. Panic had been replaced by wishful thinking. A glance at the map would have shown them how impracticable the idea of framing a union of princely states was, for the states were peppered all over the landscape of India and even in and out of each other. But even if geographical contiguity had existed, such a creation would still have been out of the question, because all history had shown that the princes were incapable of uniting. Their internal jealousies had made it possible for the British to pick them off one by one. The compulsions that governed them now, two hundred years later, were still the same. Without British protection, they would have been finished long ago. Now the British were going, leaving them to their fate. It was incredible that they could not see the writing on the wall (257).

Perhaps it was wishful thinking alone which made them visualize themselves as "the third force...as a counter-weight to the Congress and the Muslim League." There could have been other inciting factors too. "There were rumours that the political Department was actually instigating the rulers in their efforts to set it [*i.e.,* a third force] up" (237-38).[47]

One would readily concede that there is worth in the picture of the princes' plight painted from their point of view :

> The princes were hard pressed. On the one hand they were harassed by the local revolutionaries whom they were quite powerless to control, because that would have been inviting a charge of suppressing the natural aspirations of their people. On the other hand, if the preservation of law and order really broke down, the Centre had every right to intervene[48] (298).

Even after the formal acceptance of the Independence of India as a foregone conclusion, there was a lot of confusion as regards the princely states. "The government drew up a formula for the acceptance of the princes which was called 'the Instrument of Accession," But that cleared the decks only technically. "The transfer of power was to take place on the 15th August. Three weeks beforehand, the majority of the rulers had still not formally accepted the 'Instrument of Accession'" (276).[49] Here too, as in *Drum* before, Malgonkar's chronicling of post-Independence history includes one essential feature thereof : the mushrooming of bureaucracy under the guise of democracy. From the days of "rough and ready justice, on the spot and promptly delivered" (68) to a regime where a faceless hierarchy of clerks which insists on "cash even before they do anything" is too big a change for most people to swallow (355).

Ganges incorporates and assimilates a number of epoch-making individuals and incidents within its texture. Gandhi appears not only vicariously through his speeches, as in the brief quote prefixed to the novel, but also in flesh and blood. Even though this appearance is rather brief, what is most remarkable about it is Malgonkar's capture of one essential dimension of the elusive phenomenon of Gandhi the legend — his *human* existence as a mortal.[50] To the historical figure of Gandhi, Malgonkar adds substance by invoking admirably his strategy of opposing the alien rulers through the burning of foreign clothes (7) and his exhortation to oppose the government by peaceful means with "no coercion, no intimidation" (9). The novel conveys through Gian's acts of discarding his much-prized blazer the enthusiastic manner wherein thousands responded to Gandhi's call for making a bonfire of foreign clothes.[51] Not merely that, Malgonkar goes ahead to include in his tale even the rationale for this seemingly novel means of protest.[52]

> Those of us who wear clothes of British materials help to pay the administrators who are sent to rule over us, to buy the rifles and bayonets for the soldiers who hold us in captivity, to arm the police who now surround us (8).

Besides Gandhi, another real-life freedom-fighter who figures in *Ganges* is Jatin Das (74), the arch-revolutionary who is very much alive in the memory of Shafi,[53] a key character in the novel. There is a graphic invocation of the Jallianwala Bagh massacre on "a hot April day in the year 1919" with General Dyer ordering his soldiers to fire at a crowd of Gandhi's followers. The result was "379 dead and over a thousand wounded" (75).[54] The novel goes on to record the humiliation the Indians were subjected to, subsequently. "They had to crawl on their bellies because General Dyer had promulgated what was called the crawling order" (75). The specific reference to Kucha Kaurianwalan in Amritsar is another historically authentic stroke (75).[55] The strangle hold of the police and lower rungs of the bureaucracy[56] on the people in general and the poor in particular under the very nose of alien administration is graphically portrayed through the poignant frustration of Gian and Hari in their endeavour to enforce their rights.

Chronicling the stifling yoke of subjugation, Malgonkar takes his readers farther along the chequered ready to political independence, and this brings in the escalation of terrorism directed against the British rulers.[57] "A college girl had fired a revolver at the British Governor while he was addressing a University Convocation" (76).[58] However, soon this single-minded zeal for freedom got attenuated by the spread of the virus of communalism which slowly ate into the thrust of the movement for liberation. "The Congress and the Muslim League had come to a parting of ways with Hindus and Muslims separated into opposite camps, learning to hate each other with the bitterness of ages. Even their own leaders had begun to take sides" (81).[59] While the nationalist forces were thus split along communal lines, India, it seemed, was going to become the battlefield for the Axis and the Allied forces. Japan got a toe-hold over the tip of India. For the Indians living in the southernmost islands off the mainland, it was a sad day to realize how those who had liberated them from their British oppressors were far more tyrannical themselves (260). The Japanese war aim was obviously not to liberate the Indians but to disintegrate and destroy the British Empire even if it involved (as it actually did) subjecting helpless Indians to callous, wanton misery (264).

Coming back to the scene at home, Malgonkar continues his chronicling in all its human implications. With the country "ready to fall like a ripe mango into the hands of the Japanese" (282), there was seething discontent everywhere. 'Quit India' was the rage everywhere. In their anguish and frustration, "fired by their anger at the mass arrest of their leaders, goaded by the thought of the Japanese armies poised for an offensive, the people had chosen to discard their vows of non-violence" (283).[60] The repressive measures taken recourse to by the authorities, "the callous prison sentences pronounced on Gandhi and Nehru" and the show of naked aggression to stifle the upsurge 'backfired,' provoking the mobs into acts of violence. "Those who had the power to restrain the people, to persuade them to refrain from violence, were kept secretly locked up in prison" (283). The people discarded what Debi terms "bullock-cart speed and vegetable logic of the Indian National Congress" (284.) Their desperation burst forth into acts of violence.[61]

The national situation in India as well as the post-war international scene brought the tussle for independence to a decisive phase. "It was clear that the British were ready to pull out of the country. Only the terms of transfer were to be agreed upon" (295).[62] However, fissiparous forces split the nationalist movement vertically. After the elections under the Government of India Act (1935), the mutual mistrust of Hindus and Muslims was aggravated by the unwillingness of the Hindu-dominated Congress to share power with the Muslim League.[63] The "trial spell of provincial government," Shafi is convinced, demonstrated the inability of Hindus and Muslims to live together. The natural outcome of this was "the resolution of the Muslim League in which Jinnah had demanded the creation of a separate state [for Muslims] carved out of India" (295).[64] The inexorable logic of events forced itself on the people. As the stipulated day of Independence approached, "tens of millions of people had to flee leaving everything behind, Muslims from India, Hindus and Sikhs from the land that was soon to become Pakistan" (332).

Bandicoot Run, too, as its predecessors, has a significant base, a true, verifiable historical substratum. It also has a large superstructure of authentic invocation of the milieu in all its political naunces wherein the story is set. Through the reminiscences of Brian Gilchrist, a key character, is created a picture of Gandhi : his "Puckish humour," "agility of mind, scuttling behind abstract philosophy when cornered, but never without a merry glint in the eyes," a hypnotic personality, indeed (103). Later in the novel, one learns of hundreds of volunteers fired by nationalism courting arrest under the non-violent movement spearheaded by Gandhi (300). Gandhi is shown again, this time in Noakhali in Bengal, the worst affected place in pre-Partition riots where hundreds of Hindus had been done to death in one of the worst orgies of communal violence (318).[65] Moving to post-Independence times, one comes across the question "After Nehru who?" — one of the most pressing posers faced by the country in the early 1960s as the Nehruvian charisma was waning.[66]

Bandicoot also captures in small but telling strokes the abysmally low morale the Army went through in that eventful period[67] : the penchant for "Gandhian ideals of austerity" (18) among the politically ambitious in the army and elsewhere, "favouritism in high places and...politicians interfering with the promotions and postings of service officers" (62). Another familiar feature of recent post-Independence politics unobtrusively brought into the novel is the ubiquitous 'foreign hand' (read CIA) to which are attributed all the nation's trials and tribulations (312).[68]

Malgonkar not only invokes admirably the historical milieu wherein all his novels are set, he also throws in frequently actual historical personages in the background to lend credence to the picture. K.M. or Krishna Manikam in *Bandicoot* deserves special mention. He is the most obvious example of a historical character being given a fictional garb, rather transparent though. K.M. is an ambitious politician. He is the Minister of Defence. For the post of Chief of Staff, he wants "someone he can depend on...someone who owes everything to him" (154). K.M. likes to throw his weight around. He tore an Admiral to strips for a minor fault (147). The Sandhurst boys detest K.M. and K.M. delights in treating them with contempt.[69] The thinly-veiled portrait is obviously that of Krishna Menon, the Defence Minister in office at the time of the 1962 debacle on the Sino-India frontiers.[70] His opting for General B.M. Kaul as the Army Chief had been equally controversial. Here is an excerpt from what M.V. Kamath had been quick enough to observe while reviewing the book for *The Sunday Observer.* The blurb on the Orient paperback edition of the novel displays the observation prominently :

> *Bandicoot Run* is a savage and merciless attack on the late Mr. V.K. Krishna Menon and one of his favoured Generals who was promoted out of turn.

Nayantara Sahgal's novels present even more obviously a chronological account of Indian politics from the last phase of the freedom struggle to the breakdown of democracy in mid-1970s. She herself explains that politics is embedded in her "bones and marrow,"[71] and in her "emotional and intellectual make-up"[72] to such an extent that she can no longer remain a mere passive spectator to the happenings with far-reaching fall-out affecting vital human interests. The account of recent political events in her novels is imbued to the core with an acute consciousness of certain basic assumptions and values to which the novelist is committed and it is more by way of enshrining these fundamentals or bemoaning the absence thereof that she goes about setting her stories in a historically recognizable locale. The milieu invoked in all its diverse dimensions is neither mere window-dressing nor the dull, drab and soulless account of a historian.

Happy (1958) is set in the immediate pre- and post-Independence era. The novel, in small but telling strokes, creates an authentic picture of those tumultuous days. Sohan Bhai, a Gandhian freedom fighter, recreates for us the calamitous famine of 1943 in Bengal. The Quit India Movement (1942) enters the novel indirectly through the happenings in the lives of two minor functionaries in the novel. The narrative in its meandering course creates a society marked by segregation of communities (50), discrimination against Indians (55), servility among the rich and well-set people (161). However, through the narrator and Sohan Bhai, one learns of the all-encompassing movement launched by Gandhi to arouse and uplift the people. Gandhi's message, as presented in the novel, cuts across simplistic sociological, political or spiritual formulations. Equally noteworthy is the sensing of the political climate in post-Independence India with an unscrupulous scramble for power beginning to divide "even those who share the same ideals" (28).[73] There is also a covert strain of the rising trends of extremism, fundamentalism, obscurantism and populism. There are earnest, "ceaseless campaign against the evils of drinking, meat-eating and getting vaccinated against disease" (251). The clamour for prohibition and the "socialization ballyhoo" (238) also strike a disturbing note.

Morning (1965) is set in post-Independence India and it sets out to catch the dilemma of a country passing through the birth pangs of evolution. The murky note struck in *Happy* regarding the post-Independence scene is reinforced as one finds all canons of decency and decorum overthrown in the unscrupulous hunt for power. “Disorder was just round the corner, always, and no motley crew of Parliamentarians would succeed in coping with it any more than picket fences would stem a deluge” (106). With power becoming a political reality from a mere rabble-rousing slogan,[74] men of vision, such as Kailas Vrind, Abdul Rahman and Prakash Shukla, seem to be pushed to a corner while those with a ruthless approach to problems move to the centre of the stage. The winking at or condoning of such ends-oriented people with not-so-clean hands right at the peak of the era of Nehruvian idealism is a part of post-Independence political history,[75] one cannot wish away. It is this which Sahgal conveys authentically in *Morning*.

Storm focuses on what had barely been suggested in the earlier novels. It captures the bewilderment of a nation sandwiched “between...[a] dying generation and the confused youths” (*Morning,* 215); the old leaders “who feel a gnawing sense of withdrawal” and the young men, in an impatient “let's-get-on-with-it” mood (*Morning,* 198).

The ‘storm in Chandigarh’ is historical and not merely fictional — the culmination of the populist, parochial, obscurantist forces brought to a head by the government policy of the linguistic reorganization of the states of the Indian Union.[76] The novel traces the growth of abrasive political culture percolating upwards from the states to the Centre. The reference to “the Congress cracking up” (24), “the clash of personalities” (24) with “no issues left, only squabbles” (24), gives the novel a firm grounding in the post-Nehru phase.[77]

However, it is *Shadow* which brings a more complete picture of the political scenario of the late 1960s. Here the novelist chooses to cast her net wider instead of merely probing into someone aspect in its minutiae. *Shadow* depicts the post-Nehru scene with “more fever than calm” (149) in Delhi, “the belligerent new politicians[78] (3) coming to the fore, the bureaucracy shedding its anonymity to assume a vague unobtrusiveness (3). The fissiparous forces splitting the nation along parochial lines, which were subjected to scrutiny and analysis in *Storm,* here assume multifold manifestations in a conducive climate for "the government since the recent split in its own party, needed every vote it could get and the scene in the lobbies before a major debate could look like the Stock Exchange on market day" (151).[79] To catch the imagination of the people, slogan-mongering was at a feverish pitch, with socialism the newest 'catch-word' (163).[80] In this frenzied game with no holds barred, only the discerning could foresee how the "socializing ballyhoo," would gather together if not checked in time, an "avalanche in dribblets" (229) and wipe out not only the rich but also "the growing, struggling, middle class" (148).

Situation is set ostensibly in the 1960s. But in its capturing of the desperation and the urgency of the situation, it suggests the immediate pre- and post-Emergency political scene. Rather than attenuating the "mute agony" of the people, the attempt of the government was directed towards covering it up. "There is a general drift in the direction of more controls over newspapers, films, books and so on, more censorship..." (106). Through a brutal show of strength and through tracing "intricate maps of burns" (103) on the bodies of those who dare to raise their voice against the apathy of the government, the authorities seek to cow down all dissent.[81] The novel presents graphically the indifference of the Western countries to a nascent democracy. Taking it for granted that the democratic experiment would fail in the poly-religions, multi-cultural and pluralistic society in India, they "led the chorus prophesying chaos instead of supporting... [her] Herculean labours" (5-6). How they seek to support tacitly the repressive measures of the government, topping it all with seemingly wise comments in an I-told-you-so vein : "It *is* an Asian country.... And therefore we can't apply our yardsticks here" (emphasis in original) (107). "These people need a strong leader" (107). *Situation* truthfully captures the Western attitude to democracies in the Third World, especially India : the refusal to think anew, to have a close look at the situation, to help where help was needed.

Rich (1985) takes the story farther in the same setting — here it is one month after the declaration of the Emergency. The present is sought to be seen through a selective filtering of the memorable past — of a totally different flavour altogether. One is led through the epoch-making Civil Disobedience Movement launched by Gandhi (59), the fierce Quit India Movement and the communist betrayal of the national cause at that crucial hour (99),[82] the lightning 'mutiny' by the Navy in Bombay, the fall of Singapore, the INA trials (142-43). There flits before one's gaze "a skeletal and fanatic who couldn't speak his own language, [who] hardly ever wore any but English clothes" (72) — the man who single-handed brought about the partition of the country. The movement of a vast army of refugees, their pro-Jana Sangh leanings,[83] the assassination of the Mahatma, the visionary Nehru and then the underrated but equally devoted and dynamic Shastri as Prime Minister are suggested almost effortlessly to give finishing touches to the scenario before "populism burst upon us" (153). This retrospection, which is diffused all over, doesn't reduce the novel to 'a loose sally of the mind.' Rather it creates an environment wherein the present transgression — the proclamation of Emergency — is to be faced. The chronicling of the past is solely motivated by the design to demonstrate the sea-change which the leaders, their means, sense of ends and also the institutions have undergone. The Emergency in all its political and human fall-out is graphically painted: trade unions crushed, news blacked out, bureaucracy politicized, in short, the silence of suspended animation has descended on the nation. Delegations of teachers, lawyers, school children, entrepreneurs and others pass through the motion of praising the leader for timely wisdom. Congregations and conferences mushroom to take on the chant. There are also woven into the narrative factual bits like the blinding of criminals (30) and the raid on J.N.U. (185).

A noteworthy aspect of Nayantara Sahgal's political chronicling is that she captures the essence of some real historical figures so authentically and in so large a measure that their fictional counterparts immediately reveal the originals. Sohan Bhai, depicted in *Happy*, not only has been influenced by the Mahatma (87-88), he is directly suggestive of Gandhi with his spinning, his broad humanitarianism, his probing philosophizing and his crusading zeal for wiping the tears from others' eyes. The unnamed PM in *Morning* and Shivraj, the PM in *Situation,* both visionaries as well as tireless workers for their ideals, are clearly drawn from the figure of Jawaharlal Nehru. Prakash Shukla in *Morning,* with his anti-corruption zeal, resembles Feroz Gandhi.[84] Kailas Vrind, the Chief Minister of U.P. in *Morning*, in his commitment to high ideals in politics, in his concern for human values, and, in his scholarship, reminds one of the novelist's father, Ranjit Sitaram Pandit.[85] Kalyan's ego-mania, his preference for personal loyalty over ideology, his rhetorical propensity — in fact the totality of his public image — immediately brings to mind Krishna Menon, active on the political scene in the late 1950s and early 1960s. Gyan Singh, the Chief Minister of Punjab in *Storm*, with his earthiness, his zest for action uninhibited by norms is suggestive of his real life counterpart around that period, Pratap Singh Kairon.[86] Vishal and Raj Garg seem fictional prototypes of E.N. Mangat Rai, an I.C.S. officer at the Centre, who had felt on his pulse, as he himself explains in his memoir, *Commitment My Style,* the growing authoritarianism within the haloed precints of administration. Usman, the academician, bringing to politics a fresh whiff of idealism and personal involvement, resembles Jayaprakash Narain, a staunch Gandhian and selfless Sarvodaya worker who had had political limelight focused on him in early 1970s.[87]

Rich is embarrassingly abundant in such parallels. 'The Madam' in the novel who has promulgated the Emergency is Mrs. Indira Gandhi and the son who uses the official pull to make his small-car project a success is Sanjay Gandhi. The novel faithfully records quite a few of the developments historically set in motion by them : the family planning and afforestation drives, the move for Japanese collaboration in the small-car project, etc.[88] However, the novel goes beyond this to include a number of things attributed in popular imagination to the duo — nepotism, attempts to foist family rule, PM's designs to make herself President and to bring her son to power by the back-door, violation of all norms in making the PM's son an entrepreneur overnight, government-arranged rallies to hail the promulgation of Emergency and so on. J.P.'s arrest for his anti-government activities, his incarceration under Emergency provisions, his deteriorating health — all historically verifiable facts[90] — figure in the novel and they are accompanied by the apprehension that the authorities would not let him out alive — again reflection of a widespread fear.[91]

Nayantara Sahgal, in a letter to the present writer, played down some of the parrallels suggested here, laying emphasis on "the fictional roles these characters play"[92] in view of the thematic totality of the work they figure in. It would certainly be hazardous to overemphasize such resemblances and thereby oversimplify matters. It is true that in their moments of impatience with the stubbornness of their countrymen in clinging to their outworn traditions even in the face of new problems, Kalyan, Sumer and Rishad also exhibit shades of Jawaharlal Nehru. But what is significant is how such characters even though suggestive of some historical figures, do merge themselves into the narrative and represent some one easily comprehensible "approach" or another with a clear preference for definite political stands[93] which condition all their actions. Once related to a fictional situation, they round off their angularities and respond to its demands, both personal and political.

In all her novels, Nayantara Sahgal uses political chronicling for a perceptive analysis of the political process. The steadily growing unscrupulousness, the accumulating problems and the diminishing will to take hard decisions, the long term vision succumbing to short-sighted populism — all these couldn't but undermine the democratic superstructure.

Nayantara Sahgal fairly reflects the new crop of post-Independence leaders. In one respect, the leaders may themselves feel rootless but their demagogy, their "swear[ing] by the masses and not by God" (*Situation,* 20) does imbue them with a "crude, elemental attraction." As is said of Gyan and others of his ilk in *Storm,* "their very narrowness gave their arguments a crude strength...that no larger vision could ever have" (126). "Uncomplicated in...[their] functioning" (*Storm,* 78), such leaders, hold forth an apparent panacea for the perennial problems of the p eople and meet with a ready constituency in masses afflicted with a perpetual anxiety-syndrome and waiting. However, in all her works, Nayantara Sahgal seeks to explain how such attempts represent "a complete repudiation of India's assimilative, absorptive tradition...this genius for being able to contain and cradle its contradictions."[94] The novels show how this humanitarian perspective along with the political structures involved, "the climate of debate and dissent it had built, and the human give-and-take it had engendered, ...began to be eroded. The political atmosphere began to be reduced to a simple formula of for-and-against, either-or."[95] The greatest casualty was "the huge and heroic experiment of development with consent, development with compassion."[96] *Storm* and *Situation* are built around "the narrow, rigid atmosphere about us,"[97] says the author. These two novels, "reflected the mounting unease and, at times, the feelings of impending disaster I had as I wrote them."[98] *Shadow* points to the attempt to "reduce the political scene to cut-and-dried categories which are far from factual."[99] *Situation* analyses the impossibility of simple definitions, for "Left and Right cannot be divided up like sheep and goats at opposite ends of a political pole."[100] The novel records her "mounting horror of the Gulag Archipelago growing invisibly about us."[101] Even a cursory reading through any account of the current history of Indian politics, *e.g.*, Kuldip Nayar's *Between the Lines, India After Nehru, The Critical Years, In Jail,* Durga Das's *India from Curzon to Nehru and After,* would vouch for the validity of the picture drawn in its minutiae by the novelist.

What is perhaps Nayantara Sahgal's singular-most achievement is her perceptive depiction of the political scene. She gazes at the politics of the time so minutely that even mere straws in the present air spring into view as tokens of typhoons in store. "It is a tribute to her as a political novelist that she could sense and show the danger in the new trend...years before the country had actually experienced the culmination of such a trend."[102] *Storm* anticipates the "manoeuvres outside political channels and conventions, outside the party and outside the cabinet,"[103] "the street rallies and demonstrations efficiently organized...and the language of excitement and incitement...used to stir up the people"[104] — all characteristic of the Indian political scene after the Congress split in 1969. *Storm* also foreshadows the "arresting [of] the natural development of post-Nehru leadership within Congress,"[105] so that a nation accustomed to Jawaharlal Nehru's heart searching and eloquence, a party once led by towering intellectuals should now be at the mercy of what Sahgal calls "a handful of mini-brains with three-and-a-half catch phrases between them in place of a vocabulary."[106]

"Fiction often overshadows fact,"[107] Nayantara Sahgal agrees. She is herself aware of the anticipatory nature of her perceptive political analysis in her novels :

> *Storm,* based on the second division of the Punjab and the creation of Haryana State, with both...demanding Chandigarh as the capital was written a year or more before this even came to pass.[108]
>
> *The Day in Shadow* had had as an accompanying background to Simrit's divorce settlement, the growing Soviet influence on our subcontinent and definite Indian tilt in that direction. I finished writing the book in February 1971. The Indo-Soviet Treaty, a landmark of its kind embodying the tilt was not signed until August that year. The "situation" creeping upon us in *A Situation in New Delhi* — a book I had completed writing in January 1975 — was upon us in June, and I myself was hung with it.[109]

By foreshadowing the inevitable political reality through her deft portrayal of human actors, who are caught in circumstances where the political gets inextricably intertwined with the personal, Nayantara Sahgal obviously accomplishes a great deal more than what is generally expected of a novelist.

We have already seen that one significant aspect of the treatment of political consciousness in the novels of Bhattacharya, Malgonkar and Sahgal is that the narrative is frequently interspersed with objective accounts of the political developments. An examen of the artistic exigencies of such incorporation would obviously form part of this study. The account of the progress at the war-front during the Second World War is not merely implicitly related in *Hungers,* to the effect it has on the minds of the people (52). It has also been explicitly equated with the battle between the bulls and the bears closer at home (29). Nehru's statement at the Gorakhpur trial, in the same novel, again has a rationale for it sums up most effectively the mood the nation was passing through. Excerpts from the "Tryst-with-destiny" speech by Nehru on the attainments of Independence in *Gold* prepare the ground for the minstrel's explanation of the import of the *taveej* in the national context. Statistical references to the rapid increase of India's population in *Ladakh* (31), the specific mention of the achievements in diverse fields and the future prospects under the successive Five Year Plans (31) don't ring jarring at all, so well are they attuned to the presentation of Bhaskar's case. The iteration, in Chapter VII, of the experiments with truth and non-violence, undertaken by Gandhi in South Africa, appear in the novel in the shape of a vision to Satyajit when he thinks of leading a *Shanti-Sena* to the Himalayan snowlines. Bhattacharya's recourse to time-shift appears skilful for it traverses the tortuous course undertaken by Satyajit's mind before it is made : "...I will act as he would have acted even though I'm less than his shadow" (67). In the same vein in Chapter XXXVI when the Chinese aggression takes a turn for the worse, Satyajit calls to his mind the tumultuous days of World War II when faced with the threat of Japanese invasion, Gandhi had forged his weapon of resistance (337). Even the presentation of the history and culture of Tibet in Chapter IX helps make real the expansionist designs of the Chinese. The incorporation of the facts concerning the geography of Aksai-Chin (2) and Ladakh (23) helps present the strategic location of these areas.

Despite being in general agreement with Chaman Nahal that "a novelist is not interested in history *per se*"[110] and that one should go to chroniclers or historians rather than to novelists for presentation of facts, one cannot really grudge the use of such material for it contributes to instead of distracting attention from the narrative. *Drum* has given at some length vignettes of "the Indian Army from an officer's point of view"[111] in a manner marked with "authenticity with never a false note."[112] However, the account of the dressing down Kiran received as a 'Bum-Wart,' the disastrous attack on the Twin Pagoda Hill by Bull Hampton and the first successful attack led by Kiran,[113] far from rendering the novel "an extended cameo of the Indian Army"[114] provide a context wherein the Army code operates. The code comes off as a set of values tested and forged in the smithy of experience unlike abstract political ideology which only destroys and divides.

Rich quotes from "original documents with National Archives of India" to buttress the Sati-episode (6). Though it is in the backdrop, it is given a central role in providing Sonali, the protagonist, the motivation to oppose the Emergency. The repeated references to Gandhi (100, 101, 113, 114, 115) are obviously meant to highlight the sea-change in the scenario.

Obviously far from being inartistic excrescence, the incorporation of verifiable developments of the period wherein the novel is set meets the artistic requirement of contributing to the tenor of the narrative. What is of equal significance is the manner in which it establishes "the texture of the created society,"[115] which is deemed by Michael Wilding to be an important ingredient of political fiction. Orwell, writing about future, had to invent his 'documents,' to cater to this requirement of *Nineteen Eighty-four*. Bhattacharya, Malgonkar and Sahgal put history to creative use in their novels. They bring their artistic armoury to play and infuse colour and blood into the bare facts of history. Political events are charged with human emotions and history, far from remaining a lump of dead facts, merges itself into the current of human lives. From a mere chronological iteration of past happenings, history emerges in these novels as a moving spectacle of human aspirations and endeavours to realize them.

As the foregoing analysis suggests, Bhattacharaya, Malgonkar and Sahgal succeed in shaping what F.R. Leavis would have termed complete, comprehensive and enlightening histories of contemporary time.[116] For the portrayal of human reality in their novels is imbued with an acute consciousness of history as it conditions their dramatist personae. By integrating their protagonists with the political process rather than isolating them therefrom and by subjecting political platitudes and developments to a thorough scrutiny from a human angle, these novelists reflect a perceptive consciousness of the unprecedented relevance for the individual of the way the political wind blows. Politics is deemed too much of an all-encompassing activity to be left to politicians or historians alone. It is obvious how it is in this sense that Bhattacharya, Malgonkar and Sahgal play to perfection the role of a political chronicler.

REFERENCES

1. *Novelist's America* : *Fiction as History* (New York : Syracuse University Press, 1969), 262.
2. Prof. G.S. Amur takes exception and refers to the confused geography of Konkshet in *A Bend in the Ganges.* It is located on the way from Madras to Duriabad but it is also supposed to be in Himachal, north of Duriabad. *Manohar Malgonkar* (New Delhi : Arnold-Heinemann, 1973), 121. However, this lapse is just an aberration.
3. *The Ellsworth American,* November 12, 1970.
4. C. Paul Verghese, *Essays on Indian Writing in English* (New Delhi : N.V. Publications, 1975), 28.
5. "Literature and Social Reality," *Perspectives on Bhabani Bhattacharya,* ed. Ramesh K. Srivastava (Ghaziabad : Vimal Prakashan, 1982), 5.
6. *Ibid*.
7. Bhabani Bhattacharya, "Indo-Anglian," *The Novel in Modern India,* ed. Iqbal Bakhtiyar (Bombay : P.E.N. All India Centre, 1964), 47.

8. Ramesh K. Srivastava, "Bhattacharya at work : An Interview," *Perspectives on Bhabani Bhattacharya, op. cit.*, 220.
9. *Ibid.,* 228.
10. *The Ellsworth American,* November 12, 1970.
11. *The Directory of British and American Writers,* 1971, quoted by G.S. Amur in *Manohar Malgonkar* (New Delhi : Arnold Heinemann, 1973), 13.
12. Quoted by R.P. Chaddah in "A Rich Award," *The Tribune,* January 4, 1987.
13. Dorothy Blair Shimer quotes Bhattacharya claiming that "it was Tagore who convinced him that his contribution might better be made through his writing." "Gandhian influences on Bhabani Bhattacharya," *Perspectives on Bhabani Bhattacharya, op. cit.*, 22.
14. Bhabani Bhattacharya, "Indo-Anglian," *The Novel in Modern India,* 48.
15. Bhabani Bhattacharya, "Literature and Social Reality," *Perspectives on Bhabani Bhattacharya,* 5.
16. Vide Avrom Fleishman, *The English Historical Novel* (London : The John Hopkins Press, 1971), 1-3.
17. Cf. Bhattacharya's assertion about the novel. "The story was concerned with all the intensified hungers of the historic years 1942-43, not food alone; the money-hunger, the sex hunger, the hunger to achieve India's political freedom." Quoted by K.R. Chandrashekharan in *Bhabani Bhattacharya* (New Delhi : Arnold Heinemann, 1974), 31.
18. See Sumit Sarkar, *Modern India : 1885-1947* (Delhi : Macmillan, 1983), 391-92 for historical verification of this fictional presentation.
19. *Bhabani Bhattacharya,* 32.
20. See B.M. Bhatia, *Famines in India* (New York : Asia Publishing House, 1963), 321, for verification of the fictional presentation.
21. See Sarkar, 406.
22. See R.C. Majumdar, R.C. Raychaudhary and Kalinkar Dutta, *An Advanced History of India* (London : Oxford Univ. Press, 1960), 75 and Sarkar, 392-93.
23. See Bipan Chandra *et al.*, *Freedom Struggle* (New Delhi : National Book Trust, 1972), 212 and Sarkar, 375-77.
24. See Bipan Chandra, *Modern India* (New Delhi : N.C.E.R.T., 1981), 297; Sarkar, 375-77; and Bipan Chandra *et al.*, *Freedom Struggle,* 210-11.
25. For a similar account of the indecisiveness of the Congress in this phase of the freedom struggle, see Sarkar, 381.
26. For a similar account of the handling of the Quit-India Movement by the British, see Bipan Chandra, *Modern India,* 299-300 and Sarkar, 390-91.
27. *An Advanced History of India,* 75.

28. Cf. the account of the punishments given to prisoners, recorded in the diary of R.H. Niblett, the District Magistrate of Azamgarh, suspended for being 'too mild.' Quoted in Sarkar, 396.
29. For a matching account of the social composition of the Quit India agitators, see Bipan Chandra *et al.*, *Freedom Struggle,* 221. Also Sarkar, 396-98.
30. Bhabani Bhattacharya, "Indo-Anglian," *The Novel in Modern India, op. cit.*, 47. For identical views regarding the politico-historical framework of the novel, see P.P. Mehta, *Indo-Anglian Fiction : An Assessment* (Bareilly : Prakash Book Depot, 1968), 250; R.K. Badal, *Indo-Anglian Literature — An Outline* (Bareilly : Prakash Book Depot, 1975), 25 and H.M. Williams, *Indo-Anglian Literature* 1800-1970 : *A Survey* (Madras : Orient Longman, 1976), 92.
31. See Sarkar, 328.
32. Chatterjee, a lean mouse, to begin with, grew, as the temple — of which he was the *Pujari* — grew. "He bought land and his eldest son...wed the second daughter of Ganguli, the magistrate" (80). Sir Abalabandhu is not merely a rice-hoarder and black-marketeer but also the all-powerful Chairman of the Board governing the temple (125). Motichand, "a very big name in the jute business" is also a member of the Legislative Council of the state. He is accorded special privileges at the temple.
33. The women remind the constable, 'Hoosiar Singh' : "Our freedom is only a hundred days ahead" (*Gold,* 25).
34. For an account of the manner wherein Gandhi influenced the political scene in India, see Chapter II, "Indo-Anglian Novel and Political Consciousness," 20-28. For an examen of how the 'myth of Gandhi' was shaped in a predominantly illiterate society, going through a period of acute stress and strain, see Sarkar, 181-82.
35. Cf. "The Sino-Indian conflict of 1962 was restricted to a small fraction of the opposing armies; was fought in a small, remote corner of the border and lasted a mere month — with only ten actual days of fighting — and yet it is a fact that it did initiate profound changes in our international standing, domestic politics and economic progress." Brigadier J.P. Dalvi in *Himalayan Blunder,* quoted by M.J. Akbar in *India : The Siege Within* (London : Penguin, 1985), 83.
36. Cf. the account given by Gandhi himself in his *An Autobiography* (Ahmedabad : Navjivan Publishing House, 1969), 75-225 and the account given by Bhattacharya in his *Mahatma Gandhi as a Writer* (New Delhi : Arnold Heinemann, 1982), 29-97.
37. See W.H. Morris-Jones, *The Government and Politics of India,* (Bombay : B.I. Publications, 1979), 141.
38. For verification, see Brigadier J.P. Dalvi, *Himalayan Blunder* (Bombay : Thacker and Co., Ltd., 1969), 29.

39. For details of the degeneration of ideals of independent India along similar lines, see Morris-Jones, 61-64.
40. For details of political interference in Army affairs, see S.S. Khera, *India's Defence Problem* (New Delhi : Orient Longman, 1968), 70-71.
41. For the performance of the Congress in Assam and the "sordid assembly manoeuvres and floor crossings" with the help of which a Congress ministry took office there, see *Modern India,* 349-51. R.S. Singh's indictment of the 'prejudiced' presentation of history in *Combat* seems rather unwarranted against this background. See Ram Sevak Singh, "Manohar Malgonkar The Novelist," *Indian Literature,* 13, No. 1 (1970), 122-31.
42. Mulk Raj Anand's *Private Life of an Indian Prince,* the other important novel set in the milieu, is a disquieting mélange of abnormal psychology and political chronicle. See Chapter II, "Indo, Anglian Novel and Political Consciousness," 41-42. Malgonkar in *Princes* differs from both Anand and Dewan Jermani Dass (*The Maharaja*) in his presentation of princes as anything but embodiments of unalloyed evil. Obviously Malgonkar has history on his side in this respect.
43. See Sumit Sarkar, *Modern India,* 390-92.
44. See Rahul Singh, ed., *Khushwant Singh's View of India* (Bombay : IBH Publishing Co., 1982), 189-90.
45. See Sarkar, 385-88.
46. *Ibid.,* 423-25.
47. See the account of the encouragement given to such attempts by the Government of India's Political Department under Conrad Corfield, given in Sarkar, 450-51.
48. Cf. "The Congress leadership — or more precisely, Sardar Patel...tackled the situation in what had become the standard practice of the party : using popular movements as a lever to extort concessions from princes." *Ibid.,* 450.
49. See Sumit Sarkar, 451.
50. Gandhi is presented with 'a merry twinkle in his eyes,' wetting the broken thread he is spinning with saliva from his mouth. *Ganges,* 7-10.
51. See Ainslie T. Embree, *India's search for National Identity* (Delhi : Chanakya Publications, 1980), 84-86.
52. See D.G. Tendulkar, *Mahatma* (New Delhi : Publications Divn., Govt. of India, 1960), II, 55-56 and *Young India,* October 13, 1921.
53. See Bipan Chandra *et al.*, *Freedom Struggle,* 117.
54. Cf. "Official estimates...spoke of 379 killed, unofficial accounts gave much higher figures." Sumit Sarkar, 191.
55. See Sarkar, 191-92.

56. For a treatment of Malgonkar's views on the corruptability of the lower rungs of administration, mostly manned by the Indians, see Chapter VI, "The Way Out," 279-80.
57. See Sarkar, 188-90.
58. Cf. "At a Calcutta University Convocation while Sir Stanley Jackson, the new Governor of Bengal, had been presiding, he was shot at in public by a brilliant girl student of the Diocesan Women's College, Bina Das..." Bipan Chandra *et al.*, *Freedom Struggle,* 188.
59. See Sarkar, 233-37.
60. See Sarkar, 394-96.
61. See Bipan Chandra *et al.*, *Freedom Struggle,* 219-22.
62. *Ibid.*, 226-27.
63. See Akbar, *India : The Siege Within,* 30-34.
64. See Sarkar, 378-80, for historical verification of the picture painted here. Meenakshi Mukherjee's dubbing the novel "an *erratic* national calendar" (emphasis added) in *The Twice-Born Fiction* (New Delhi : Arnold-Heinemann, 1971), 61, seems rather a harsh judgement in the light of the evidence adduced herebefore.
65. See Sarkar, 437-39.
66. See Tariq Ali, *The Nehrus and the Gandhis — An Indian Dynasty* (London : Picador, 1985), 102.
67. See Dalvi, *Himalayan Blunder*, 29; B.M. Kaul, *Untold Story* (Delhi : Allied Publishers, 1967), 208; and Khera, *India's Defence Problem,* 70-71.
68. See Khushwant Singh's *We Indians* (New Delhi : Orient Paperbacks, 1982), 152.
69. For a real-life picture of Krishna Menon which meshes with the fictional projection here, see "My Days with Krishna Menon," *Khushwant Singh's India,* ed., Rahul Singh (Bombay : IBH Publishing Co., 1969), 1-33. Also see page 58 of this chapter.
70. See Kaul, *Untold Story,* 204-5; Khera, *India's Defence Problem,* 70-71, 222; and C.P. Bhambhri, *Bureaucracy and Politics in India* (Delhi : Vikas Publication, 1971), 177.
71. Nayantara Sahgal, "The Book I Enjoyed Writing Most," *Bhavan's Journal,* 20 (January 6, 1974), 41.
72. *Ibid.*
73. See W.H. Morris-Jones, *The Government and Politics of India, op. cit.*, 90-92.
74. Morris-Jones, 73.
75. Cf. "Most of this [corruption and bribery] was known to Jawaharlal. He realized that this was the price that had to be paid and concentrated his attention on what he believed were more pressing matters." Tariq Ali,

The Nehrus and the Gandhis — An Indian Dynasty (London : Picador, 1985), 88.

75. See Morris-Jones, 95.
77. See Tariq Ali, 163-65.
78. See Morris-Jones, 206.
79. For the Indian political scene after the Congress-split, see Tariq Ali, 165-68.
80. *Ibid.,* 169.
81. For an account of the Naxalbari incidents and the Government reaction, see Tariq Ali, 178-80.
82. For details along similar lines, see Sarkar, 384-85.
83. For the political affiliations of the erstwhile refugees, see Tariq Ali, 80.
84. For Feroz Gandhi's crusading role in exposing corruption, especially in the "Mundhra Affair," see Lok Sabha debates, November 9, 1957, columns 2886-89, December 16, 1957, column 5741, 5748 quoted in C.P. Bhambri, *Bureaucracy and Politics in India, op. cit.*, 114, 115.
85. See the autobiography of the novelist's mother Vijay Lakshmi Pandit, *The Scope of Happiness* (Delhi : Orient Paperbacks, 1981), 56-59.
86. For details of Kairon's political profile see G.S. Bhargava, *After Nehru* (New Delhi : Allied Publishers, 1966), 243-46. Also Kuldip Nayar, *India After Nehru* (Delhi : Vikas, 1975), 199 and C.P. Bhambhri, 20-21.
87. Tariq Ali, 183-84.
88. *Ibid.,* 188-92.
89. See Darbara Singh, *Indian Politics* (Delhi : Sandeep Prakashan, 1978), 60-61.
90. See Mary C. Carras, *Indira Gandhi — In the Crucible of Leadership* (Bombay : Jaico, 1976), 205-6.
91. See Darbara Singh, 78.
92. Letter dated November 15, 1981.
93. *Ibid.*
94. Nayantara Sahgal, *Voice for Freedom* (New Delhi : Hind Pocket Books, 1979), 51-52.
95. *Ibid.,* 52.
96. Sahgal, *Voice for Freedom,* 64.
97. *Ibid.,* 12.
98. *Ibid.*
99. *Ibid.,* 62.
100. *Ibid.*
101. *Ibid.* 18.

102. G.P. Sharma, *Nationalism in Indo-Anglian Fiction, op. cit.*, 272.
103. Nayantara Sahgal, *Voice for Freedom,* 57.
104. *Ibid.*
105. *Ibid.,* 58-59.
106. *Ibid.,* 14.
107. Sahgal, *Voice for Freedom,* 100.
108. Nayantara Sahgal, "The Book I Enjoyed Writing Most," *Bhavan's Journal, op. cit.*, 41-42.
109. Sahgal, *Voice for Freedom,* 20.
110. "Telling of Time Past," *The Hindustan Times Weekly,* March 15, 1981.
111. William Walsh in his review in *Encounter, October* 1964, 82.
112. Major C.L. Proudfoot, in a letter to Malgonkar quoted by G.S. Amur, in *Manohar Malgonkar, op. cit.*, 57.
113. Malgonkar himself mentions how the account could be of any of the battalions of the 17th Indian Division. *Drum,* 6.
114. *Edinburgh Magazine,* June, 1961.
115. Michael Wilding, *Political Fictions* (London : Routledge & Kegan Paul, 1980), 10.
116. Cf. "It is the great novelists above all who give us our social history; compared with what is done in their work — their creative work — the histories of the professional social historian seem empty and unenlightening." F.R. Leavis, *Lectures in America* (New York : Doubleday, 1969), 7.

□□□

4

The Contours of A Crippling Creed

ONE OF the main aspects of the works of Indian English novelists in general and Bhabani Bhattacharya, Manohar Malgonkar and Nayantara Sahgal in particular is their concern with religion and religious attitudes which, they believe, go a long way to explain both the personal predicaments and the political plight of people. The acute political consciousness with which their novels are imbued makes them go beyond a mere chronicling of the political scenario to probe into what conditions people's political reflexes. An important component of their political consciousness is the awareness of religion as a motivating force of action or otherwise. However, to understand and evaluate the role of Hinduism and religious consciousness in the social and political context, we have to look at Hinduism, the dominant creed which has influenced the ethos of the land, in a wide perspective, both historical and contemporary.

Hinduism defies definition. The word 'Hindu' doesn't appear in any of the original scriptures of the Hindus. Whereas in Christianity and Islam, truths are believed to have been revealed in a defined form by God to a particular person at a particular time and place, in Hinduism religious truths were realized and expressed through a gradual process of reflection by many individuals spanning over centuries. Through ages of gradual evolution, a wide spectrum of beliefs and rituals, ranging from primitive animism through polytheism to lofty, abstract philosophical monism, have got assimilated into the body of Hinduism. The idea of godhood is indefinable in Hinduism. Thus creeds or cults from whatever source are taken to be divine manifestations complementing each other, all oriented to the infinity of truth and the well-being of mankind, and hence deserving of admiration and reverence. The basic truth of Hindu religious evolution is : Truth is one, its statements many, each one open-ended but pointing to an ascending order of experience and apprehension. In relation to doctrinal religions such as Islam or Christianity, Hinduism is vague. But in spite of its doctrinal vagueness, Hinduism does postulate certain key concepts. At the root of Hindu metaphysics lies the idea of *Brahman, i.e.,* an eternal, infinite, immanent and transcendent cosmic reality which embraces the forms of the abundant variety of beings in the universe.[1] Man is an intelligent part of the variety of cosmic reality. As against the one Eternity, this variety is existent, mutable, mortal and *maya* — from the absolute point of view. The return of the human spirit to the Absolute by way of *moksha* lies in realizing and merging the identity of the individual self with the Cosmic Self and it is towards the attainment of this goal that the whole life is oriented. *Moksha* is attained by transcending the world of change through active but detached contemplative living and religious practice which help man to awaken to his true origin and rise to his nature. *Moksha* also means rising from a state of ignorance (*avidya*) to knowledge (*vidya*) and realization of the Infinite and the Eternal.[2] In this pursuit, what is desirable is a deep introspective experience of the individual's oneness with the Absolute.

Closely allied to the idea of man's return to the Absolute is the doctrine of the cycle of rebirths (*samsara*). By the sixth century B.C., belief in metempsychosis had developed into the doctrine of the transmigration of soul and the law of *karma* (literally 'deed'); the law that one's next life is a causal extension of one's deeds performed in the past and present lives. All living beings are thus deemed to be self-trapped in the eternal cycle of birth, death and rebirth (*punarjanma*) until *moksha* is attained through intelligent action and meditation. The universe and its subsystems including human society were seen as organic wholes in which each *jati* (on the cosmic plane a form of life, on the social plane a class or community) has a specific task (*dharma*) to perform. Only in the faithful, dispassionate performance (*nishkam karma*) of this duty can an individual acquire merit and a higher station in the next life.

However, it is the popular practice of Hinduism rather than the standard version of its core which gets reflected in the responses of particular persons in specific situations in different phases of Indian history. The two often differ very substantially and for that reason Milton Singer thought it fit to organize the diversity found in Hinduism along a continuum ranging from 'Sanskritic Hinduism' to 'Popular Hinduism.'[3] S.C. Dube in his pioneering anthropological work on the actual practice of the faith points out :

> Hinduism...as it is practised is not the Hinduism of the classical philosophical systems of India, for it possesses neither the metaphysical heights nor the abstract content of the latter.[4]

The popular practice of Hinduism in the earlier stages came to value the inherent flexibility and inclusivism of the pristine creed on the one hand, and the other-worldly attitude on the other. But the orderliness of its social organization slowly gave rise to community stratification so that in course of time the *status quo* assumed a sort of divine sanction. Consequently temporal distress got mystified into supernatural ordinance with a distortion of priorities between action and sufferance. What is true of popular Hinduism is true of most of the religions belonging to what can be termed as the Hindu family of religions, which includes Jainism, Buddhism, Sikhism and Hinduised-Islam. While the religions belonging to the Hebraic family of religions, embracing the Jewish, Christian and the Muslim faiths, lay greater stress on man's duty towards other men, the Hindu family of religions lay greater stress on man's duty towards himself and the individual's God, and both usually were subsumed under the concept of the individual's duty to "the inner self."[5] Hence later, especially since the medieval times, the otherworldliness, evasiveness, the instinct to regard the real as illusory, fatalism, smug acquiescence, inaction, patient wait for an *avatar,* self-centredness, discrimination and, as the extension of discrimination, even exploitation.

How far has Hinduism affected the adherents' potential for action, initiative and enterprise has engaged the attention of quite a few discerning observers of the social scene. Max Weber,[6] while attempting to explain the difference in rates of economic growth in Europe and in the great civilizations of the East, finds an answer in the fundamental difference in the religious creeds of the people. While the Reformation and Protestantism in Europe fostered economic competition and development, Hinduism led to essentially negative effects. However, it was the spirit of the whole system, rather than the particular rituals of Hinduism which, according to Weber, inhibited entrepreneurship and endeavour. This 'spirit' Weber found in the Hindu concepts of *samsara, karma, dharma* and *moksha.* A host of sociological studies have corroborated Weber's findings in this respect. Nair,[7] Kapp[8], Saran,[9] and Eisenstadt[10] attribute the lack of enterprise among Hindus to their traditional rejection of economic incentives. Such motivations, by being characterized as nothing more than materialistic, are ignored. Among other causes are listed lack of achievement motivation and lack of 'the killer instinct.' Elder[11] found Hindus less in control of the empirical and social events in their lives and less motivated to achieve than Muslims and Christians though he found Muslims and Christians to be no less fatalistic here. Though Fliegel and his associates found in a social survey that the notion of fatalism was more a method of rationalizing past failures than a determinant of present behaviour,[12] even this rather limited scope of fatalism would affect an individual's inherent ability to act. We meet many such characters in the novels of Bhabani Bhattacharya, Manohar Malgonkar and Nayantara Sahgal.

Bhattacharya, Malgonkar and Sahgal repeatedly find their characters inhibited in acting decisively and responsibly in all walks of life, private or public. These novelists seek to relate this self-imposed helplessness to the inadequate creed that these people live by. In diverse ways, religion affects human action, and, far from becoming a creed of action, Hinduism becomes a creed of negation.[13] At times, in the hands of the unscrupulous, it becomes a tool of exploitation.

Bhattacharya, Malgonkar and Sahgal trace the root cause of the people's fettered political existence to the inadequacies of their faith as it is practised. By breeding escapist or indifferent attitudes to the pressures of the present, Hinduism becomes an ally of exploiters — social, economic and political. It is proposed to examine here some such attitudes presented in the novels under study and to see how far they inhibit action in the political field.

Hinduism in its essence is "neither a creed nor a religion but a way of life sprung from the soil, the stones, the mountains and the rivers of India" (*Morning,* 25). Religion in this sense reflects in every aspect of life in India. There would have been nothing improper about this pervasive influence of Hinduism, if it had been less of a philosophers' religion and more of the ordinary human beings', if the popular practice of it hadn't fostered a number of contradictions and anomalies.

Trivedi in *Storm* is disturbed by the amorphousness of Hinduism, its "lack of definition." The abstract nature of the creed encompasses "baffling uncertainty"; it is "boundless enough" to incorporate mutually exclusive virtues within it. "You could not accept [popular] Hinduism in its entirety without harbouring ignorance and superstition too" (*Morning,* 42). There are "two opposite tendencies that create the pattern of Indian life : a forthright sensuality existing side by side with a stark and stoic resignation" (*Happy,* 164). Similarly other opposing tendencies exist side by side : violence and non-violence, materialism and spiritualism, acquisition and sacrifice, enjoyment and abnegation.[14] As the narrator in *Happy* explains, the central philosophy of *Karma* itself can be seen as encouraging passivity if man's present life is seen as the result of his past actions.[15] However, the doctrine can also be taken as a challenge for it is within human capability to shape a better future (*Happy,* 161).

The philosophic but non-specific nature of Hinduism made it easy for priests to pervert it down the ages. Sahgal believes that religious leaders are squarely to blame for deliberately trying to confuse issues by equating caste with *karma* and investing this mode of stratification with divine sanctity. This confusion made the Hindus resign themselves to their fate and made mockery of "the Hindu view of evolutionary development with the good life, constructively lived as its central purpose."[16]

In a society characterized by widespread ignorance and illiteracy, with fatalistic and other-worldly attitudes, religion becomes a tool of exploitation. *Rich* suggests how the priests came to their own as middlemen between the people and the mysterious, divine power (127-28). Self-appointed seers and interpreters have a vested interest in perpetuating themselves. That explains why they dole out superstition, fatalism and other opiates to consolidate their hegemony. How priests can market religiosity in a business-like manner and prosper at the believers' expense is aptly suggested in the growth of Chatterjee, "a lean mouse," "the poorest Brahmin in the community" (*Tiger,* 80). It was made out that "the great god...spoke to him [Chatterjee] at night." He started a temple. The temple grew and Chatterjee grew with it. "He bought land and his son...wed the second daughter of Ganguli, the magistrate of the district" (80). Here is a classic case of what C.D. Narsimhaiah has termed in his study of *Kanthapura* as the 'cultural elite' transforming itself into the 'governing elite.'[17]

Kalo in *Tiger* reveals another aspect of the abuse of religion. Biten tells him how anybody in a saffron loin-cloth, with his body smeared with ash and a red-paste trident of Shiva on his forehead would have his alms bowl filled in no time (40). Kalo plans to make a "milch-cow of religion" (41). He has a fake Shiva idol installed and he himself becomes Mangal Adhikari, the priest. The way he conducts himself reveals the changes the rebel in him has undergone. He humiliates and silences the owner of the land where the temple is being built unauthorizedly by referring to the landowner's low-birth. Thus he puts the owner straightaway on the defensive (88). He exploits "the clash of interests among the great ones, their mutual jealousies and hatreds" (136). He masters the art of coming out with economic strategies of adding to the temple's income.

In *Tiger,* Bhattacharya uses religion as an instrument of social revenge. Kalo is transformed from a rebel to an exploiter who sides with his erstwhile tormentors to defeat them at their own game. As a priest, Kalo has to patronize unscrupulous businessmen and exploiters such as Motichand and Sir Abalabandhu, for without their patronage the temple can't be established, nor without such business tactics, can it be run effectively. Once the temple is established, such men have to be paid back in the same coin by being accorded a place at the top in the hierarchy of believers. Kalo plays this game of commercial religion with more than the customary élan for "the counterfeit coin needed more glitter than the real" (*Tiger,* 115).

So much do Mangal Adhikari and the commercial instinct dominate in Kalo that his mission of revenge upon the self-styled saviours of faith fades into the background. This end-displacement strays Kalo so much from his mission that Biten, his mentor, has to ask him pointedly if "there was in the fraud no purpose larger than filling your own belly and your purse?" (*Tiger,* 191).

Religion is used even to counteract political urges. Sir Abalabandhu reveals the unholy nexus between unscrupulous businessmen, toadying to the alien rulers, and the priests using religion to quell discontent. It is not insignificant to note that at the time of the *yagna* before the installation of Kalo's daughter as the Mother of the Sevenfold Bliss, the pavilion was reserved for guests of rank which included black-marketeers, hoarders and Motichand, a speculator and a member of the State Legislative Council. For their comfort, "thick cotton *satrenji* woven on handlooms in the city's central jail was spread all over" (*Tiger,* 234), the jail having been packed with poor, hungry protesters for food. Sir Abalabandhu had used business tactics to 'sell' Kalo's daughter as the Mother. He had used his paper, *Swadesh* to float false stories about her mystic powers. Motichand now plans to marry her so as to make "a partnership of her divine role and continue it together" (*Tiger,* 235). Religion, obviously comes in handy for the realization of the nefarious power-aspirations of men like these.

Through a rigid stratification along caste lines, religion facilitates discrimination and the exploitation of those lower down the hierarchical order.[18] Jhanak in *Ladakh* and Kalo in *Tiger* feel the sordidness of this inhumanity. Kalo's daughter, despite her brilliance, is "still a *Kamar's* daughter" (5). It was only because of the old Mission lady that she could be admitted to the school. Kalo, a mute witness to the blind prejudices against the low-born, vows to fight "the centuries-old tradition from which had come the inner climate of his being" (71). He had not only to "deny but to eradicate the values by which he had been bred" (71). However, once he enters the fold, he too thinks that by accepting him, a *Kamar,* as the priest, and a fake Shiva idol, people would be "committing sacrilege and desecrating caste sanctity" (161-62). Interestingly, Kalo himself unconsciously bows to the callous logic of social stratification. As Mangal Adhikari, he subscribes to the same meaningless discrimination which he had set out to demolish. He gives his daughter a suitable horoscope showing "the star conjunction of a girl of high Brahmin birth" (179-80). The only reservation he has against Biten, whom his daughter loves and would like to marry, is that he is not a Brahmin. Rather than rebel against the religious discrimination and exploitation, he comes out with patchwork solutions within the system. He plans to float the idea that only the rich devotees would be required to make offerings (186). Even his daughter, Lekha, realizes how "instead of undermining society by challenging the age-old system of caste-stratification, he had become part of it" (221).

Popular Hinduism emphasizes not merely self-denial and austerity but also an unhealthy distrust of enjoyment, self-fulfilment and pleasure. Satyajit's Gandhigram subscribes to this creed of self-denial by which people are made to live. Any deviation from the pattern is termed vice. Bhaskar, the votary of modernism, is given by his creator an insight into what ails Gandhigram and, by implication, India at large.

> Vice in this country lay choked in taboos, inhibitions — the rickety props of spiritual India. (*Ladakh*, 57)

Bhaskar also comes to realize how Hinduism makes people lackadaisical, uninvolved and uninterested in what happens to them or to those around them. "A zest for living — *that* was vice" (emphasis in original) (*Ladakh*, 57). Consequently, the youthful ones were looked at with suspicion. They were called 'impulsive.' "In India you came of age when you reached your fiftieth year" (*Ladakh*, 56). Ramkishan, in *Shadow*, realizes how such a negative attitude marks the disuse of one's best self. Making of renunciation a prized virtue means turning an individual into "a sadhu with his arms held above his head until they could never be lowered again. It was eyes blindfolded until they lost their sight" (175).

Bhattacharya, in *Tiger*, reveals how by exhorting people to sacrifice themselves for some cause, unscrupulous procurers can even ask women to sell themselves to save their kinsfolk from the famine :

> What virtue is greater than self-giving for a true cause? Does not all our tradition sing the great glory of self-giving? Saving their dear kinsfolk from a terrible doom — there could be no higher cause — those young women will attain glory (38).

Motichand, in the same novel, exploits his wives by arousing their inborn instinct for self-abnegation and forcing them to live away from him. He could then marry again.

Hindus view life as part of a continuum. It puts them in a frame of mind which makes them seek answers to their present problems in terms of either the past or the future. Mona, in *Rich*, rather than blaming her husband for marrying again, resorts to "calling upon the Almighty to spell out what she had done in this or past lives to deserve such outrageous treatment" (54). The villagers in Behula in *Music* let a dangerous crocodile thrive in Shiva's pond for they believe that it is a "devotee of Shiva" and that it was "a Brahmin in a pre-birth, apparently doomed by his *karma* to brute form" (155).

The account of the sati of Comor, taken from the file of Sonali's father in *Rich*, reveals how "this victim of superstition" had committed that act of self-immolation under the belief that "the present…[was] the third time of her soul's reincarnation" and that "she would be recompensed…hereafter" (126). Rather than demolishing the system which facilitates their exploitation, Kajoli's mother prays that the punishment should be hers alone if Kajoli and her brother, Onu, are "guilty of wrongs in past lives" (*Hungers*, 202). Jasoda blames her barrenness on the sins which she must have committed in her past life rather than her husband who deserts her (*Tiger*, 141). Abhay's mother in *Princes* attributes her desertion by her husband to her destiny, 'the slipping of a star' (173). Prabha Mathur has reconciled herself to the second marriage of her husband, muttering, "Everything depends on Providence." She uses the Hindi word '*honhar*' which means "what must be" must be (*Happy*, 201). The same defeatist logic is employed by Biten's parents in *Tiger* to explain the suicide of their daughter, though they were themselves squarely to blame for causing it. They had married her off forcibly to an aged widower with children and grandchildren. When she drowned herself in a well, they attributed it to their *karma*, "the fruit of sins they had committed in life or in a past life" (169). The same resignation prevails among the villagers in *Combat*. A rogue-elephant has run amok and killed a number of people. Rather than doing something to nab it, the fatalistic people regard the animal as a god and believe :

> …its victims were sure to have committed some unforgivable sins during their previous lives and [therefore they] were being punished in this one (75).

Obviously, opposing and killing this elephant, a reckless killer, is deemed sacrilegious.

It is easy to see how fatalistic and superstitious beliefs render people vulnerable to social and political exploitation. Seth Shamsunder in *Gold* exploits people's faith in *punarjanma* and the theory of *karma* to make out that Meera's grandfather is the reincarnation of Atmaram, a devoted disciple of a yogi (110). The Seth and Meera are partners in making gold out of copper with the help of the Grandpa's *taveej*. People's faith in Grandpa and the *taveej* would help the Seth not merely economically but also politically for he plans to contest the elections soon. Kalo, as Mangal Adhikari, in *Tiger*, can consolidate his hegemony over the credulous only by means of the "Brahminic lore" he has imbibed. All worldly suffering is "the fire of punishment," for "there is no faith in our hearts" (119). A trader in Kalo's village had said, "God has sent this mighty hunger [the 1943 Bengal famine] to teach the low-born people a true lesson" (16). Now Kalo's verdict as a priest is that the famine is "the fire of punishment" for "purification" (119). All this is highly ironical and Bhattacharya exposes scathingly the use of religion as a means of exploitation. There was a ring of sincerity in what Kalo had realized before his 'fall': "The real evil doers seemed untouched by *karma*; they ate well and spoke the name of Shiva and the name of Rama and slept in beds of peace and comfort" (120).

Popular Hinduism breeds attitudes which make one reconciled to the *status quo*.[19] One comes across attitudes which sap initiative and ignore the role of the individual in the scheme of things. Ram Kishan in *Shadow* realizes sadly how millions have missed the lesson of non-attachment, interpreting it to be a submission to fate. When he watches Simrit in the role of a victim, he bemoans the fact that it is resignation not resistance which comes easily to the Hindu mind. Gobind Narain in *Happy* "clung...tenaciously to his comforts" (15), ignoring vital issues like racial discrimination which had affected his own daughter (56). Savitri Sahai brushes aside the colonial exploitation of India by alien rulers to find some vague pride in the fact that "the realm of the spirit continues inviolate, soaring above the crushed hopes…" (188). Even the murder of her son, Sahdev, by a Tommy fails to arouse her. Her only comment is fatalistic : "Each man can live only to his appointed hour" (192). Similar is the reaction of Kajoli's mother to Kishor's incarceration during the movement for freedom : "Poor boy! Five hard months in the jail-house! It is Fate's writing…" (84).

A passive view of religion forestalls soul-searching and self-questioning, for those who succumb to their vulnerabilities through their passive conduct shelter behind the excuse that it is their fate. Neeri's mother explains Neeri's selling herself to ward off starvation by lifting her hand to her forehead, saying, "The lines here" (*Hungers*, 129). In *Tiger*, a procuress comes to fetch Lekha with a false message about her father's accident. The old aunt sends her, "trusting her to her fate" (64).

The persistent obduracy with which Hindus in general ignore individual initiative and attribute everything to fate is remarkably displayed in the manner in which the Seth in *Gold*, belittles the role of Meera in saving his son from drowning in a well. "Everything is worked out by fate. Nago could not die before his time. The star-conjunctions give him a fairly long life. Those women were the tools of fate" (45). The honourable decision reached by Kajoli by herself that she would work hard to make a living and never sell herself is attributed by womenfolk to her fate. "What fate Bhagwan! A golden lotus wasting in mud and filth" (*Hungers*, 188).

One who regards human beings as "toys and tools of Fate, tied by the writing on the brow" would do nothing but call himself 'luckless' if he "turns thirsty eyes on a full stream and lo! the stream goes dry" (*Music*, 49). The firm conviction in such persons is that for mortals "there is no escape from one's wheel of destiny. Even a guru must accept the fruit of his *karma*" (*Hawaii*, 95). The Behula Mother warns Mohini, "Let the scrawl of destiny be ever in your mind" (*Music*, 145) for "who can see what lies round the future's bend?" The warning indicates destructive passivity reducing one to the stage where one can do nothing but wait for "the crumbs fate will throw" (39). It is this tendency to resign to one's fate which breeds passivity, apathy and unconcern.

Unaccustomed to think for themselves and move out of the grooves of tradition, the people have got accustomed to accepting blindly whatever is around them, be that the insensitivity of husband or the corruption of a Chief Minister as their destiny. Vishal in *Storm* feels that the worst part of the tragedy in Chandigarh was the apathy of the people. "The problem was not even that there was a crisis, but that people now took it for granted" (75). Vishal in fact, saw in Chandigrah "the funeral march of Hinduism" (92). "The Hindu race — mute acquiescent, letting things happen to it, from a country to the mind and body of a woman" (*Shadow*, 37).

Typical Hindu apathy is seen as the root cause of suffering at both the personal and the public levels. Sahgal describes the two levels. She makes 'critical insiders' like Ram Kishan and Simrit and 'objective outsiders' like the Christian Raj see through the superficial façade. Raj is sceptical of the capability of Hindus to oppose evil in the political or personal realm. "What did people like Shah or Simrit believe in? What if anything would they fight to defend? (*Shadow*, 145). They simply represent acquiescence in the face of evil, political and personal. Vishal in *Storm* bemoans "the absence of the courage to hold up what we call sacred to light and examine it to throw it away, if necessary" (92). He feels exasperated with the situation where "no one was enthused about anything. People functioned without spirit" (72). Raj in *Shadow* reveals his insight when he tells Simrit: "The type [the religion of] ours produces doesn't face up. It puts problems into cold storage" (233-34).

It is resignation, inertia and paralysis that Vishal comes across in Chandigarh where everybody seems to be waiting masochistically for hell to break loose. "This was not a taut situation. One could come to grips with a stir, an aspiration of some kind — and there had been plenty of those — but what could one do with paralysis?" (41). Unscrupulous politicians like Gyan Singh, the Chief Minister of Punjab, unabashedly exploit this passivity ruthlessly by spreading a cult of violence. There is awareness of the nefarious designs of such demagogues in a significant section of the people but they do nothing. They wait for the situation to correct itself. They are passively waiting, as they "waited for the rains, for the harvest, for the birth of unwanted children, for death" (*Storm*, 6).

In the face of passivity, Rishad and his revolutionary friends discover to their chagrin how the theory of revolt against circumstances is utterly irrelevant. Neither the quarry workers nor the farmers feel worked up against their lot. They wait, "rooted to their patches of soil, for the rain to come...." Rishad realizes "to stir, to break and rebuild that mentality was beyond him and his group" (*Situation*, 68). The student from Nehru University, incarcerated during the Emergency, has much the same to say of his experience with peasants in Bihar (*Rich*, 180). They had been so much used to accepting everything doled out to them as their destiny that it never crossed their mind that they could, by organizing themselves, demand something. Bhattacharya's explanation of this riddle, when he is faced by the starving destitutes, in *Hungers*, is that the people have their "hands menacled with their antique moral tradition. The rice robbers were safe from peril because of the peasants' tradition" (111).

Far from being a credo of hope and action, faith in India pushes the people down to passivity and subservience. Looking up to the gods for divine benediction often leads to passivity, acquiescence and bowing to whatever is meted out to one in life. In *Rich*, Sahgal explains how fatalism comes to be the final answer to all the questions with its 'irrefutable iron logic.' When Sonali's father sought to explain to the family barber that drought is caused not by a curse but by lack of rain, pat came the question : "What makes lack of rain?" When it was explained that rainfall was dependent on certain atmospheric conditions, the query was still the same : "What causes those?" until the smug conclusion was unilaterally agreed upon : "There was definitely a Reason which chose to bless or to punish"[20] (127).

Biten's father is waiting for the "new *Avatar*...the Supreme one's eleventh reincarnation in earth-form" (*Tiger*, 165) to sort out the mess he himself has created. To the people suffering the excesses of the English rule, Hitler appeared to be "the new *avatar*," "the saviour with his short moustache and staring eyes" (*Ganges*, 174). He would do for them what they couldn't do themselves, that is, save them from the foreign yoke. Towards the close of *Tiger*, the Brahmins are outraged by "the godless *kamar* who had made a mockery of the Supreme deity," But they very well know that his punishment "would have to come from the divine hand" (244).

Belief in the overseeing gods makes Hari await "Shiva's *kaul*" to know if he should appeal against the court verdict. "If the flower falls to the right, we should appeal, if it falls to the left, we should give up" (*Ganges*, 43). A similar spiritualism paralyses Lekha's Old Aunt in *Tiger* :

> What evil destiny had broken up their home? Old Aunt had tried to avert it by puja and prayer. She rose long before, sunrise, sat cross-legged on a little carpet of scented Kusa grass and spoke the prayers, all her spirit crying for mercy to the gods in heaven. She had even brought incense at the price of the day's meal, for the gods would readily bless a home where the sweet-smelling sticks were burned (58).

The saffron-robed Buddhist monk, Sanghamitra, in *Ladakh*, had his eyes closed in prayer after reading the shocking account of the Chinese attack on India "as though prayer would change its content" (3). Another vignette of patient wait for the gods to descend, is, ironically enough, a crowd of hungry people looking with hopeful expectation at the fake Shiva installed by Kalo, the *kamar*. "Would not the Coming bring them relief? Perhaps the great God was rising out of the Earth to put an end to the misery of the land?" (*Tiger*, 81).

One aspect of this passivity is the break into impulsive action. "Hinduism couldn't be turned into action at all, worse, it could become inhuman action" (*Shadow*, 13). In *Situation*,

Usman, the Muslim Vice-Chancellor of Delhi University, and an 'objective outsider,' finds an inherent duality in the basic moral of the *Bhagwad Gita*. The performance of duty in a detached manner could evoke the best in man. However, it could also lead to the most brutal and inhuman action (78-79). Usman opines that the unchannelized energies of the young, shorn of constructive guidance which their faith could have accorded them, lead them inevitably to impulsive, often violent action. "They'll storm into buildings, stab and rape on campus and kill Vice-Chancellors because they're so bored" (78). Vishal in *Storm* bemoans the fact that "either we sit paralysed waiting for heaven to send us a sign or we charge like bulls into the ring and call it action" (79).

It is a cruel dilemma : those who are good-intentioned are inert and cannot achieve anything worth-while, while those who act, do so in a thoughtless and violent way. This dilemma is acted out in *Storm* in the virtuous inaction of Saroj (who has to be coaxed out of Inder's hold) and of Harpal (who is aware of a feeling of withdrawal in his own self and a sense of frustration) and in the vicious action of Inder and Gyan. It would certainly bode ill for society at large, for both rank opportunism and servile conformism corrode social and individual needs and aspirations.

In the stagnant imagination of people, smug under the crux of passivity, anybody who breaks that shell and assumes control of the situation, gets invested with a divine halo irrespective of what he stands for.[21] It certainly is an ironical distortion of *Bhagwad Gita* that rather than setting their house in order themselves, under the impact of their faith, Hindus become "nostalgic for kings, or charismatic leaders" (*Situation*, 22). If they are lucky, they may have visionaries like Shivraj with "an imperial touch" (*Situation*, 48) or, may be, "the young idol on his white horse who had led Indians in a pledge of Independence on a river bank in Lahore" (*Rich*, 157) or "the man in the loin-cloth who had urged, "Let's free ourselves without the barrel of a gun" (*Rich*, 157). But a community cannot bank on luck alone. Craving for gods might as well breed tyrants. *Rich* illustrates this possibility most poignantly. During the Emergency regime, the

PM is termed "a many-armed goddess." She forms with "her father, and her son, a regular Holy Trinity" for the people (155). This deification fulfils an internal need of the Indian psyche as is shown by the way Nishi reacts to the imposition of the Emergency.

> The idea of a Leader, someone to look up to, made her pulse beat faster, fulfilled a yearning for tidiness.... (*Rich*, 73).

In the face of 'divine' dispensation which makes people feel safe, the only reaction can be conformism. The delegations of teachers, lawyers, school-children which went everyday to the PM to congratulate her for declaring Emergency and the group of intellectuals — a chief editor, a professor from Delhi University and a lawyer — in their sophistic justification of "the dictatorship around us" (82) reveal a significant cross-section of Indian society rendered spineless by its faith. Malgonkar presents such conformism in Sarkar Babu (*Combat*) who doesn't protest even when he is superseded by an untrained teacher at the school. Winton, the tea-estate manager, feels confident because of this conformism :

> Oh, yes; Sarkar was going to be dead easy to deal with. He was the typical babu; grinning, servile, grovelling, almost dog-like; he was the ideal Indian subordinate, the kind of man who was totally incapable of thinking in terms of hitting back — in the last analysis, the kind of man on whom the business of the Empire rested (76).

Winton is proved absolutely correct in his appraisal of Sarkar Babu. Malgonkar reports the latter's reaction when his much-belated promotion does materialise : "Sahib is *bhery* kind" (152). Shafi in *Ganges* has this inborn conformism in mind when he terms Hindus "pacifists at heart" and "soft" (296). What he actually implies is 'compromisers,' *i.e.,* lovers of peace in the sense that they would put up with anything.

Not only is spineless conformism indicted, even the blind faith that gods will whatever happens is exposed as debilitating. Despite the shock which Kalo administers to his audience towards the close of *Tiger,* when he confesses all, the people see the unseen hand of God in all this. They believe that it is God who has "forced the blacksmith to vomit his foul confession" (244). They also come to the specious conclusion that the punishment to Kalo will also come from God. They themselves don't have to do anything about it. Such paralysing faith in gods is effectively rebutted by Bhattacharya in *Tiger* itself. This is how he reports the reaction of gods to the fervent prayers of the famished :

> For days and months, they [the starvelings] had prayed hard, prayed to all the gods in temples and in heaven. The gods would not listen. They would not even bless the slow-dying with death's quick thunderbolt (23).

Gian realizes sadly in *Ganges* how despite all the elaborate *mahapoojas,* "the god of the Little House" — a Shiva idol — "had been powerless to save it from destruction" (165). Gian's brother and grandmother look up to Shiva to save them from being exploited by a combination of feudalists and corrupt and in-human bureaucracy. The net result is the murder of Hari, Gian's brother, and later the confiscation of their movable and immovable property. The aged grandmother is left to die, shelterless and helpless. Malgonkar underscores the futility of an exclusive reliance on gods most trenchantly as he presents the gods totally unmoved, immobile at the sight of the communal frenzy unleashed by Shafi and his goons (338). A similar realization of gods not being there to intervene on behalf of the suffering and the humble ones is presented by Bhattacharya through the questioning of Old Aunt in *Tiger;* she had devoted hours to *puja,* spending money extravagantly out of her frugal means on the "emblems of worship." "But where were the gods?" (58).

It would be pertinent to comment on one aspect of Malgonkar's treatment of this popular belief in gods. With his prerogative as an omniscient narrator, he presents, at times, events in such a sequence that they reinforce some popular convictions like belief in fate, in gods, etc.[22] By way of a flash-back, Malgonkar relates the hardships heaped on Gian's grand-parents,

Dada and Aji, at the Big House. Aji was subjected to blatant discrimination, for she was of the weaver caste. Then comes the following :

> Damodar's wife, the one who had rejected Aji's cotton wicks for the lamp in the prayer room, acquired some wasting disease (38).

The narration would leave one in no doubt that the suffering was no coincidence. It was justice doled out by gods. In a similar vein is this explanation given in *Princes* for the disintegration of the princely states : "The fate that overtook the Indian princes was ordained" (280). The underlying fatalism would not leave one unaffected.

There is an overpowering instinct among Hindus to brush aside the real as illusory, especially if it happens to be unpalatable. "The Hindus have such a fully developed assurance that everything will always be as it was, for ever and ever, amen" (*Shadow*, 19). Whatever disturbs this smug complacence is dubbed unreal. "The whole tumultuous, actual world," according to Hindus is an illusion. "Even your hand was not your hand, your pain was not your pain in that indisputable, flawless monstrous logic" (*Shadow,* 105). Such an attitude doesn't lead to the facing of any problem. It rather leads to evasion. Tek Chand in *Ganges* feels a persistent urge to escape from the scene of communal frenzy unleashed by Shafi and his murderous goons even though his own family is at the mercy of the hired assassins. This is how he rationalizes this evasion :

> I have had a good life and a full life, and it would be improper for me to go on hanging on to it — indecent, almost, according to our philosophy. At my stage in life, a man should be prepared to turn his back on *sansar* — the involvement of the world... (347).

It is this instinct to evade the issues which makes Satyajit attribute the Chinese incursion into Indian territory to merely a misunderstanding on maps (*Ladakh,* 24). "Must we see an evil motive [in the Chinese action of advancing into Indian territory]?" Satyajit wonders.

The refusal to see and face evil is termed "the ostrich syndrome" by Swami Yogananda in *Hawaii* (33). Sonali in *Rich* reads in the MSS of her grandfather how his whole faith in Hinduism was shaken by this evasiveness implicit in the faith. His mother was forced to perform *sati* and all his and her suffering would be termed illusory in Hindu thought.

> If the universe is an illusion, and eternity is a split second, and there are eternities of life to come, then in terms of the cosmos, my mother's agony is nothing. And all suffering is nothing. But it is that twitch of time in the cosmos when I saw her there, when I would have given my life to drag her out of the fire, and killed those about me who had consigned her to it, that I want explained. And if evil has led us to where we stand then the ground beneath our feet...is far from firm (136).

By camouflaging the real under a façade of *maya,* the unscrupulous exploit the gullible and, at times, individuals also deceive themselves. It is this "antique tradition" of neglecting what the senses perceive to focus on what lies beyond the senses that we find in Kajoli too. It deadens Kajoli's consciousness of her being criminally assaulted. "She walked on as in heavy sleep, led by the other's will, barely aware, for her body was a bit of a rag to cover her soul, and the rag was of no account, a mere encumbrance" (*Hungers*, 150).

This sense of illusion breeds in the people "a conspiracy of silence" on the political plane. Sonali in *Rich* explains why people in India accepted even the repressive regime during the Emergency : "We are blind from birth, born of parents blind from birth. We do not see what we do not want to, and when we cannot avoid a nasty sight it still can't do much to hurt us" (25). Sonali believes that it was her Hindu upbringing which had given her this insularity.

Sahgal in her novels shows the breeding of corruption in public life as the direct consequence of the non-concern of Hindus with their immediate problems. Dhiraj Singh, Kalyan and Hari Mohan (all from *Morning*), Gyan Singh (*Storm*), Sumer Singh (*Shadow*), the sham ideologues, the so-called 'intellectuals in the Cabinet' (*Situation*) and the thoroughly rotten set of people basking in official favour during the Emergency (*Rich*) — all can be seen as inevitable products of the atmosphere generated by such indifferent attitudes, born of philosophic insulation from the world of fact.

Debjani, herself a student of philosophy, thus opines on the primary preoccupation of people in India : "Indians were somewhat overly occupied with what they reckoned as the deeper values" (*Hawaii*, 77).[23] This prepondering concern with what is believed to be the deep value, the spirit of things, seems to emanate from Vedanta's prime concern with "the spirit of man, which was beyond the intellectual" (*Hawaii*, 164). Swami Yogananda speaks of the "quest of Brahma" to be attained at the World Centre at Hawaii. This preoccupation with the remote to the neglect of what is immediate is heightened when placed against the background of an American like Dr. Vincent Smith. Dr. Smith is "a practical man" who "will not let any time be *wasted* on abstractions" (*Hawaii*, 57) (emphasis added).

According to the novelists under study, what baffles and incapacitates an individual is the excessive concern in Hinduism with philosophic intricacies which, for an ordinary person, constitute incomprehensible verbiage. Hafiz in *Ganges* quotes Gandhi's 'enigmatic' assertion : "In the midst of darkness, light persists; in the midst of death, life persists." He finds here "the peculiar escapism of Hindus" into, what is at best verbal jugglery for a person confronted with a crisis. In *Ladakh,* Satyajit's smug complacence that the Chinese incursion into the Indian territory is only a mistake (24), is, according to Bhaskar, a form of 'delusion' (128). Satyajit shies away from confronting the issues by mouthing pious abstractions. However, Bhaskar himself comes out in *Ladakh* with statements like : "Virtue and vice together give life its colour, savour…. One without the other could easily destroy us" (29). The hapless peasants in *Situation* can't be shaken from their fond belief that "good and evil are part of the cosmos and each man's destiny his own to work out within that cosmic pattern through all eternity" (71). What actual help are such statements for a man in search of something tangible in his faith to hold on to and to resolve the conflict between good and bad, virtue and vice? Mere dabbling in hair-splitting will give no clear-cut commandments goading the believers to action.

So well-entrenched is this practice of treating everything as a distant and mysterious riddle, where what is, is not and what is not is, that Kalo's audience refuses to take him at the face value. He has given them a straightforward confession — a plain account of his faking the Shiva-idol with no scope for any ambiguity whatsoever — but the assembly refuses to see the obvious. The general impression is that "there is a deep meaning behind the meaning" (*Tiger*, 237). Michael, an objective appraiser of the Indian scene in *Situation*, is baffled by this preoccupation with multiple, allegorical layers of meaning in even the most obvious things. He believes that "this Trimurti business, three faces to every action will be the ruin of the country" (79). These abstractions pull the individual into passivity, forestalling any possibility of decisive action. No wonder, men like Rakesh in *Morning* and Usman in *Situation* find Christianity and Islam (respectively) less ambiguous religions, spelling out clearly what they believe in, while the impression persists that Hinduism itself has been devoid of "clear compelling commandments" (*Morning*, 41). No wonder, Kalyan who has had close brush with stark poverty feels alienated and impatient "in this strange land which was and yet was not his own" (*Storm*, 25).

Despite its philosophic view of evil, the basic issue of evil in its actual manifestation is not resolved in Hinduism. Keshav, in *Rich* realizes now evil in the abstract engages the attention in Hindu thought whereas its manifestation in worldly forms, where it afflicts the individual, is just brushed aside as insignificant in the context of the universal. This disregard of the personal and the social for the impersonal and the universal, of detail for a general theme, according to Keshav, makes Hinduism a debilitating faith. It fails to measure up to the diverse desperations of an individual. It can thus give one no sustenance in a crisis. The story Mona relates to Rose relating to the two-fold concept of time, cosmic and temporal (208-9) reveals one in-built 'defence mechanism' whereby temporal distress can be made to look insignificant against a cosmic background. It is this lesson which Chandralekha in *Tiger*, as 'the Mother of Sevenfold Bliss' is made to grasp in her new role. From the heights of godhood human misery is too insignificant and insubstantial to move and stray one from the set grooves of fixed rites.

Another aspect of popular Hinduism which facilitates evasion, acceptance and acquiescence is the Hindus' other-worldliness or excessive concern with the hereafter to the total neglect of what lies here and now.[24] Bindu's mother in *Music* subjects herself to undue suffering by investing a year's wages in having one inset slab, with her name engraved on it, installed in the Jagannath temple. "Here soul would be saved for ever," the moment some great yogi steps on her name (104). It is by invoking this hankering in his old wife that the ageing Seth, Motichand, in *Tiger*, succeeds in getting rid of her and marrying a sixteen-year old beauty : "Why not take to the way of devotion and tell the name of the Supreme one on your rosary beads, a hundred and eight times every day? Why not seek release from the self?" (143).

With uncanny precision, Bhattacharya traces the root cause of exploitation of the poor and the starving to their hankering after the spiritual. Those who were starving and dying daily on the streets of Calcutta "would not rise in revolt that their stomachs could be soothed — a selfish personal end! They would fight and die over a moral issue" (*Hungers*, 111). A group of destitutes would pause near a cookshop, "sunken eyes avidly gazing at the array of eatables behind the plate glass." When they are asked why they do not break the glass and snatch the eatables, the answer is :

> *Chich*! My sons, *Chich*! How can you take by force what is not yours? Have you no true principles of living? Are you wild beasts? (*Hungers*, 111).

When they are questioned further, someone from the crowd gives a morsel to quieten the sceptic and then murmurs, lifting his hands in grateful salutation, "He is saved from the evil in him" (111). Sujata and Anami in *Hawaii* have run from such an atmosphere of deadening debility, for "The opium Varansai gave them was not what they had longed for" (140).

Popular Hinduism abounds in superstitions. Born of ignorance, such beliefs do grievous injury to both the individual and the body politic by delimiting people's capability for autonomous action. It is the expectation of "gold mine luck" in his forty-fifth year, according to a reading of his horoscope, which motivates Seth Shamsunder in *Gold* to think of realizing his greedy desires in politics. He keeps on making mental calculations of the money 'invested' in electioneering, hoping to earn his flat ten per cent cut on all contracts he will give as a minister after elections. Political power will become his gold-mine and confirm the truth of his horoscope.

Even though the novels of Bhattacharya, Malgonkar and Sahgal abound in both overt and covert indictment of many ill-founded, ignorant and superstitious beliefs by linking the plight of their protagonists with these inhibiting convictions, it would be pertinent to see how some such beliefs and practices get reinforced because of the manner wherein certain events are presented. Sahgal's *Rich* is a case in point. Down to earth and matter-of-fact as Sonali is presented to be, within that realism is introduced a streak of superstitiousness, thereby sanctifying it. This is the anagnorisis she is depicted to have come round to :

> I can no longer ignore the supernatural since the day my father suddenly died at the age of fifty, in apparent good health, as the clock's hands reached the hour and the minute of the prediction. What is not wildly improbable — the earth is round, machines will fly — until the future makes it fact? (130).

What sounds much more disturbing is the tacit nod Malgonkar seems to give to certain beliefs which make Winton appear but a nincompoop in having striven to act in defiance of his destiny. The impression left is that silent acquiescence in the face of 'the inevitable' would have been a more honourable course than his fretting and fuming.

All the factors contributing to Winton's successive failures and ultimate death come to him unexpectedly, by chance : his father's demise, depression, which had his business folded, Gauri, Jugal Kishor, Rosie, Eddie, the one-tusker. His own life may appear to be filled with successive failures to make him expiate past sins. He himself has the feeling that the elephant-god is seeking him out (244) to punish him for his gross dereliction of duty leading to the death of his tracker, Kistulal. Then there is Bichwa-Baba and the mysterious powder he gives to Rosie which actually helps her win over Winton.[25] There is presented an unmistakable lull in the air as Winton goes to kill the rogue-elephant on the night of *Sankranti*, which "belongs to the goddess of destruction" (238). The result is all but too predictable : Winton himself is trampled to an inglorious death. So inextricably are myths, miracles and omens intertwined within the narrative that they all seem to play an integral part in leading the protagonist to his denouement. The taut organization of all these bits certainly does credit to craftsman in Malgonkar[26] but still the novel would go to reinforce the credulous, the superstitious and the fatalistic streaks in the make-up of his readers.[27]

In popular practice, rituals, far from remaining mere means to an end, assume importance in themselves. They even facilitate exploitation of the individual by inhibiting and incapacitating him. The socio-political matrix is relegated to the background and gods become the ultimate point of reference. In *Princes*, gods are thanked through the holding of a *mahapooja* for the failure of the Cripps Mission (231). Aji purifies her grandson, Gian, in *Ganges*, with sandalwood paste and by showering popped rice in fistfuls "to propitiate all the evil spirits that might be lurking around" (29). Far from saving Gian, this elaborate paraphernalia leads all concerned to a false sense of security, forestalling individual endeavour. The "Little House" in *Ganges* has obviously been victimised through forgery in the records of land-revenue. Whether to appeal or not against the adverse court judgment is a matter Hari, Gian's brother, leaves to Shiva's *kaul* (43). Hari in *Ganges*, arranging a *mahapooja* he could ill-afford to thank Shiva for the victory in the court (33), Onu in *Hungers* paying the few coins he has for jasmine flowers and butter-lamp to be offered at the goddess's feet, the destitute Ratandas in *Tiger* offering the five pieces of copper he has — all exemplify religious dissipation of individual energy and endeavour. In *Tiger*, the young and vivacious girl in Purnima gets stifled in the straitjacket of such inhuman rituals as are ends in themselves.

> Since her twelfth birthday much of her time outside the school hours had to be given to religious rites at home. It was not enough that she had to help with the daily preparations for *puja* — their Brahmin parents spent hours everyday in the prayer-room chanting hymns or reading from the scriptures — but there were the special rites for an unmarried girl, the observance of which would ensure her happiness in marriage. When Purnima complained that she could not do her school-work because of this preoccupation, Mother threatened to stop her schooling (*Tiger*, 164-65).

"While kindliness dried up, religion was more in demand. It was only the outward form of the religion, the shell of ritual, empty within" (*Tiger*, 116). It is the blind force of such perverted faith which deadens all sensitivity and even leads to a brazen defiance of all norms — social or political — with the firm conviction that with adequate show of religiosity, with the holding of *mahapoojas*, everything done here can be rectified. A grand *mahapooja* on an unprecedented scale is arranged at the 'Big-House' in *Ganges* after Vishnu Dutt, the young master of the House, murders Hari. It is "the force of [such a] faith" that makes Purnima's loving parents in *Tiger* not merely "blind and devastating" (167) but murderous too. Their role in what passes as her suicide cannot be doubted in the least.

The "violent acts of ancient origin, rooted in mythology" (*Rich*, 119) facilitate the brazen exploitation of women, feels Keshav. Even the myth of earth's opening up and receiving the long-suffering Sita is interpreted by him as the murder of Sita by society. "Why would a lovely princess cry out for the earth to swallow her if life hadn't become a wilderness?" (67). For Keshav, the pernicious custom of *sati* is a re-enactment of the old myth. *Rich* depicts a woman's being forced to perform *sati* so that her dead husband's relatives can claim the estate of the deceased, unhindered. When the fake Shiva rose from the ground in *Tiger*, as per the ingenious scheme which is Biten's brain-child, there was a mad rush of people to pay ritual obeisance to the god. "Children were knocked out. Women screamed. The weak, half-suffocated, struggled, panting to make their way out.... The helpless old people waited in despair" (84).

Those whom religion brutalizes thus would stop at nothing. *Tiger* reveals how even as hundreds of children were dying daily of starvation in famine-stricken Calcutta, there were scores of donors registering themselves in advance for offering the ritual milk bath to the stone god. None of the registered donors was prepared to accommodate a dying man who wanted to perform the rite before his death, even if it implied denying him a peaceful death. A big hue and cry was raised when it was discovered that the used milk, after the ritual bath, was being taken to the starving children instead of being cast into the Ganga with fit ritual. The donors protested that the rites be fully observed. "Tens of thousands have died of hunger. What difference would a few more or a few less make? The issue at stake is bigger than those useless lives" (134). There is rice aplenty to be scattered on the street as a flower-decked bier is carried, but no rice to feed the starving millions (51). At funerals, lots of foodstuff can be wasted in ritual feasts where the whole community is fed in a land where millions have been reduced to "dehydrated sticks of humanity" (*Hungers*, 140).

The cloistered mental horizons of Hindus have had no new light for centuries. "Nothing new has entered their mental orbit for hundreds of years" (*Situation*, 78). Raj in *Shadow* believes that the Hindus are content to draw their credentials from an old, deep source. They are 'out of step' with life. Vishal Dubey in *Storm* considers the Hindus obsessed with a backward-looking tendency which makes them excessively dominated by the past :

> I think our great grandmother does have a formidable influence on what we do. In a number of ways she is still alive. Sometimes I think it will need a tearing up by the roots to get her out of the way (66).

For Mara in the same novel, the Hindu heritage is suffocatingly limited :

> It's ours all right, but some of it is rotten. We'll die if we go on like this. Sometimes I Think we are already dead (138).

Usman, the Vice-Chancellor of Delhi University in *Situation* thinks that Hindus, bogged down by the albatross of such worn-out heritage, are "a frighteningly bored lot" (78). Roopa, half-American and half-Indian, believes that the rub lies in the inherent inability of Indians (read Hindus) to change, to learn from experience. "Deep down in him, an Indian remains what he was in the times of yore" (*Ladakh*, 331). A Hindu may go to America, but he'll bring back only "the industrial know-how. Not the know-how of life,"

> He goes West and becomes a new person. He returns home and at once he is a complete Indian (31).

This unwillingness as well as inability to grow, to change, to make one's past of use in confronting an uncertain future, to mould one's strategies according to the need of the hour, makes of Hinduism an anachronistic creed which hinders more than it helps.

Of what use is this old heritage if it has no positive contribution to make to ordinary life, Trivedi wonders in *Storm* :

> What use was this heritage to ordinary men? What did it create but quietude? Did it toughen fibre, give emotional satisfaction? Did it help the soldier to fight better, the businessman to do his job better? (78).

Misguided faith, Jayadev realizes in *Music*, functions like a great lamp of oil which gives "little light but a great deal of smoke" (79).

The dead weight of stagnant ideas seems to be a negation of real Hinduism. Swami Yogananda in *Hawaii* is aware of "an aura of corruption, an enveloping vapour which threatened to suffocate the system itself" (105-6). Down the ages, "the core, the spiritual content had been choked by centuries of evil overgrowth," laments Jayadev in *Music* (179), rendering Hinduism to be merely "a religion of cooking pots," as Sonali in *Rich* puts it (120).[28] Thrown behind the bars in solitary confinement during the Emergency, K.L. realizes that to counterbalance the pervasive opiate in religion, "Hinduism needs antidotes" (*Rich*, 172). It is this opiate in Hinduism which makes persons like Sujata and Anami in *Hawaii* and Keshav and Sonali in *Rich* opt out of the fold.

Bhattacharya, Malgonkar and Sahgal present in their novels, as has already been made out, a critique of Hinduism through the presentation of a number of characters whose passive existence is a sad testimony of their fettering faith. Thoroughly unaware of what ails them, they merely exist and don't live in the real sense of the term. Such characters include Gobind Narain, Prabha Mathur and Savitri in *Happy*, Aji in *Ganges*, Abhay's mother in *Princes*, Jayadev's mother and the villagers at Behula in *Music*, the destitutes in *Hungers*, the silent, suffering peasants in *Situation* and *Rich* and the villagers in *Combat*, the list not being exhaustive. The unthinking acquiescence of these characters is successfully contrasted with the instinctive, healthy manner wherein another group of characters functions. The members of this group don't pause to ponder what true Hinduism should or shouldn't be like. But their conduct is their theory. Some prominent characters here would be Kusum and Veena in *Happy*, Rahoul, Monju and Kishor in *Hungers*, Meera, her grandmother and the members of the 'Cowshed Five' in *Gold*, Kiran in *Drum*, Debi in *Ganges* and Mohini and Harindra in *Music*. However, we do have theorizers also in these novels.

Hinduism is looked at from different points of view in the novels of Bhattacharya, Malgonkar and Sahgal. Many characters realize on their pulse the glaring gaps where Hinduism proves wanting. Those who expose the debilitating deficiencies include not merely 'objective outsiders' but also 'critical insiders.' Believers in other faiths like Mclvor (*Happy*), Raj (*Shadow*), Winton (*Combat*), Usman (*Situation*), Shafi (*Ganges*) and Rose (*Rich*) provide a perspective wherefrom the harmful implications in the attitudes bred by popular Hinduism can be seen. There are also a fair number of Hindus who subject their faith to critical scrutiny. Some such critics are the narrator in *Happy*, Rakesh, Kalyan and Kailas in *Morning*, Vishal, Trivedi and Mara in *Storm*, Ram Kishan in *Shadow*, Sonali and Keshav in *Rich*, Jayadev and Mohini's father, the Professor in *Music*, Bhaskar and Roopa in *Ladakh*, Devjani, Yogananda, Sujata and Anami in *Hawaii*, and Biten and Kalo in *Tiger*. All these characters are not merely aware of the fetters of their faith. They also seek to make them snap through their active involvement in their immediate environment.

The novelists make it amply clear that Hinduism, to be a living force, requires constant renewal. It is only through a continuous reappraisal of what constitutes a desirable virtue in the present context and what doesn't that a code of action can be formulated "at this particular juncture in our history when we have to act and be responsible for our actions" (*Ladakh*, 117). Linking the fetters without with the faith within constitutes a condition precedent to such an appraisal. It is such an awareness which precipitates in Biten in *Tiger* :

> Belief in this country could be likened to its mighty rivers.... The swollen waters burst the banks and flooded the countryside, destroyed lives, eroded the soil and went to waste, while great areas of dry corn land thirsted and crops failed; harnessed, put to proper use, the rivers could irrigate, produce power, add to the country's riches. In the same way, the people's belief was a great force which could be guided in good ways, made creative. When this great force had ceased to go to waste, it would no longer be a curse, blighting lives. It would be the country's truest asset (181).

This potentially great force was duly harnessed for constructive political ends by Mahatma Gandhi by breathing new life into the stagnant faith. How this was done and how Bhattacharya, Malgonkar and Sahgal value the Gandhian endeavour in the present context is sought to be taken up in the following chapter.

REFERENCES

1. See Manu, XII, 112, rendered in Durga Prasad, *Light of Truth — An English Translation of "The Satyarth Prakash"* (New Delhi : Jan Gyan Prakashan, 1970), 11. Also *Gita,* IX, 4-8; XIV, 3-4.
2. *Ishopanishad,* 9-12; *Gita,* II, 11-30.
3. Vide *When a Great Tradition Modernizes : An Anthropological Approach to Indian Civilization* (New York : Praeger, 1972), 45-46.
4. *Indian Village* (Ithaca, New York : Cornell Univ. Press, 1955), 93.
5. That is precisely why ancient Indian, Greek and Chinese religious traditions are termed 'man-centered' as against the Semitic creeds which are God-centred. See Prof. Pratap Chandra, "Two Religious Traditions," *The Times of India,* January 6-7, 1987. It is significant, however, that while 'God-centred' religions emphasize man's duty to the community (household of God or *'Millat'*), 'man-centred' religions emphasize man's duty to God through his duty to 'the inner self.'
6. *Religions of India : The Sociology of Hinduism and Buddhism* (Glencoe : Free Press, n.d.).
7. Kusum Nair, *Blossoms in the Dust* (New York : Frederick A. Praeger, 1962).
8. K.W. Kapp, *Hindu Culture, Economic Development and Economic Planning in India* (Bombay : Asia Publishing House, 1963).
9. A.K. Saran, *Hinduism and Economic Development in India,* Archives de sociologie des Religions, 15, 87-94.
10. S.N. Eisentadt, *The Protestant Ethic and Modernization* (New York : Basic Books, 1968).
11. J.W. Elder, "Fatalism in India : A Comparison between Hindus and Muslims," *Anthropological Quarterly,* 39, 227-43.
12. F.C. Fliegel *et al.*, *Innovation in India — The Success or Failure of Agricultural Development Programmes in 108 Indian Villages* (Hyderabad, 1967).
13. Cf. "The crisis in India is not political : this is only the view from Delhi.... Nor is the crisis only economic. These are only aspects of the larger crisis, which is that of a decaying civilization...." V.S. Naipaul, *India — A Wounded Civilization* (New Delhi : Vikas Publishing House, Pvt. Ltd., 1977), 174.

14. Cf. "In Hinduism, order rests upon a tension between polar forms : between good and evil, and between the forces of degeneration and regeneration. Resolution lies not in the conquest of one by the other but in the merger of both back into the one source of their being." Wendy O' Flaherty, *Asceticism and Eroticism in the Mythology of Shiva* (London : Oxford Univ. Press, 1973), 109.
15. V.S. Naipaul describes this defeatist attitude thus : "...*karma,* the Hindu killer, the Hindu calm, which tells us that we pay in this life for what we have done in past lives : so that everything we see is just and balanced, and the distress we see is to be relished as religious theatre, a reminder of our duty to ourselves, our future lives." *India — A Wounded Civilization,* 25.
16. "Majorities and Minorities," *The Sunday Standard,* November 12, 1972.
17. *Raja Rao* (New York : Humanities Press, 1973), 58.
18. Cf. "A ritual law in which every change of occupation, every change in work technique, may result in ritual degradation is certainly not capable of giving birth to economic and technical revolutions from within itself...." Max Weber, *Religions of India : The Sociology of Hinduism and Buddhism, op. cit.*, 111-12.
19. Sudhir Kakar, a psycho-analyst, opines that the Indian ego is 'underdeveloped' and this underdeveloped ego is created by the detailed social organization of Indian life. "The mother functions as the external ego of the child for a much longer period than is customary in the West, and many of the ego functions concerned with reality are later transferred from mother to the family and other social institutions. Caste and clan are more than brotherhoods; they define the individual completely. The individual is never on his own; he is always fundamentally a member of his group, with a complex apparatus of rules, rituals, taboos. Every detail of behaviour is regulated. Relationships are codified. The need, then, for individual observation and judgment is reduced and blind unthinking conformism assumes the character of a prime virtue." See V.S. Naipaul, *India — A Wounded Civilization*, *op. cit.,* 102-3.
20. According to Sudhir Kakar, a psychoanalyst, "generally among Indians there seems to be a different relationship to outside reality compared to one met with in the West. In India it is closer to a certain stage in childhood when outer objects did not have a separate, independent existence but were intimately related to the self and its affective states. They were not something in their own right, but were good or bad, threatening or rewarding, helpful or cruel, all depending on the person's feelings of the moment." Quoted by V.S. Naipual in *India — A Wounded Civilization*, 102.
21. For the view that Indians need a King-Emperor to look up to, see Girilal Jain's lead article in *The Times of India*, January 7, 1987. Also

T.K. Oommen, "Charisma and not King Emperor," *The Times of India*, January 22, 1987.

22. Malgonkar's story "Two Red Roosters" in *Rumble Tumble* (New Delhi : Orient Paperbacks), 45-48, is another good example of the reinforcement of superstitions. Sonba has failed to propitiate the *churail* who lived in the palas tree and this leads to the death of his big buffalo. Chastened, he promises to sacrifice two red roosters to appease the *churail* and requests her to help him plough his field somehow. There come *kheti-Sahibs* in the village, who, in order to demonstrate how effective new farming methods are, plough the field with a tractor by way of demonstration. On the night of the new moon, there are seen two headless red roosters under the palas tree, encircled by a garland of marigold flowers.
23. Sudhir Kakar's psychoanalysis of Indians is that they have an 'underdeveloped' ego, 'the world of magic and animistic ways of thinking lie close to the surface' and that 'the Indian grasp of reality' is 'relatively tenuous.' "We Indians...use the outside reality to preserve the continuity of the self amidst an ever changing flux of outer events and things." Men do not, therefore, actively explore the world, rather they are defined by it." See V.S. Naipaul, *India — A Wounded Civilization*, 102-3.
24. V.S. Naipaul finds that among Indians "the inward concentration is fierce, the self-absorption complete." They are not concerned with whatever happens around them. "I may be proved wrong, but in all the great length of *My Experiments with Truth* I believe there are only three gratuitous references to landscape," so busy Gandhi has been with the 'battle inside.' *India — A Wounded Civilization*, *op. cit.*, 101.
25. It is only after having the lemon tarts Rosie had sent — on these she had sprinkled the powder Bichwa-Baba had given her — that Winton has his obsession with the one-tusked elephant broken. The way is paved henceforth for Rosie to obsess his thoughts (*Combat*, 104-7).
26. "The ending of *Combat of Shadows* has the perfect symmetry of a Greek nemesis," G.S. Amur, *Manohar Malgonkar* (New Delhi : Arnold-Heinemann, 1973), 75. Asnani calls the ending "a serious flaw of the otherwise well-contrived plot" but the view ignores the basic thrust of the narrative right from its beginning. See Shyam M. Asnani, *Critical Response to Indian English Fiction* (Delhi : Mittal Publications, 1985), 48.
27. The title of the novel is an adaptation from verse 27 of 'The Path of Knowledge' in *The Bhagwad Gita*; the verse itself is quoted at the very beginning of the novel : "Desire and aversion are opposite shadows. Those who allow themselves to be overcome by their struggle can't rise to a knowledge of reality." From this philosophic perspective, all of Winton's life, his fretting and fuming, would seem mere shadow-boxing.

28. Cf. "There is a danger of our religion getting into the kitchen. We are neither Vedantists...nor Puranics, nor Tantrics. We are just 'don't touchists.' Our religion is in the kitchen. Our God is in the cooking pot, and our religion is 'Don't touch me I am holy.' If this goes on for another century, everyone of us will be in a lunatic asylum." Vivekanand, quoted by Bipan Chandra in *Modern India* (Delhi : N.C.E.R.T., 1971), 218.

□□□

5

The Ossifying of the Gandhian Panacea

WE HAVE seen that Hinduism is characterized by heterogeneity, flexibility and tolerance. Paradoxically, in spite of (or is it because of?) such pluralism and inclusivism, there have been a number of attempts down the ages to reinterpret and fashion Hinduism to make it meet the challenge of times. With a remarkable tenacity and resilience, Hinduism has grown with such changes in emphasis and assimilated reorientations of its basic values in response to the changing environment. Buddhism and Jainism challenged the supremacy of the Brahmin priests and stressed agnostic materialism, ethical behaviour and sensory control for attaining liberation. In ninth century A.D. Shankara and Ramanuja introduced the concept of *Bhakti* which offered liberation from the endless cycle of rebirths to all on the basis of personal devotion to the Absolute Brahman. The *Sufis* or mystics, coming close on the heels of the Arab invaders, challenged the ritual hierarchy and social caste system of Hinduism with their emphasis on the brotherhood of men. Under the stress of new challenges, Bhakti movements that were born in the south, and syncretistic movements in the north, between the thirteenth and the sixteenth centuries, sought to make Hinduism more compatible with Islam. Coming to recent times, the encounter with Christianity led to an awareness of the need for social reform. The nineteenth century Renaissance sought to project the Vedic synthesis of idealism and action. Gandhism can be seen as the latest and one of the most significant attempts to reinterpret and reinvigorate Hinduism in the new context.

Gandhi turned religion from an inhibiting legacy to a rejuvenating and revolutionizing component of the life of an individual. He fused together abstract religion with a concrete socio-political plan of action.[1] He was convinced that "those who say that religion has nothing to do with politics do not know what religion means."[2] If he got himself "entirely absorbed in the service of the community, the reason behind it was my desire for self-realization."[3]

Gandhi deemed the *Gita* to be "an infallible guide of conduct"[4] and his "dictionary of daily reference."[5] He was essentially an action philosopher, not an idealist in the Weberian sense of the term. Man's struggle for truth all his life was for Gandhi the whole of man. Whereas the orthodox schools of Hindu-thought religiously equated *maya* with the external world, Gandhi corrected the distortion by using 'untruth' as the term equivalent of '*maya*,' and thus facilitated a pursuit of truth unhampered by outmoded notions of objective reality. Gandhi also dispensed with the distorted tradition of individual *nirvana*. *Moksha* divorced from the service of the masses was not for him. Even in its political ramifications, Gandhism builds on Gandhi's essentially religious views. His espousal of enlightened humanism, freedom as a means to that end, and fearless adherence to truth and non-violence are but a corollary of the way he interpreted Hinduism wherein action was a prime value in this life itself.

Gandhian ideology encompasses the whole gamut of human existence. It consists of six major concepts, according to one eminent Gandhian.[6] These are *satya, ahimsa, satyagraha, swadeshi, sarva dharma samanata* and *sarvatra bhayavarjana*. In its political ramification, Gandhian ideology postulates clear and consistent answers to important questions : What is a just social order? What is the aim and nature of State? What is freedom?, etc.

Gandhi indicted in no uncertain terms the alienation of the individual from political power and those who exercise it. People's periodic participation in the electoral process alone cannot, in any way, diminish it. The essential attribute of Gandhi's notion of democracy was its participatory character down to its humblest constituent. N.K. Bose reports[7] how Gandhi explained that he would oppose the tyranny of Indians as much as he had opposed that of the alien government. "I mean the welfare of the whole people and if I can secure it at the hands of the English, I should bow down my head to them."[8] Political consciousness percolating to the very grass-roots was essential in Gandhi's scheme of things.

The Gandhian concept of freedom in all its humanitarian and egalitarian nuances gets faithfully represented in the thinking and aspirations of the positive heroes[9] of Bhattacharya's and Sahgal's. In Malgonkar, it is this criterion with which the *bona fides* of politicians and other public men get tested. The minstrel in *Gold*, referring explicitly to Gandhi, maintains that the political freedom of the country is to be the sum total of the freedom of each of its constituents (301). However the purpose of freedom is thus expressed, with reference to Gandhi again :

> An old man whose voice has filled this country for thirty years has a curious wish in his heart. It is to wipe every tear from every eye (75).

Satyajit in *Ladakh* is positive that the ultimate end is the welfare of the people (377). In such a Gandhian *swaraj/Ramrajya*, says Sohanlal in *Gold*, "The very face of India will change," for "the people are going to be the masters. It is they who will own everything, the land, the rivers, the railways..." (114). Gandhigram, established by Satyajit, is intended to be a realization of Gandhi's ideals. "The new community of people was creating a new social order in which all were truly equal" (25).

Far from being an 'open sesame,' freedom is only the opening of the avenues to the attainment of greater heights. The Grandma in *Gold* is convinced that "freedom is to be built with our own hands" (124). Sohanlal in the same novel is positive that "we must demand what should be ours, the right to live as human beings" (176). *Gold* illustrates the frustrations of banking on charity for changing people's lives. There is no alternative to hard grinding, *Gold* maintains. It is this which Jayadev has in mind when he tells Mohini in *Music* : "Our political freedom is worth little without social uplift" (127). To enable freedom to reach the remotest corner of the country, "social slaveries" have to be uprooted. The roots of these are in "economic bondage." "A hungry man could not be free in spirit" (139). "India must reorient her national life on a new social basis" (124). The participatory nature of Gandhian freedom comes out in Abhay's frequent references to a sense of belonging and the people's involvement with the process of administration, though, in particular instances, the system Abhay longs for with nostalgia may not meet the idealistic Gandhian norms.[10] As general axioms about the relationship between the rulers and the ruled, these sentiments of Abhay's are perfectly in harmony with Gandhism :

> We may not give our people prosperity but we give them roots, perhaps happiness; a cause to live for and die for (101).

Gandhi knew India to be predominantly an agrarian community. With his own illustrious example, he steered political concerns to a proper order and priority on a universal scale :

> No single fact had done more to reorient the thinking of an entire nation than Gandhi's semi-nakedness. It had shifted the political spotlight from town to village, jolting the town dwellers into a awareness of the peasants' existence and plight.[11]

Except in *Hawaii*, in every novel of Bhattacharya's, a village provides the essential background against which matters personal and public are reflected and resolved. The narrative is set in a village; the protagonists confront political issues affecting the lives of millions. The novelist thereby demonstrates political consciousness percolating to the grass-roots. Devata and Rahoul (*Hungers*), Jayadev and Harindra (*Music*), the minstrel, Meera and Sohanlal (*Gold*) are Gandhian emissaries of light who jolt the villagers to an awareness of the vital issues of the day. The political programme of Davesh's in *Hungers* — like that of the narrator in *Happy* — is Gandhian in nature, encompassing the spread of nationalism as much as mass literacy. The narrator in *Happy* was awakened to the need of his participation in the mission of nation-building by Gandhi's words about village India and its poor people, their desperate plight and their crushing burdens of debt (9). Kailas in *Morning* functions as political activist, "teaching people the laws of hygiene and encouraging the art of spinning during the months when the fields lay fallow" (37). Jayadev's blueprint for rural reconstruction includes eradication of "the inequities of caste and untouchability; the ritualism that passed for religion; the wide-flung cobwebs of superstitious faith" (80).

Not merely are the villagers to be brought round to an awareness of their role in the polity, the village has also to be established as a functioning autonomous unit. Devata in *Hungers* is given an awareness of the interdependent economy of the village which would be jeopardized by unscrupulous external deals. His forbidding the villagers to dispose of their stocks of grain to hoarders from the cities (64) is a testimony to that awareness. Usman in *Situation* is a Gandhian advocate of decentralization. A coercive state is no solution to any socio-political problem. Rather, it is in itself the root cause of a host of problems. Usman is convinced "we'll never be properly self-governing in this country until we vest power in little units, in people at the base" (80). Even communism of his choice would be Gandhian, a native Indian communism with its roots in the village and its inspiration drawn from the Indian heritage" (27).

What precisely does improvement in the lives of the people imply? It is more than material welfare. Satyajit in *Ladakh* is well aware that it is "fullness of life that makes one happy, not fullness of possessions" (10). This could be ensured only by providing everybody with opportunities for soul-fulfilling work, not the work that alienates the worker from himself, from others and also from the product of work itself. Biten in *Gold* opts for a creative vocation which could be meaningful rather than stifling. He chooses to work "as a *mishtri* when…he could be employed at a respectable desk [as a clerk]" (156). He knows that, "a craftsman honest with his iron and fire is as good as the best of folks. He can hold his head high because of the skill of his hands, his special knowledge" (113).

Gandhi was clear on the role of machines in a new India. He was neither a technophile nor a technophobe. His view of technology is related to social justice and man's value system. Therefore, he aimed "not at eradication of all machinery but limitation."[12] In a labour-surplus State such as India, the problem is "not how to find leisure for the teeming millions, inhabiting our villages. The problem is how to utilize their idle hours…."[13] Gandhi refers approvingly to the sewing-machine. Rather he goes to the extent of saying, "I would favour the use of the most elaborate machines…if thereby India's pauperism and resulting idleness can be avoided."[14] Another proviso Gandhi added was that "the machine should not tend to make atrophied the limbs of man";[15] it is "to help and ease human effort."[16] Man must not be put in a condition where he gets alienated from either his work or his produce. Even

> the heavy industry for work of public utility which cannot be undertaken by human labour has its inevitable place but all that would be owned by the state and used entirely for the benefit of the people.[17]

Bhaskar in *Ladakh* is a Gandhian employer as well a worker himself. He is "a kind of steel that can think" and feel too (125). He is convinced that steel holds the key to the betterment of the destiny of the millions in the country. "Steel means economic progress. Machine tools, tractors, big industrial plants, locomotives" (27). The way he looks after the interests of his workers, fully involving himself in their well-being, makes him a different kind of employer. Such work with a single-minded zeal, fired by nationalism and inspired by the personal example of the employer, would be most fulfilling.

Bhaskar has another, less perceptible, Gandhian facet about him. Despite his swearing by industrialization, he hides within himself a "queer discontent" (228) with materialism : "He was, he thought, journeying from exhaustion to exhaustion" (228). This makes him opt for "seeking something beyond" (229). Taking our cue from another novel by Bhattacharya, we see what Bhaskar could have been but is certainly not. Unhindered and uninhibited growth of the industrial culture is indicted unambiguously through one interpretation of Prof. Walt Gregson's poem, "The Dead Rate," in *Hawaii*. The explanation, given by a student, is worth consideration for its evocation of the true Gandhian spirit :

> The dead rat — I call it technology. Up to a point, technology is good for mankind. It's a tool of civilized living. Beyond that point it turns anti-social and defeats its original purpose. While it goes on hitting at every aspect of traditionalism, technology, super-technology becomes an end in itself. Machines with monstrous power take over the functions of the human brain, control human action. As machines get humanized, men get dehumanized (124).

Satyajit in *Ladakh* is convinced like Gandhi that in India, small machines like the spinning wheel were the answer. A spinning wheel was ideal in that it "helped an individual to add to his efficiency without turning him into its helpless slave" (26). Big machinery, on the other hand, was "ugly, repressive." "It uprooted masses of people from a healthy, rural environment. Simplicity has to give way to sophistication. The craze for speed grew, speed for its own sake, an end in itself. And the glamour of endless gadgets" (71). Unabashed consumerism would lead a society to ever widening inequality, inequity and tensions. The spinning-wheel on the other hand had been in Gandhi's hand an "instrument of social philosophy.... It was an emblem of unity between all classes of the people; the manual effort of plying the wheel was an obligation for all" (63).

Satyajit stands for the Gandhian crusade against the stifling, soul-killing, consumption-oriented and needs-escalating ramifications of mechanization as well as the puritanical insistence on *brahmcharya* for social activists. Bhaskar, on the other hand, is committed to the sensible use of technology for the eradication of want and misery — a goal essentially Gandhian. It is obvious to see that in *Ladakh* both Satyajitism and Bhaskarism are presented as but two facets of Gandhism, sharpened for dramatic effect : the Gandhi of *Hind Swaraj* vintage and the latter-day Gandhi, who himself had unabashedly declared that he was "evolving from truth to truth."[18] By oversimplifying and exaggerating the political, economic, sociological and philosophic stances of Gandhi during the *Hind Swaraj* interlude, Bhattacharya makes Satyajitism what his wife, Suruchi, most pertinently dubs "strident revivalism" (301). By exaggerating the later posture of Gandhi in its political and economic dimensions, the novelist makes Bhaskarism a hypothetical projection of Gandhi in time and space. By rounding off the angularities of both Satyajitism and Bhaskarism, as they are portrayed in the novel and by presenting them as "complementary" (359) to each other, Bhattacharya leads only to a vindication of Gandhism in its inherent complexity. The conscious amalgam Bhattacharya leads to by the end of the novel involves the shedding of Satyajit's holier-than-thou and I-know-it-all exclusivism. Even as Satyajit vindicates "the spirit's supremacy over the flesh" (367), there is a new mood of acceptance in him (367). In Bhaskar, too, there is almost a *volte-face* from the haughty impatience which had made him term Gandhigram "a toy workshop out of the eighteenth century" (38) to a heightened fascination with the use of 'soul-force' to make others fall in step.

Freedom in Gandhian thought is an opportunity for alleviation of misery and growth of the humblest constituent of the polity; the individual is the fulcrum of the political system. The individual, according to Gandhi, is "the one supreme consideration."[19] The State is a means for the development of individuality, "which lies at the root of all progress."[20] "Just as a man will not grow horns or a tail, so will he not exist as a man if he has no mind of his own,"[21] declared Gandhi. He would wonder what would happen to society if an individual ceased to count.[22] However, the individual, in Gandhi's vision, was always seen in his social milieu, never in isolation from it. Hence the need for social restraints in the interest of social good. Gandhi was emphatic that the individual must learn "to adjust his individualism to the requirements of social progress."[23] He maintained that willing submission to social restraints for the sake of the well-being of the whole society enriched both the individual and the society.

Davesh Basu in *Hungers* iterates the exact position taken by Gandhi regarding the position of the individual in society. He is fired by love for the common people. In distrusting sole reliance on statistics for assessing human condition, Davesh, like Gandhi, echoes Ruskinian sentiments. "Facts never tell much unless they are seen in terms of human experience" (22). His advice to Rahoul at a critical juncture in India's struggle for freedom — during the Second World War — is to relegate other considerations to the background. The call of the country comes first. Rahoul, who had all along hungered for fulfilment "at an individual level,"[24] himself comes to realize how "the welfare of society…is not…apart from the welfare of the individuals that constitute it."[25] In a typically Gandhian manner, he comes to know how "self-realization is impossible without identification with, and service of the poorest."[26] The minstrel in *Gold* is an inveterate believer in man, in the "secret goodness in everyone" (63). Satyajit in *Ladakh* recalls to his mind Gandhi's hopeful words as he finds himself confronted by the harsh reality of the Chinese aggression :

> Not to believe in the possibility of permanent peace is to disbelieve in the godliness of human nature (80).

This concern for the role of the individual in the body politic links Sohan Bhai (*Happy*), the mythical Shivraj (*Situation*), and the visionary Prime Minister (*Happy*). Sohan Bhai has first-hand contact with "the agony of the people in the street" (88). He espouses the cause of what has most appropriately been called "saintly politics."[27] The relationship of the unnamed Prime Minister in *Happy* and Shivraj in *Situation* with their countrymen goes "far beyond political bounds" (*Situation*, 54). Shivraj in his concern for the all-encompassing welfare of the masses, most appropriately reminds Michael in *Situation* of the Sermon on the Mount (46).

In his vehement espousal of the cause of the individual, Kailas in *Morning* appears most Gandhian. In questions regarding the choice of ideology or a system of government, he believes, "The only thing that does matter is the human being, his calibre, his...dedication" (130). "The central consideration to any problem was the man who faced it" (88). Therefore, the goal for Kailas is that of "raising a people to modern times with their own consent. In tackling the onerous task of nation-building, "the tools will be our power of persuasion and the limitations will be the men and women of India" (201). There can be no other way. For Kailas, "The balance between morality and expediency" and "the imperfect circumstances that must be accepted in the game" (188) were mere euphemisms for unbridled despotism and therefore "travesty of truth" (187).

In *Situation*, Sahgal indicts forcefully the ahuman and unscrupulous perspective of "the Cabinet Intellectuals" and poses the million-dollar question : "How could a pluralistic society be made to toe one hypothesis, unshakable, unquestionable" (16).

> We are a society at crossroads, all right, as the Professors in the Cabinet keep saying.... But they don't realize how many different crossroads we are at, some in yesterday, some in tomorrow, some in the Middle Ages (41-42).

It is this realization of the individual factor that Rishad comes to have towards the end of the novel. He comes to a Gandhian anagnorisis, one that Usman has known all along : "Revolution begins with oneself, is not a lesson given to others" (146). "Revolutions, if they had any meaning, meant putting oneself into the crucible of change" (30). Usman is the most reminiscent of Gandhi. His idea of government, with "maximum power to the small community" (83-84), his awareness of non-violence being "the only way most people in his country understand" (116), and his working for a revolution from the ground, a hunger and thirst for justice in all forms" (117) represent a Gandhian endeavour to put politics on a 'saintly' keel by restoring the human factor to its proper eminence in politics. His success in reaching the inner core of people (158) is a vindication of Gandhism.

What characterizes all the positive protagonists of Sahgal's is their unshakable and inveterate faith — essentially Gandhian — in the people whom they would like to call, like Shivraj, in *Situation*, the "multitude" and not the "masses," for the latter term "lumps humanness into a thing, like a mass of clay, for *someone else's use* (emphasis in original) (80). Kailas Vrind in *Morning* speaks for all the positive heroes of his creator's when he explains what he means by government : "Government will begin" when even those remotest from the centre of authority arouse concern and "are given a chance to live like human beings" (42-43).

Malgonkar's positive heroes also exhibit their concern for people. Brigadier Kiran Garud in *Bandicoot* is presented as one really interested in those who work with him. He has a human, personal rapport with them. Values like loyalty to a person or a cause, decency, steadfastness and perseverance are qualities which Kiran values the most in his life (207). In pursuit of such values, he can even flout harsh political realities. Army for him is a forum to practise, to preach and to pass on the values he holds dear (251). Barkat, the second son of the Maharaja of Tilkatta, is conspicuous for his democratic credentials, his regard for the individuality of others and the absence of the sort of snobbery displayed by upstarts in the Malgonkar would like Rawal Singh, K.K. and others. It is the absence of this consideration for others as individuals which becomes one factor responsible for the damnation of Henry Winton in *Combat*. With his arrogance, Winton creates potential enemies in Jugal Kishore, Gauri, Eddie and Jean and each of them contributes to the denouement.[28]

If the individual is the cornerstone of the polity and the central consideration in any political/ideological premise, then he must feel free and fearless in seeking to herald a political system wherein he may realize his potential fully. Following Gandhi's message of *sarvatra bhyavarjana*,[29] the minstrel as well as Davesh in *Hungers* forge people into an unbeatable combine by giving them the *mantra* of fearlessness. "Do not be afraid.... Do not step back, whatever happens" (75), advises the minstrel. Fearlessness and unity constitute his recipe for success. The minstrel breathes fire into the leaden nerves of the people, shaking off their age-old habit of submission. Using religious terminology and a religious platform, fully reminiscent of the Father of the Nation, the minstrel inculcates fearlessness in the people through the recitation of the stories of Rama and Seeta and the Demon king.

Rahoul in *Hungers* expresses best the metamorphosis brought by Gandhi in the psyche of even an average Indian through "the catalysis of experience"; the soul of the nation grew more in those moments than it had grown in years (69). Rahoul is emphatic that "India after August [1942] will never be the India of before..." (69). *Hungers* closes with vanloads of prisoners awaiting long sentences or the gallows, singing with "no defeat in the[ir] voices, but a secret, excited triumph" :

> The more their eyes redden with rage,
> the more our eyes open;
> The more they tighten the chains,
> the more the chains loosen (215).

In *Gold* one comes across the memories of Meera, barely a kid then, and other men and women of Sonamitti, facing "lorryloads of Red Turbans as if they were mere goats" (8).

Bhattacharya artistically weaves in his novels another important facet of Gandhian political ideology, *viz*., the consideration of women as equal citizens of a state and hence the exhortation to them to come out of their sheltered existence and play their essential political role in a fearless manner. *Hungers* is the story of the political education of the Gandhian variety of not merely Rahoul but also of Kajoli, the peasant girl and Monju, Rahoul's wife. Kajoli is a representative of women in general who are objects of oppression and exploitation. However, under the Gandhian impact of Davesh Basu, Kajoli is imbued with fearlessness. She passes through a lean phase and just as she is on the verge of selling herself, the Devata's Gandhian message of fearlessness opens her eyes and shows her the way. In Monju, Rahoul's wife, we have another woman who rises to self-awareness under the Gandhian movement for freedom wherein her husband participates. Gone is the vulnerable Monju who was at her wits' end with embarrassment and discomfiture at being winked at by an Englishman. She is no more "the silly thing... she used to be." She coolly tells her husband as he rings her up before courting imprisonment as part of the Civil Disobedience Movement : "I too shall go your way soon..." (213). Towards the close of the novel, Monju reveals herself as another representation of *Shakti*,[30] that dynamic female energy. Rahoul understands all this :

> Yes, he knew, she had grown fast. Once the process started, women grew faster than men (213).

The women in the later novels by Bhattacharya : Mohini in *Music*, Meera, her Grandma and 'the Cowhouse Five' in *Gold*, and Sumita and Suruchi in *Ladakh* highlight the freeing of women from conventional barriers of home and hearth to sacrifice and participate in the holy *yagna* for freedom under the inspiring guidance of the Father of the Nation. Lakshmi in *Gold* speaks for womankind in general when she says : "Gandhiji touched our spirit as it slept. Wakened, we became the equals of our men folk. Proud, chins up, we marched in a column of our own..." (6).

Another parameter of the Gandhian redemption of the individual as the carrier of the divine spark is the humane consideration of even the supposedly irredeemable sinners. In the true spirit of Gandhian humanism, Bhattacharya and Sahgal present even their negative characters in a sympathetic light, focusing on the sin rather than on the sinner concerned who is generally the inevitable product of a set of circumstances. Such a presentation not merely humanizes their villainy, it also implicitly engages one's attention to the rot which is to be stemmed rather than the individuals who have got infected. One minor character in *Hungers* best illustrates this humanization of persons straying to the wrong side of the fence. This is how the novelist describes the soldier, who, critics allege,[31] raped Kajoli :

> The soldier was a man of feeling. But he desperately needed a woman. It was over a year since he had seen his wife. And in this instant he was back home with his wife. He could barely see Kajoli's face in the dark — the clean woman smell, like rain-wet earth that was part of her. He spoke words of caress, words lain buried in his feelings. The soldier was lost in a twilight, half dream, half reality… (150).

Rahoul's father, Samarendra Basu in *Hungers* and Seth Sham Sunder in *Gold* have been humanized to make their avaricious, amoral present seem the inevitable outcome of a past marked by fruitless toil. Samarendra is a finer study for not merely are we told how he hoards grain only to ensure a trouble-free future for his sons but we are also shown how he is undergoing pangs of conscience.[32]

Kalo's turning into a trickster in *Tiger* is only the last phase of a long tale beginning with the honest *kamar* being discriminated against simply because of his 'low' birth. Law deems him a nobody because of his poverty. He sees respectable people dabbling in illegal and immoral activities and going scot-free, rather adding to their respectability by their dishonourable deeds. This gives birth to the rebel in Kalo and henceforth his aim becomes teaching the so-called 'pillars of society' a lesson the hard way.

In the fictional universe of Sahgal and Malgonkar, the villains are generally professional politicians. However, in Sahgal's novels such public figures are rendered as less of ogres fired by 'motiveless malignity.' They appear as human beings whose actions and ideological platitudes make sense. Presenting their public postures as the external manifestation of internal compulsions, Sahgal succeeds in humanizing the demoniacal contours of most of her villains or negative heroes. In *Happy*, Nootan's public posture of a revolutionary is depicted as a means to gratify his inner craving for fame (85). Politics became a bore to him when he couldn't attract that kind of publicity again in post-Independence India. He "tried to regain the thrills of his student days by becoming a communist" (86). Sir Harilal Mathur in the same novel has his anglomania on the public front shown as the direct consequence of his indebtedness to the English for releasing him from an inhibiting inferiority complex. Kunti Behn's "ceaseless campaigns against the evils of smoking," etc. as well as her "scornful unconcern for appearance by refraining from combing her hair or cleaning her nails" (59), is the psychological result of a long life of forced renunciation and repression. Her husband "was a close follower of Mahatmaji's" and, therefore, her "marriage was not consummated" (60). Kunti Behn does try to give an ideological garb to her psychological aberrations when she expresses her "contempt for women who attended to their toilette while rural India cried out for assistance" (50-66). Her political platitudes are but an attempt to sublimate her repressed desires.

Kalyan's portrait in *Morning* also has psychological pertinence in its political and personal dimensions. Having been orphaned in tragic circumstances during the stress and fury of World War I, "he had grown up without the ordinary marks of identity" (135). Hence his feelings of insecurity, his rootlessness, "his hunger for identity" (135), for recognition. His contempt for non-violence is the outward manifestation of the scars of non-violence he carries on his soul. "Caught stealing once, every nerve in him had screamed, srike me; but the man had given him a long scornful look and left him" (77). The stark poverty and starvation of his early life, leading to his mother's death of hunger, has made him impatient for results irrespective of the means adopted.

In *Storm*, Gyan Singh, an orphan, had been brought up by his uncle, a man of rough morals, after his father had "killed a man and then was killed by his relative" (119). Fascinated by the "primitive colourful reality of his uncle" (120) (and perhaps also of his father), "Gyan had been bred in a turbulence where honour had more meaning.... Conscience was invisible, hidden under secret layers of bafflement and doubt" (123). Gyan's insensitivity to feelings and emotions, his violent impatience and narrow, parochial, communal and populist policies seem the inevitable outcome of such an upbringing.

In *Shadow*, the ex-zamindar, pseudo-radical and demagogic Sumer Singh is also humanized. The 'heady wine' of victory in the parliamentary election has gone into his head and now after having had the 'fiery touch of power,' he is "too hell bent" in everything he does, "even in bed" (130). The impression is created that it may be sublimation of something he has been missing in his life.

However, in Malgonkar, one comes across a one-dimensional presentation of his negative heroes[33] as seen through the perspective of the protagonists. Malgonkar's politicians and other antagonists reveal only their political facets. They thus come off only as inexplicable irritants when they are too trivial or too distant from the centre of the stage to be the beneficiaries of a fuller probe. That is precisely where the rub lies as regards personages like Lala Vishnu Saran Dev (*Drum*) and Krishna Manikam (*Bandicoot*).

There are other novels by Malgonkar where the antagonists exist in both the personal and the public realms of being. Here we do discern a linking of their private and public selves but with totally different results. In *Combat* and *Princes*, what we must guard against is the temptation to go along with the controlling voice and thereby oversimplify the characters of the antagonists. It is obvious that both Winton and Abhay wish to see in the public postures of Jugal and Kanak respectively a mere extension of their private selves. Their politics is seen as but an attempt to settle personal scores. It is obvious that this simplistic view of their public activities would deprive them of the complexity of being which they potentially have. Jugal and Kanak have a mesmeric hold over the people they lead. The possibility of their having genuine ideological predilections which make them arouse the people against their exploiters — Winton (*Combat*) and Hiroji (*Princes*) respectively — cannot be brushed under the carpet easily.[34] It is obvious that by placing the political against the background of the personal, what is achieved in Malgonkar's novels is not the humanization of the public postures — as is the case in Bhattacharya and Sahgal — but, in effect, their diminution.

In the novels of Bhattacharya, Malgonkar and Sahgal, the unambiguous indictment of some seminal concepts of Hinduism is artistically integrated along typically Gandhian lines.[35] Gandhi's deep attachment with Hinduism was matched by his intense impatience with the way parts of the Hindu creed were seen by Hindus. We have already seen that Gandhi made the individual the lynchpin of his philosophy. He also considered the fulfilment of the individual's basic needs in his physical existence as the very criterion with which to judge the desirability of a particular form of government. This obviously brought a much needed reorientation in the hierarchy of priorities sanctified in Hindu thought. The contemplative, non-active bias implicit in popular Hinduism made Gandhi exclaim, "If I had the good fortune to be face-to-face with one like him [the Buddha], I should not hesitate to ask him why he did not teach the gospel of work, in preference to one of contemplation. I should do the same thing if I were to meet...these saints [Tukaram, Jnyaneshvar and others]."[36] In their indictment of the fatalism, status-quoism, obsessive other-worldliness, inaction, complacency, mute acquiescence and evasiveness inherent in the popular practice of Hinduism,[37] the novelists under study dilate upon what is essentially Gandhian, though in a germinal state.

Bhattacharya, Malgonkar and Sahgal make their protagonists come to grips with the ills the body politic is afflicted with, rather than leaving them sitting back in abject surrender to whatever they find around them. Davesh Basu, Rahoul, Kajoli and even Monju in *Hungers*, and Jayadev, Mohini and Harindra in *Music* are all 'doers.' The minstrel in *Gold*, by himself agreeing to be a candidate for the forthcoming elections in immediate post-Independence India, underscores the need for right thinking persons to come out of their self-imposed hibernation and participate actively in the task of nation-building. Abdul Jamal and Kiran Garud in *Drum*, fighting successfully the menace of communal riots in old Delhi, reveal how those committed to action in defence of the ideals they cherish, can make all the difference.

Bhaskar, too, like Gandhi is a *karmayogi*, impatient of abstract intellectualization and a staunch votary of social activism. He represents "not the heritage of philosophic inanity but the dynamism of technology" (157) — technology with a human face. Sumita herself is ultimately converted to Bhaskarism, if that term be coined, when she, too, clamours for action.

> We cannot sit still and wait for the Messiah to come. If we do, we shall be sitting on our haunches forever. Even when the Messiah comes to our doorstep, we'll not see him, for our eyes will be fixed expectantly on the far horizon. And the Messiah will go back unanswered like a lone beggar (345).

However, action irrespective of the means, is not what Gandhi advocated. Sahgal exposes the view that the Gandhian heritage makes a virtue of passivity and that for action, means have not to be bothered about. The political scene as Sahgal sees it is marked by two forces : the Gandhian and the non-Gandhian. The line of distinction is not that one is given to speculation and sermonizing, and the other to action. The line of distinction is the nature of means adopted and the place accorded to human being in the ultimate scheme of things. The people in these two camps "belonged to different lines of thinking and the future of Asia would depend on which line won" (*Situation*, 155). We have thus in each novel of Sahgal's, characters cast in the Gandhian mould, endeavouring not merely to expose but also to stem the rot percolating to the very core of the polity.

Kailas in *Morning* represents the Gandhian mean of purposeful action coupled with proper means. Neither is he bogged down to passivity with speculations and abstractions nor does he throw all norms to the winds in the zeal for action. Other 'doers' of this nature, besides Kailas, are the President in *Morning* who "had founded a home for handicapped children that had been built on a trickle of small donations" (86), and Prakash Shukla, in the same novel, "something of an institution in the Lok Sabha" (86), who can lumber up an "undeniable procession of incriminating data" (221) to expose unscrupulousness and corruption. Harpal in *Storm* is another Gandhian doer. His work for the Congress party had been "fanatical" in its devotion (38). He worked tirelessly for the rehabilitation of the refugees and the reconstruction of a new Punjab. In *Shadow,* it is through lone crusaders like Raj, an Independent M.P. with a feeling "for India" (15), that the Gandhian tradition is kept alive. He fights single-handedly against the "shadowy beginnings of a vast alliance" (152). Usman's blueprint outlining "a new pattern that stood education down in its own cultural milieu and envisaged experiments where it became a two-way process between the teacher and the taught" (*Situation*, 114), is another dimension of such constructive action. In *Rich,* too, Sonali is brought round to involve herself in the situation rather than seeking to withdraw herself therefrom.[38]

For Gandhi, truth was God. He preached the pursuit of truth in all walks of life. Truth was the end and non-violence the means. "They are like the two sides of a coin, or rather a smooth unstamped metallic disc. Who can say which is the obverse, and which is the reverse?"[39] Ahimsa or non-violence implies the largest love, the greatest charity, applying "the same rules to the wrong-doer who is my enemy or a stranger to me as I would to my wrong-doing father or son."[40] In a non-violent struggle, there is no personal enmity, it is the wrong which is resisted. Non-violence rather than the use of violence "would at first dazzle… the adversary and at last, compel recognition from him, which recognition would not humiliate him but would uplift him."[41] Translated in political terms, the doctrine implies that *Satyagraha* is to be directed against the English rule rather than the English men themselves and there is no personal hatred or ill-will involved.

The minstrel in *Gold* is unequivocal that "you cannot right one wrong with another. You cannot fight malice with malice" (62). We learn that Satyajit will fight Steeltown in such a manner that :

> no hate will be involved...to give hate for hate is only to make the evil grow stronger. To hate is to be defeated in the moral struggle (12).

The strategies Satyajit comes out with to counter the twin threats from Ladakh and Steeltown are essentially Gandhian. Satyajit is convinced that a negotiated settlement of all the differences in the perception of the two countries can be found. Bhaskar, too, like Satyajit is convinced that it is evil which is to be fought and not the evil-doer (266). The same Gandhian message is reiterated by Davesh in *Hungers* as he forges the people together to uproot the English rule.

In the fight against evil (in the political context, 'the English rule'), Davesh is emphatic that violence in any form, in word, in deed or even in thought is taboo. Davesh admonishes the villagers for harbouring violent thoughts :

> There is violence in your thoughts : that is evil enough. Do not make it worse by violence in action (73).

The foreign rule, well-entrenched with time, cannot be overthrown with violence, "If we use the weapons of our enemy, we play into their hands" (73). There is a graphic description of the Gandhian magic of Davesh's working on the masses who had grown violent impulsively but the thought of their leader in penitence for them makes them regret their momentary surrender to their impulses. They "thought how he would grieve if he knew; they had disobeyed him and sadness was heavy in their bones" (76).

On the public plane, suffering and atonement for a lapse committed by some constituent of the community is the Gandhian way of reforming the wrong-doer the non-violent way. Like the five-day fast undertaken by Gandhi as penance for the lapse on the part of a resident of Tolstoy Farm in South Africa, Satyajit, too, does the same for much the same purpose. Again when he was faced with the threat of Steeltown's expansion towards Gandhigram, Satyajit "forced himself" into a Gandhian stance and gained victory over himself" (366). He went on a fast-unto-death. Even in meeting the threat of external aggression, Satyajit is determined to forsake all violence in thought and deed and to use 'soul-force' to arouse the inherent goodness (though momentarily subdued) in the adversary. He proposes to take a *Shanti Sena* to Ladakh (64). Satyajit's strategy seems to be inspired by Gandhi's conception of World Government, which may have a police force functioning as a *Shanti Sena* rather than as a fighting force.[42]

Whereas Satyajit failed with the Great Uncle's grandson whom he couldn't bring to repentance with his fast (48), Bhaskar succeeds remarkably with the Chinese girls (298). The hatred and suspicion in them for Indians is transformed into compassion and love. Moreover, under the leadership of Bhaskar, Steeltown's battle against Gandhigram is totally devoid of any aggression or force. By enabling Gandhigramians to have a glimpse of Steeltown, Bhaskar intends to give them the chance to choose either. The exposure to Steeltown fascinates Sumita who discovers the wonders of electricity and comes to feel that there is nothing bad in using it (144). Suruchi, with her 'intuitive understanding,' rightly guesses that Bhaskar's objective is to be "achieved by peaceful penetration.... A conquest by non-violence" (84-85). Bhaskar's strategy of exposing the people of Gandhigram to the culture of Steeltown is approved as Gandhian by Chittaranjan, an elderly member of the tribe of Satyajit. Quoting Gandhi, he says :

> No culture can live if it tries to be exclusive. I do not want my house to be walled on all sides and my windows to be stuffed. I want all cultures to flow freely about my house. Mine is not a religion of the prison-house (158).

Non-violence for Gandhi was not as much philosophy or ethics as it was action. "It took you by the guts and steeled every nerve and fibre of you. It trimmed and toughened you" (*Morning*, 45). Non-violence presupposes ability to use force to defend the right with conscious restraint and use of 'soul-force' against the wrong-doer. "Where, however, there is only a choice between cowardice and violence, I would advise violence.... I would rather have India to arms in order to defend her honour than that she should in a cowardly manner become or remain a witness to her own dishonour."[43]

It is significant to note here now Gandhi himself gave his 'tacit consent' to Government of India's defence measures in Kashmir in 1947, and advised the Czechs and Poles to fight the German invaders during World War II. In fact, he went so far as to characterize the resistance of the Poles as almost 'non-violence' because the Poles had given proof of rare national self-respect and valour by standing up against a vastly superior power and because the Poles were unprepared for the way in which the enemy swooped down upon them.[44] Gandhi was certainly a pacifist but he had "no use for peace that served to maintain the *status quo*, by the perpetration of existing inequalities and injustice; he wanted peace that resulted from the realization of justice and ensured equality and independence for all."[45]

It is revealing to study the character of Satyajit, who is taken to be a Gandhian in all respects in the light of Gandhi's views on non-violence. Not only does Satyajit deviate from Gandhism in his attempt to hide the unpalatable aspects of his wife's experience as a member of the Indian delegation to the Peace Congress at Moscow (6), he also propagates and practises, during the crucial period of external aggression, a version of Gandhism which Gandhi himself would have repudiated. Satyajit's unwillingness to face the harsh reality in the light of the unmistakable signals is a type of escapism, a sort of 'ostrich-syndrome,' which is at the farthest remove from Gandhism. It is 'delusion,' as Bhaskar terms it (128). Satyajit laughs away the misgivings his wife, Suruchi, entertained after her encounter with members of the Chinese delegation in Moscow. He says :

> Must we see an evil motive? The Himalayan border is well demarcated. Local Chinese guards have acted wrongly on their own initiative. What both the sides need is a cool dialogue to settle this petty dispute (52).

While the reference to negotiations for the solution of international problems is truly in accord with Gandhian political ideology, one still feels uneasy with such smug, bland optimism, flying in the face of facts. However, what takes the plum is the following. Satyajit

> waves aside the legalistic attitude of New Delhi. He was all for a new understanding. *Friendship of the Chinese people was worth more than a bleak wasteland between snowclad cliffs* (emphasis added) (70).

This meek submission, indeed rank cowardice, leading to certain degradation of the soul is not really Gandhian. Gandhi would have advocated "fighting non-violently to the last man…without any bitterness or hatred against the invader." This is the advice Gandhi had given to the Indians in Assam and Indo-Burmese border at the time of the Japanese invasion of these regions during World War II.[46]

Malgonkar is sceptical of the Gandhian belief in the inherent goodness and divinity of each human being. He is chary of the idealistic platitudes of a Bhattacharya or a Sahgal, for he finds the tribe of humanity peopled by outright charlatans, impulsive beings vulnerable to the frenzy of passions or inconspicuous fit-ins who cut themselves according to the slot wherein they are pushed, never daring to stand out. In such a scenario, the only version of non-violence would be sham non-violence and that is indicted as a philosophy of political behaviour in Malgonkar. His work is freely interspersed with such indictment through different characters who carry the mantle of the author.

There is no scepticism at all in Malgonkar about Gandhi's own sincerity of purpose or his total belief in non-violence. Gilchrist in *Bandicoot* represents the high approbation wherein Gandhi as a practitioner of non-violence is held. Only a saintly being like Gandhi could have attempted such an idealistic and exalted concept. However, it is precisely for this reason that in *Ganges,* an impression is created that it is impracticable and unrealistic to expect whole masses of people at the receiving end of colonialism, oppression and exploitation to metamorphose themselves overnight into sages sans rancour, ill-will or hatred. Basu in *Ganges* equates Gandhi's sincerity with delusion, "something brought by wishful thinking endowing the human race with virtues it does not possess" (291). For it is "merely a pious thought, a dream of the philosophers" (291). Hafiz finds the non-violence in vogue to be sham :

> In the midst of Gandhi's non-violence, violence persists. Violence such as no one has ever seen. That is what awaits this country : the violence bottled up in those who pay lip-service to non-violence (93).

The statement attributed to Gandhi, with which the novel is prefaced, is explicitly sceptical of the general adherence to non-violence :

> This non-violence...seems to be due mainly to our helplessness. It almost appears as if we are nursing in our bosom the desire to take revenge the first time we get the opportunity. Can true, voluntary non-violence come out of this seeming forced non-violence of the weak? (5)

Violence persisted, not merely without but also within the self-proclaimed believers in the Gandhian creed. Malgonkar himself buttresses the argument with the irrefutable proof of history, as he declares,

> Only the violence in this story happens to be true : it came in the wake of freedom, to become a part of India's history. What was achieved through non-violence, brought with it one of the bloodiest upheavals of history : twelve million people had to flee leaving their homes ; nearly half a million were killed; over a hundred thousand women, young and old, were abducted, raped, mutilated (6).

For most of the people swearing by non-violence, it was only an expedient to "shelter their cowardice," as Singh, the arch-revolutionary, cynically believed (19). Even otherwise, for most of the people who are "mixed-up, shallow and weak" (128), a strict compliance with the norm is obviously too demanding. The omniscient author in *Ganges* presents the discarding of their vows of non-violence by people as inevitable in the face of escalating World War, the repressive measures of the alien government and the incarceration of their leaders (283). The impression is created that the forsaking of "their proverbial restraint by the British" (283) could only lead to the conversion of "the non-violence of the leaders of India into the violence of the terrorists" (284).

Malgonkar gives the impression that non-violence as an ideal is unrealistic; it can never by fully adhered to. With relentless logic, he gives the impression that only in specifically defined circumstances with a specifically defined adversary can non-violence be an efficacious strategy. The following exchange between Debi and Basu is significant in this context :

> 'Non-violence is all very well, if the other party too plays by the rules. It may prove an effective weapon against the British because of their inherent decency. How far would it have gone against Hitler?'
>
> 'I don't know,' Debidayal said weakly. 'The Jews are said to have tried it.'
>
> 'Yes, and what happened to them. Did you see the pictures of Buchenwald? Of Belsen? Read the accounts? They were exterminated like some kind of pest…' (291).

This interpretation of the inefficacy of non-violence underscores the context in which *ahimsa* is to be practised. If the Nazi or the Chinese context is ignored and we expect every adversary to be decent, we are asking for annihilation and also glorifying annihilation. Non-violence is not a closed myth. It must be interpreted in the light of the context.

If non-violence is a strategy of limited applicability, preachers of non-violence are making their disciples 'soft.' The revolutionaries accuse Gandhi of "emasculating the population" (72). The Congress, as "a milksop organization" (282) is accused of "bullock-cart speed and…vegetarian logic" (284). *Ganges* creates uneasy doubts about *ahimsa,* as it is practised, as a total creed of life for it presents self-professed Gandhians using it as a mere "political expedient" without any "deeper significance" (333). Coming from Dewan Bahadur Tek Chand, who has no ideological axe to grind, this lament is imbued with force. Non-violence was used "as an effective weapon against British power" and discarded "the moment the grip of British power was loosened" (333). Even as the political ideology of a sovereign nation, non-violence is found wanting. Debi Dayal, the positive protagonist, has nothing to say and Basu's rhetorical query on this score goes unanswered : "If non-violence is the bedrock of our national policy, how is the fighting spirit to manifest itself only in our services?" (292)[47]

Not merely is non-violence in *Ganges* indicted for its inadequacies in practice, the Gandhian tenet is discredited in a more subtle manner by making 'the unheroic hero,' Gian, use it as a ploy to cover up his inherent imperfections. Gian discards his imported blazer into the bonfire, lit by the Gandhian *satyagrahis*. Malgonkar, however, peeps into the working of his mind :

> Was is merely a moment of weakness — the heady glow brought on by an act of sacrifice.... Or the sight of a beautiful woman throwing away her fur-coat into a fire? (18)

Gian wears khaddar because it is cheap but he secretly dreams of affluence. "The gap between the world he secretly longed for and he world he fitted into was wide enough" (23). Nevertheless he is "thankful that khaddar has now become synonymous with nationalism" (23).

Malgonkar thus makes a distinction between non-violence as faith and as a practical political or individual creed. Non-violence can be a strain, a burden, even a scar on an average man. Gian strains like Kalyan Sinha in *Morning* under the burden of an essentially Gandhian gesture. He resents the sacrifice of his elder brother, Hari, who had him educated :

> What right had anyone to burden another with so much that could not be repaid, making him powerless, breaking down his defences with unwavering kindness, saddling him with lifelong self-denial? (27)

Repeated peeps into the psyche of Gian reveal how his non-violence is sham. Gian is shown wondering why he has "embraced the philosophy of non-violence...from physical cowardice, not from courage? Was his non-violence merely that of the rabbit refusing to confront the hound?" (50). And yet, Gian is found often muttering, "The path of *ahimsa* is not for cowards" (10), as if the reiteration of it would make the same valid for him too. This early impression of Gian is borne out by the role he is assigned to play in the narrative later : his toadying to the English to secure petty comforts for himself in the Andaman prison even as Debi Dayal suffers in lonely splendour; his resigning himself to living for ever in the Andamans even as Debi Dayal makes a heroic attempt to flee. Gian is made to undergo further deterioration, to worsen the worst he was deemed capable of, revealing his selfishness, amoral conduct and rank indifference to anything he himself is unconcerned with: extracting the sovereign from the dead body of the Ramoshi, using the family idol of Shiva as a pawn in his selfish designs, betraying the confidence of Sundari, Debi's young sister. However, Gian is to learn and to grow and what is highly significant in this context is the manner wherein he asserts himself. His sticking to the docks in the face of the ravaging fire would win acclaim for courage and devotion to duty even from the staunchest Gandhians.[48] He does have 'the suburban rectitude' which helps him get over "the corrosive damage suffered in the Andamans" (277), before he finally succumbs to temptation and falsehood. When Sundari exposes him, Gian sounds convincing :[49]

> I had just begun to believe in myself taking courage in the fact that somewhere in spite of all his weaknesses, there is in every man something that he can value. You have now destroyed that faith (330).

From a fake Gandhian, covering up his cowardliness with a garb of non-violence, Gian grows into a truly Gandhian fighter with non-violent weapons like love, sacrifice, the willingness and the capacity to fight evil, even with violence, if need be, in his armoury. Gian is given an eminently Gandhian motive at this juncture : "To try and prove, if only to myself that there can be some good in the weakest of human beings" (351-52). Gian reveals his new-found qualities — quintessentially Gandhian — in his encounter with Shafi and his communalist goons, as he measures up to them and gets the better of them eventually. It is also not without significance that whereas Debi Dayal, the idealized proponent of violence dies (albeit martyr-like), it is the grown and matured Gian who survives and drives the convoy to safety.[50]

Whereas *ahimsa* in *Ganges* comes off as complicated, abstract, idealistic, impracticable and only partly valid in its usually practised half-baked form, *himsa* appears more real, more natural. This presentation of *himsa* is as much material in the consideration of the treatment of Gandhian political ideology in Malgonkar as is the sceptic note in the presentation of *ahimsa*. Debi Dayal, the positive protagonist in the novel, holds the view that *himsa* would have been a 'cleaner' alternative to *ahimsa* for fighting a war for freedom. Then the resultant bloodshed would have been "an honest sacrifice, honest and manly — not something that had sneaked upon them in the garb of non-violence" (355). The recourse to *himsa* in Debi and Shafi is not merely inevitable, it is also a means of self-fulfilment. The urge in Debi to be strong and to value force dates back to the day when he was "lifted bodily by that enormous bull-necked soldier from the Scottish Borders" whom he had caught making love to his mother one day (69). Shafi, the other advocate of violence, has his own reasons. "As a boy of seven, he had been taken to identify the body of his father, flung obscenely on a heap of other bodies, in the enclosure of the Jallianwala Bagh" (74). Since then, "Shafi had a good deal to avenge" (74).

Not merely does the recourse to violence in these two look

legitimate, the association of Shafi with positive symbols tends to give him a halo, strengthening the case of *himsa* thereby. As Gian prays to Shiva in the prayer room, he finds Shiva's face replaced by the bearded face of Shafi, "pronouncing words charged with malevolence : A million shall die, a million" (32). Debi Dayal, as he participates in the terrorists' plans to blow up trains, looks at Shafi's face. Here again, the description of Shafi, the emissary of *himsa*, comes to have images with positive connotations :

> ...he looked like the statue of Buddha in repose...a bearded Buddha in deep contemplation, radiating inner peace — a Muslim who had become a Sikh and looked like Buddha, transcending the religious insularity of ageless Indias (77).

Recourse to violence brings a certain fulfilment in the lives of both Debi and Shafi. What is much more significant is that such fulfilment looks a legitimate recompense. Debi and Shafi, looking at the plane they had set fire to, experience an exhilarating "joy of some secret fulfilment" (82). Whereas Bhattacharya's arsonists in *Hungers* had been remorseful after burning a *dak ghar*, here in *Ganges,* there is a note of tacit condoning on which the episode concludes :

> ...both of them were conscious that this crawling itself was some kind of an answer on behalf of the men and women who had been made to crawl in the streets of Amritsar, twenty years earlier (82).

Gian had experienced a similar sense of fulfilment in the feudal set-up at Konshet earlier in the novel. When all avenues of justice had been blocked by a wanton display of heartless miscarriage of justice and corruption, the only way Gian could feel himself a man again was to take the law in his own hands and murder his brother's murderer.

Along with the subtle manner wherein recourse to 'honest' violence is handled by the novelist, there are other means, equally subtle, to convey the ideological point. The Englishmen, themselves, primary target of the terrorist nationalists, are shown not merely understanding but also praising the zeal of such terrorists as Shafi and Debi, even though they call them 'misguided.' The people, we are told, are "sympathetic towards them" (131). They "almost hero-worship some of them" (131). Malgonkar himself seems to have hero-worshipped Debi, so much is his portrait idealized and overblown. He is given a plausible motivation for his actions, untiring selfless dedication, an endless capacity to suffer without yielding, abhorrence of cringing and crawling before his tormentors and, to top them all, almost superhuman physical prowess — all this with Gian serving as his foil in the Andamans. Most surprisingly, he is given proficiency in Japanese too when the need demands it (205)! His death is that of a martyr, the way Malgonkar describe it, investing the event with poetic and symbolic overtones. The last thing he ever saw was "the rising sun in the land of the five rivers on the day of their freedom" (369).

The 'greatness' of the propagator, *viz*. Debi, certainly reflects on *himsa*, to some extent at least. More important is the manner where in the insistent use of the Shiva idol — both as an object and as an integral part of the myth of Trimurti — enables *himsa* to draw exclusive attention to itself, to the detriment of *ahimsa*. The idol is put to use both as a weapon of offence and that of defence by Gian in his new-found role of a saviour towards the closing stages of the novel. It is the idol that disarms one of the goons, Inoos; it is the idol that comes between Gian and the bullet that Shafi fires at him. It is the idol that catches Shafi squarely on the side as he shoots at Sundari's mother. Last but not least, it is the idol which comes down again and again on Shafi "as though killing a scorpion or a spider, crashing in the dead man's skull until it cracked open and blood and brains spurted out in a red and white mess" (379). The Senecan ending of the novel surely seems brought about by Shiva through a *tandava nritya* to eradicate evil.

The change wrought in the character of the idealized protagonist, Debi Dayal is as significant as is the one in the character of the 'negative hero,' Gian. It is significant that both

Gian and Debi, though they set off from divergent points, converge finally at something which represents a truly Gandhian posture. Gian's inculcation of the Gandhian tenets has already been commented on. Debi, too, "was conscious of some great change that had come over him. He felt weak, like someone waiting for outside guidance." "He wondered whether all the exposure to what Gandhi had described as man's inhumanity to man had converted him to the doctrine of non-violence?" (268). The form of revenge against Shafi which Debi chooses is indeed 'inexplicable' and is in striking departure from his violent ways of yore. The manner wherein he falls in love with Mumtaz, the flame of Shafi's, whom he had taken away, shows a new Debi emerging from the wreckage of the past. Both Gian and Debi come under the mystifying fold of love and they have their better selves awakened thereby. In their love for each other and in their attempt to save each other from the frenzy of communalism, both Debi and Mumtaz fall victims in a cause dear to Gandhi. It is obvious that these representatives of the Gandhian force of love may temporarily have been overpowered, what they have lost is a mere battle and not the war as such.

It would be improper to describe *Ganges* as 'anatomy of non-violence,' as G.S. Amur does.[51] It is not merely *ahimsa* which is anatomized, and found wanting in certain respects, *himsa* also comes to be, in the final analysis, self-destructive. It is tempting to find here Malgonkar's debunking of ideological panaceas in his espousal of apolitical, personal bonds a la *Drum* where Kiran and Abdul had flouted all 'irrational' political regulations to toast to each other's health. However, in Debi's adherence to love, understanding, self-introspection and willingness to make the supreme sacrifice for a cause he cherishes, and even more than that, in Gian's new-found role as a selfless crusader against evil, one simply can't help detecting unmistakable shades of Gandhism.

For Gandhi, the idea of freedom and democracy flowed from religion. His view of democracy was humanitarian and egalitarian. "A nation that runs its affairs smoothly and effectively without much State interference is truly democratic. Where such a condition is absent, the form of Government is only democratic in name."[52] Gandhi dreaded a coercive State masquerading as a democracy where the masses are left high and dry. Gandhi could see such 'limited democracy' degenerate into either anarchism or authoritarianism, given the patchwork agglomeration that the Congress was. He had suggested the creation of institutions of parallel polity, which would exist in the form of an 'oceanically' spread Panchayat system to forestall the concentration of power at the Centre.[53] However, after the sad reality of the Partition, Gandhi was a disillusioned man. He planned to approach the people directly for they had been by-passed by their leaders. "What did it matter if there were two Indias instead of one? In both, those who ruled were not the masses, but the educated minority."[54] N.K. Bose refers to Gandhi's "last will and testament" [55] wherein Gandhi had desired that the Congress organization must wind itself up and send all Congress workers to educated and organize the people politically and also economically. "...the first step and the necessary step was understandably political freedom. But it was no more than the beginning; the hardest was yet to come."[56]

Like Gandhi, the minstrel in *Gold* is not content with the mere attainment of freedom : "Freedom is the beginning of the road where there was no road. But the new road swarms with robbers" (119). Expounding these words of the Grandpa, Sohanlal rightly speaks for him :

> There was the money-Seth...to whom freedom meant a chance to seize fields of trade vacated by the aliens. Then the Seth of politics, ready to dupe the people with the power of his glib tongue. The official Seth, a man of arrogance, ready to change masters without a change of mentality, human chattel open to the best offer. The Seth of religion with gods for sale (119).

A telling example of the pernicious manner in which Gandhian exhortations for *sarvodya* are put to practice in independent India is suggested by Jayadev in *Music*. The cause of the so-called untouchables was dear to Gandhi. The

Constitution gave them special privileges and reservations. But these soon became "a vested interest!" What would happen to leaders in the District town if there were to be no untouchables!" (142).

In *Gold*, the picture Sohanlal draws of what free India may turn out to be like, gives shape to the apprehensions voiced by Gandhi. "Those men who were the prison guards of yesterday's slavery" may present themselves as "the guardians of tomorrow's freedom" (120) to perpetuate their hegemony. For a proof of the forebodings echoed here through Sohanlal, one has to turn to Malgonkar and Sahgal.

Sahgal deeply bemoans the inexorable retreat from Gandhism, so much so that if the spirit of the Mahatma survives anywhere in the world, she says, "It is certainly not India.'[57] The Gandhi image sits "farcically on the ruling party"; but it is one legacy none can dare dissociate oneself from publicly, for "no one could capture and hold the masses without it" (*Shadow,* 10). This reversal of values in politics and the consequent forsaking of Gandhism, has been brought about equally by insincere leaders and an apathetic public. The people failed "to be aware, to respond fearlessly and intelligently to some of the challenges our society now faces."[58] As one moves from the rambling tone of *Happy* to the drumbeats of *Situation* and the topsy turvy world of *Rich*, one finds not merely Gandhian protagonists but also Gandhism yielding to populism, parochialism, jingoism, fundamentalism and obscurantism.[59]

The professional politicians of Malgonkar are rather oversimplified and exaggerated beings carried over their feet by the abrupt change in the political scenario in 1947. Malgonkar seems to echo Gandhi in the latter's prophecy that Independence granted to an unprepared nation in an abrupt manner, would lead merely to a change in the colour of the skin of rulers.[60] Lala Vishnu Saran Dev in *Drum*, Kanak Chand in *Princes*, Jugal Kishor in *Combat* and Krishna Manikam in *Bandicoot* are persons catapulted to the pinnacle of political glory all of a sudden, the result of the British withdrawal from the scene, much in the same manner as their counterparts in Army, *viz.*, K.K., Rawal Singh, Shanti Lal and Behl had come to the top after the departure of the senior British officers in the Army. Puran Das in *Bandicoot* with "political astuteness," a "spotless record of honesty" without the contrivance of Gandhian self-abnegation about him in his demeanour, is the only picture of a politician painted positively in Malgonkar (58-59).

Malgonkar reveals his contempt for unscruplous politicians[61] — and here his criterion is essentially Gandhian—as he introduces Lala Vishnu Saran Dev stamping into Kiran's office with a three-day growth of beard on his chin and his mouth full with the juice of *pan*. The Lala takes a chair uninvited and announces belligerently : "I yam the Chairman aff the District Caangrus Committee" (59). He wants the Regimental shamiana "shent to the shity haal garden" where a "resheption" is to be held. When Colonel Garud points out that the regimental shamiana is never lent for political functions,[62] the politician in the Lala bares his fangs :

> Coynelsaab...the political party aaf which you taak so lightly is ruling thish country today. The days aaf treating us as a sheditious aarganization are gone. Now the party and the gournment are the shame (60).

Despite the linguistic distortions to suggest unsophisticated and comical use of language, the menacing tone can't be mistaken. Lala Vishnu Saran Dev can't be brushed aside as a comical creature. That he is no more heard of in the novel is merely an indication of Malgonkar's fond belief, at this stage, that the nuisance value of such upstarts is minimal and it can be successfully met through a show of official rectitude. In Jugal Kishor and Kanak Chand, we are to meet what the novelist conveniently lets fade here.

In *Combat*, in his description of what he chooses to call 'babu politicians,' Malgonkar gives a fairly accurate account of the amoral, unscrupulous and power-crazy politicians, a phenomenon brought about by prospects of impending freedom :

> Politics are his business, just as growing tea is yours and mine. We grow tea for no other reason than because it gives us the wherewithal to live according to our standards: he goes into politics for much the same reason (225).

Jugal Kishor, being such a practitioner of politics, is "wholly amenable…to reason, particularly when reason is accompanied by the tinkle of rupees" (226).

With relentless logic, Malgonkar lays bare the machinations of professional politicians and politicized army men, the latter provide the staple dramatis personae of his fictional world. In this exposè is easily discernible the exacting Gandhian yardstick which the novelist uses consistently to separate his men from monsters. There is a very long list of Army men in Malgonkar who dabble in politics and have their career as army officers advanced thereby. The list includes K.K., Lt. Col. Namdar, Major Rawal Singh (*Drum*), Major General Shantilal, General Behl (*Bandicoot*) and also Mr. Kagal, an Under Secretary.

A Gandhian examen of the current political scenario inevitably shows the rot. Gandhi had a totally different conception of politics and power. For Gandhi, both politics and power were value-oriented. He was not against State power but he insisted on much greater dedication, austerity and exemplary behaviour and sacrifice, otherwise those who wielded power couldn't enjoy legitimacy with the masses. Essentially the power-elite had to live at the level of masses and with them. Gandhi's entire emphasis on decentralization and the preservation of human values was designed to avoid the alienation of man from man and from his environment.[63]

The Gandhian insistence on the mass-elite dynamics has been well incorporated in the novels of Bhattacharya, Malgonkar and Sahgal. All their positive characters are either well integrated with the masses already or they arrive at the stage of such integration in due course. Gandhi himself was an example *par excellence* of what he expected a leader to be. Yogananda in *Hawaii* brings out the secret of Gandhi's power :

> Gandhi renounced all and clad in a peasant's loin-cloth, he lived as one of the poor and humble, that was the secret of his power over a hundred million people (188).

Kajoli and her mother in *Hungers* are presented by the novelist as inseparable part of the masses. They have no compunctions in sharing their meals with their "kisan uncles" (79). Even in the face of the famine and the imminent starvation, her mother is firm. "If we eat, our kisan brethren and their kin shall eat" (105). Rahoul's grandfather, Davesh Basu, has got so well-integrated with the villagers that he has started living with them. The villagers call him their own. He has become the *de jure* head of Kajoli's family after the imprisonment of her father for his having participated in Civil Disobedience Movement. Rahoul himself moves from a mere enchantment with his Dadu's Gandhian ideals to an actual involvement with the destiny of the masses. He feels guilt-ridden for his insulated, luxurious life in fashionable Calcutta, for his Western mode of life appears to him mere self-indulgence.[64] He grows into a truly Gandhian fighter for freedom as he casts off his "intellectual snobbery" and feels himself "as of one clay with the common people of the soil" (102), in the joint crusade for the liberation of the land. Though he is a member of the upper stratum of society, he addresses Kishor, a mill-hand, as his brother (101). The shift from his "intellectual blanket" (19) to the fret and fury of the political struggle occurs as he, significantly enough, leaves the laboratory for the public place where the peaceful processionists are being callously lathicharged by the alien police. He leaves the place of distinction at the laboratory and merges with the multitude.[65]

Mohini and the Big House in *Music*, too, are fully integrated with the masses. The Big House has already made itself the guide and guardian of the whole village. During the famine in Bengal, "Many precious jewels and some two hundred sovereigns dating back to the Mughal days" had been sold to "feed the starving people" (101). The master of Behula had done best to prevent the sale of paddy to grain profiteers during the war, knowing well that this would starve the people (122). He himself was drowned while attempting to evacuate stricken villagers inundated by Meghmala in spate (122). Mohini herself, even before she discovers the fine heritage of the Big House, promises to her husband, Jayadev, "You'll see how soon and easily I become Behula's own" (77). On her way to Behula after her marriage, she shares her meals with the cartmen (78). She feeds the children of the farm labourers who come to bring their ration to the fields (118).

The minstrel in *Gold* offers villagers spiritual guidance and political leadership. He has a certain aura of mystery and greatness about him. Yet he has an intuitive feel of the people he meets and addresses. He is easily accessible and feels perfectly at home with the villagers. As a matter of fact, the novelist himself endeavours to divest the minstrel of his halo by presenting the ironic banter between the old man and his wife as he comes home after a long time (60).

In Meera (*Gold*) and Kalo (*Tiger*), Bhattacharya validates the Gandhian dictum by making these characters retrace their steps and tread wary of the means they adopt, however good in itself may be the goal they aim at. Even as a young girl, Meera had revealed her strength of will and her determination, and her concern for others. However, towards the later part of the novel Meera loses this rapport, this camaraderie with the folks as she allows herself to be coaxed into a dubious partnership with the Seth. She is dazzled by the vision of immense wealth. Even though she dreams of bettering the lot of the whole community and not of personal aggrandizement, it is wrong to have faith in wrong and improper means however good the ends they seem to promise. As Sohanlal explains to her : "It is the fight with the Seths that will save India, not a miracle, not armfuls of gold" (197). This short-cut to prosperity without blood and sweat cuts Meera off from the people completely. But then she discards the amulet and the schemes she had woven round it. She finally comes round to the conviction that there can be no easy way and human suffering can't be solved with the help of a miracle, but only through a determined effort (270). It is thus that she regains the love and respect of the village-folks.

In Kalo, the blacksmith from Jharna (*Tiger*), we discern a similar pattern. An honest, sincere, hardworking blacksmith, "his heart was truly with his own people whose life he shared. His roots were in the age-richened soil of his own caste" (12). However, after he reincarnated himself as a priest, he grew alienated from all, including his daughter (112), and his new-found community of Brahmins. It is only towards the close, when he unburdens himself of all his machinations, that he feels *en rapport* with the people. They listen and hail him as a legend. Kalo's reintegration and his return to truth are a vindication of the Gandhian protester in him.

Satyajit and Bhaskar from *Ladakh* appear contrasting studies from this perspective of elite-mass dynamics. Bhaskar has never embraced the form of Gandhism even though his inner being is permeated with its essence. His workers remember how their C.E. worked with his own hands to help a petty worker who was having trouble with his electric welding set. They exclaim, "He has always been our friend. He has known our mind, our feelings" (370). Bhaskar is a dedicated leader with saintly ingredients. Mrs. Mehra, his Private Secretary, testifies: "Twelve years in the land of fabulous wealth, and he comes back empty-handed. He is a saint, I tell you" (35-36).

Satyajit in *Ladakh* leads an austere life in a mud house. However, he has travelled far from the Gandhian link with his people. He has an aura of intellectuality like Rahoul's (*Hunger*), a halo of sanctity and sainthood like the minstrel's (*Gold*), but unlike these two :

> Satyajit towered over all the others. He was unequalled among the equals. With each passing year, he had shut himself up more and more in a loneliness where none could enter (47).

Suruchi finds him engrossed in Sartre when she would like to discuss her Moscow visit with him (51). She is true to a large extent when she calls him "an egoist" (324). He is referred to as "the stone god" too (20). It is this which prompts Bireswar, his friend, to ask him to lead a normal life rather than allowing himself to be "vested with...saintliness" (360) which distances him from the people. Bireswar himself, an independent M.P., is presented as leading a life unencumbered with such saintly baggage and perfectly in communion with those around him. Towards the close, Satyajit recalls his friend's words and promises to himself that he will come down from his high pedestal to be one with the masses. "His new won release would seek expression in the honest acceptance of every human need" (367). Satyajit, thus, far from being a Gandhian from the beginning, develops during the course of action, into a true follower of Gandhi.

The elite-mass dynamics in Sahgal is taken up in some of its baffling dimensions, especially in her later novels. *Happy* admittedly delineates the relationship in the Bhattacharya-vein. Sohanlal, the idealized Gandhian in *Happy* takes to politics as a mission. He has no other identity, no marks of distinction from the masses. The narrator and Maya in the same novel turn their backs on power and money to lead a life of dedication and service to the masses. Sanad, too, towards the end of the novel, decides to efface his anglicized background and strive towards greater involvement with the people. Later characters like Kailas Vrind, Abdul Rahman and Prakash Shukla in *Morning* are maturer beings in their avowal of this Gandhian dictum. In the long term perspective, they take their political role like that of a parent in relation to their children. It is this which makes them nurture freedom like young trees which "grow in time, and if the roots aren't strong, they can't grow at all." Leaders of such vintage realize that their responsibility as public men is to check and divert popular aspirations in proper channels rather than let them be carried over in the current.

But where to draw the line between legitimate voicing of popular will and populism, between responsible statesmanship and irresponsible playing to the gallery? Kalyan, Hari Mohan, Som and 'the Cabinet Intellectuals' raise this problem in differing ways time and again.

Kalyan in *Morning* objectifies the phenomenon of charisma.[66] Charisma is an aberration in the healthy flow of the elite-mass dynamics insofar as it stifles the two-way Gandhian traffic between the power-elite and the masses. It draws people to a leader, irrespective of his inner worth. The leader becomes the end, the people the means.[67] Kalyan knows how to use people and their weaknesses for the fulfilment of his "hunger for identity" (132). Celia wonders how Kalyan possessed this 'fascination' "against all the rules" (62). Perhaps one component of this 'fascination' or 'charisma' is Kalyan's populist rhetoric. His queries like "Whose ego is so sacred that it must flourish at the expense of the community" (63) hide conveniently the disproportionate shadow his own ego casts on everything. Barbara is right when she complains how Kalyan "needs people but there is no tenderness in him" (61).

Gian Singh in *Storm* is another study in distorted elite-mass dynamics. With his roots in the soil, his unabashed rusticity, his avowal of the preternatural code of honour as against conscience ("Conscience was no match for it," 107). He is the self-styled spokesman of the people. He exploits their helplessness, whether they are Partition-scarred or tied down instinctively to their region, religion or language. It is ironic that while such leaders carry the day, men like Harpal with secularism, humanism and impeccable Gandhian credentials fail to make an impact.

It is in Usman and Rishad that Sahgal presents the positive aspects of her view of the elite-mass give-and-take. Usman and Rishad come from the academics and the upper middle class. Both are insulated from the harsher realities of life. But the novelist implicitly avers that for close integration and empathy with the masses, what is essential much more than physical proximation is emotional and intellectual involvement and concern. Whereas 'the Cabinet Intellectuals' in *Situation* believe in division of the masses into "the Poor and the Small against the Rich and the Big" (129), Usman and Rishad go to the roots of the malady which afflicts the people: they go to the humblest constituent of the masses, the least common multiple, to stir what lay moribund into action. Both Usman and Rishad make it a personal, individual crusade in their differing ways, unlike 'the Cabinet Intellectuals' who act as a group, following the most vocal amongst them, the minister of Minerals and Metals.

Malgonkar feels uneasy in the company of 'charismatic' leaders, voicing loudly what they term as the popular mandate. *Combat* and *Princes* reveal his contempt for such demagogues who are flashy without but shallow and hollow within. The positive protagonists in his novels like Kiran (*Drum*), Abhay (*Princes*), and Puran Das and Nadkar (*Bandicoot*), provide intellectual leadership but keep themselves at a safe distance from the pulls and pressures of those they profess to guide.

Malgonkar exhibits another dimension of Gandhism in his indictment of bureaucracy for its red-tapism which distances the people from those who exercise power on the basis of the mandate from the people. When rules, regulations and administrative channels become ends in themselves rather than means to action and efficiency, it signals the death-knell of grass-roots democracy and the cohesion between the power-elite and the masses.

> It was all governed by what everyone called baboo-logic…a state of mind in which officials had begun to use procedure not to avoid mistakes, but to avoid decisions. The tendency was to seek shelter behind some obscure but impregnable bastion of procedure and strenuously resist the need to make a decision…only when that was no longer possible, when a decision could no longer be delayed, they tried desperately to make someone else responsible for taking it (*Drum*, 123-24).

Kiran realizes how, in New Delhi, the 'Head-Quarters people' "make you feel like a Bum Wart all over again" (*Drum*, 82). Nadkar in *Bandicoot* feels indignant and terms the 'H.Q.' "the monkey house" and the bureaucratic procedure "muddled thinking compounded by foggy prose" (50).

Bureaucratization Malgonkar sees as an evil attendant upon the misconceived notion of welfare polity[68] wherein the people are dealt with as errant children and the State a schoolmaster.[69] This is how Abhay creates the impression of the people's response to Independence from the princely domination :

> Freedom from foreign domination was less tangible than the fact of being transferred from the rule of a Maharaja to the rule of the petty official, from the rule of flamboyance to one of niggling austerity and total prohibition, from one of direct, easy access to the source of all authority, their ruler, to the faceless hierarchy of clerks (*Princes*, 67).

It is the 'faceless,' impersonal functioning of bureaucracy lacking intimacy and understanding, which hurts, as Abhay's ex-subjects tell him (355). Abhay himself experiences this lack of 'finesse' and 'civility.' He knows that the merger of princely states into the Indian Union is politically inevitable (280). But what he minds is the callous and heartless manner wherein haughty bureaucrats go about 'accomplishing' it[70] (310).

One aspect of Gandhism is well-suggested by Bires in *Ladakh.* "Gandhiji always offered every possible opportunity to his adversary to win. His own personal stand was never important" (358). The openness with which views antithetical to Gandhi's are pronounced in Bhattacharya, Malgonkar and Sahgal has something of the liberality of the Gandhian political ideology.

Gandhi was undoubtedly all for action and not passive contemplation. However, because of the inherent philosophization of issues in Gandhism, the creed itself becomes vulnerable to the charge which Gandhi levelled against the popular practice of Hinduism — the seeming advocacy of passivity.

Mulk Raj Anand's protagonist, Lalu in *The Sword and the Sickle* had been lulled into listlessness "as if suffocated" by the Mahatma's philosophizing and his "egoistic confessional talk of self-purification."[71] It is against this background that in *Morning* Kalyan's impatience with passive resistance seems well-founded. Kalyan regards undergoing long terms of imprisonment as political strategy to register one's opposition to some government measure as so much waste of time and energy which can be put to more productive use[72] (136).

Kailas Vrind in *Morning* believes that Gandhism is to be seen as a dynamic faith rather than a closed myth. This would necessarily involve a constant reappraisal of the creed. Such an exercise, according to Kailas, is overdue so that the incidental may be isolated and only the essential concentrated on. How the whole edifice of Gandhism is to be revitalized to sharpen its efficacy in solving the problems the country is faced with, is sought to be taken up as one of the ways out in the next chapter.

REFERENCES

1. Pyarelal attributes the definite social colouring in Gandhi's religious thought to the influence of Tolstoy's writings on him. See Pyarelal, *Mahatma Gandhi : The Discovery of Satyagraha on the Threshold* (Bombay : Sevak Prakashan, 1980), II, 171. Kalidas Nag is of the view that unlike Tolstoy, Gandhi put his religious and spiritual convictions to explicit social and political uses. See Kalidas Nag, *Tolstoy and Gandhi* (Patna : Pustak Bhandar, 1950), 136.
2. M.K. Gandhi, *The Story of My Experiments with Truth* (Ahmedabad: Navjivan Publishing House), 383.
3. *Ibid.*, 118.
4. *Ibid.*, 198.
5. *Ibid.*
6. J.B. Kripalani, "Gandhian Revaluation of Values," K.P. Misra and S.C. Gangal, eds., *Gandhi and the Contemporary World* (Delhi : Chanakya Publications, 1981), 24. The six concepts, however, overlap.
7. N.K. Bose and P.H. Patwardhan, *Gandhi in Indian Politics* (Bombay : Lalvani Publishing House, 1967), 18.
8. *Ibid.*, 25.
9. The term is an extension of the coinage, 'negative heroes' by Paul Hollander in "Models of Behaviour in Stalinist Literature : A Case Study of Totalitarian Values and Controls," *American Sociological Review*, 31 (1966), 353.
10. See Chapter 6, "the Way Out of the Labyrinth," 183-84.
11. Nayantara Sahgal, *From Fear Set Free* (London : Victor Gollancz, 1962), 40.
12. *Young India*, November 13, 1924.
13. *Harijan,* June 5, 1937.

14. *Young India,* November 5, 1925.
15. *Young India,* November 13, 1924.
16. *Harijan,* June 22, 1935.
17. *Harijan,* January 2, 1938.
18. *Harijan,* September 19, 1939.
19. Nirmal Kumar Bose, "An Interview with Mahatma Gandhi," *Modern Review*, June-December, 1935, 411.
20. *Ibid.*
21. *Harijan*, February 1, 1942.
22. *Ibid.*
23. M.K. Gandhi, *Sarvodya* (Ahmedabad : Navjivan Publishing House, 1958), 52.
24. Vide Jasbir Jain, "The Human Dimensions of Statis and Growth," *Perspectives on Bhabani Bhattacharya*, ed. R.K. Srivastava (Ghaziabad: Vimal Prakashan, 1982), 54.
25. Paul C. Verghese, "Indian English and Man in Indo-Anglian Fiction," *Indian Literature*, 13, No. 1 (March 1970), 15.
26. *Collected Works of Mahatma Gandhi* (New Delhi : Ministry of Information and Broadcasting, 1958), XXXI, 511.
27. W.H. Morris-Jones, *The Government and Politics of India* (Delhi : B.I. Publications, 1979), 59.
28. For the values crucial in the Malgonkar world, which Winton sadly lacks, see Chapter 6, "The Way Out of the Labyrinth," 176-83.
29. Vide J.B. Kripalani, "Gandhi's Revolution of Values," in *Gandhi and the Contemporary World*, eds. K.P. Misra and S.C. Gangal, *op. cit.*, 21-24.
30. Vide Marlene Fisher's "The Women in Bhattacharya's Novels," in *Perspectives on Bhabani Bhattacharya*, 12-18, even though Fisher ignores Monju.
31. K.K. Sharma believes Kajoli was raped. See *Bhabani Bhattacharya — His Vision and Themes* (New Delhi : Abhinav Publications, 1979), 22. But Bhattacharya himself is non-committal. See Ramesh K. Srivastava, "Bhattacharya at Work : An Interview," *Perspectives on Bhabani Bhattacharya*, 220.
32. K.R. Srinivasa Iyengar finds in *Hungers* the belief highlighted that "People's follies are greater than their crimes and we sin because we are blind." *Indian Writing in English* (New York : Asia Publishing House, 1962), 413-14.
33. The coinage is Paul Hollander's in "Models of Behaviour in Stalinist Literature : A Case Study of Totalitarian Values and Controls," *American Sociological Review*, 31 (1966), 353.

34. See, for example, G.S. Amur's explanation of what motivates Kanak, the politician. "...it is the humiliation that he and his class suffered which turns him into a revolutionnary and not just the imagined treachery of Abhayraj or the punishment he receives at the hands of the Maharajah." *Manohar Malgonkar* (New Delhi : Arnold-Heinemann, 1973), 94-95.
35. See Chapter 4, "The Contours of A Crippling Creed."
36. Harijan, November 2, 1935. Among some important studies of Gandhian thought wherein this emphasis on action has been highlighted could be cited : Lloyd I. and Susanne Hoeber Rudolph, *The Modernity of Tradition* (Chicago : University of Chicago Press, 1967), 157-210 and Raghavan N. Iyer, *The Moral and Political Thought of Mahatma Gandhi* (Delhi : OUP, 1973).
37. It is interesting to note that Jawaharlal Nehru echoes Gandhi's impatience with popular Hinduism. He was convinced that such religion "does not help, ... [it] even hinders the moral and spiritual progress of a people." "It had little conception of human values and social values and social justice." See *Towards Freedom — The Autobiography of J.L. Nehru* (New Delhi : Allied Publishers Pvt. Ltd., 1962), 377, 507.
38. This is what Nayantara Sahgal wrote about Sonali in a letter to me, dated April 5, 1987. "Sonali, far from being subdued, faced a difficult situation with great courage. She was thrown out of her job during the Emergency and she did not submit or kowtow to the government. She stayed out. At the end, she realizes she can build a new life for herself, and this without benefit of marriage or a man's protection. She stands alone."
39. M.K. Gandhi, *Yarvada Mandir* (Ahmedabad : Navjivan Publishing House, 1945), 8-9.
40. *Speeches and Writings of M.K. Gandhi* (Madras: G.A. Natesan & Co., n.d.), 252.
41. *Young India*, October 8, 1925.
42. Pyarelal, quoting Gandhi, observes how Gandhi conceded that "there might be a world police in the absence of universal belief in non-violence," but in Gandhi's view, it would function more as a *Shantisena* (or Peace Brigade) than a modern fighting force. See "Gandhian Analysis of the Causes of International Tension and War," in *Gandhi and the Contemporary World*, *op. cit.*, 101-4.
43. *Young India*, August 11, 1920.
44. See K.J. Shah, "Gandhi's Non-violence : Its Bases," and S.C. Gangal, "Gandhi and World Order," in *Gandhi and the Contemporary World*, 54-55 and 167-69.
45. Pyarelal, "Gandhian Analysis of the Causes of International Tension and War," *ibid.*, 104.

46. See S.C. Gangal, "Gandhi and World Order," in *Gandhi and the Contemporary World*, 165-68.
47. Here obviously the point is not well taken. Gandhi's advocacy of a sovereign state without an army was a sort of 'Euclid point' which is of imperishable value, "even though [it is] never realizable in its completeness!" A centralized state, eschewing exploitation altogether and having internal harmony, would not excite the envy and greed that ostentatious concentration of wealth excites. Hence, such a state would run less risk of foreign invasion. But that is an ideal to strive for. See Narayan Desai, "Gandhi's Answers to Central Problems," and Pyarelal, "Gandhian Analysis of the Causes of International Tension and War," in *Gandhi and the Contemporary World*, 31-40, 101-10.
48. Cf. "No matter how weak a person is in body, if it is a shame to flee, he will stand his ground and die at his post. This would be non-violence and bravery." M.K. Gandhi, *Harijan,* August 17, 1935.
49. R.S. Singh's scepticism on this score is without foundation. He believes that "It was another lie Gian was giving to cover up his personal interest in Sundari : he was not morally regenerated." See *Indian Novel in English — A Critical Study* (New Delhi : Arnold-Heinemann, 1977), 135. However, the emphatic manner wherein Gian is depicted redeeming himself towards the close of the novel is enough to set at rest all such misgivings.
50. To say, as Robertson does, that Malgonkar, through the ending, indicts the post-Independence scenario ("a nation of Gian's") is to ignore totally the change in Gian, the novelist has taken so much pains to highlight. See R.T. Robertson's review of the novel in *Richmond News Leader*, February 7, 1965. To put Gian and Debi into the neat slots of 'corpus' and 'animus' respectively and say, as does Haydn Moore Williams, that the ending shows how the intellect kills, is, again, to ignore the life-like complexity of being which these characters come to have in the novel. See "The Doomed Hero in the Fiction of Khushwant Singh and Manohar Malgonkar," *Explorations in Modern Indo-English Fiction*, ed. R.K. Dhawan (New Delhi : Bahri Publications Pvt. Ltd., 1982), 197.
51. *Manohar Malgonkar*, 103.
52. *Harijan*, January 11, 1936.
53. Vide Naryan Desai, "Gandhi's Answers to Central Problems," in *Gandhi and the Contemporary World*, 47-49.
54. N.K. Bose, *Gandhi in Indian Politics*, 50.
55. *Ibid.*, 53.
56. N.K. Bose, *Gandhi in Indian Politics*, 53.
57. "Murder of Gandhiji Continues," *The Sunday Standard*, November 23, 1969.
58. "Failure of the Educated," *The Sunday Standard*, July 22, 1973.

59. For an account of how Gandhism has been dealt with in the country after Independence, see Chapter 3, "Chronicling the Political Web," 53-61.

60. See N.K. Bose, *Gandhi in Indian Politics*, 18-19, and *Young India*, December 19, 1929. Also Bhabani C. Bhattacharya, *Mahatma Gandhi : As A Writer* (New Delhi : Arnold Heinemann, 1982), 218.

61. Calling it only Kiran's contempt — for the story is presented through his perspective — could only be technically true. Malgonkar has *Drums*, *Princes* and *Bandicoot* presented through the perspective of protagonists like Kiran, Abhay and Nadkar respectively, precisely because they speak for their creator.

62. Kai Nicholson reads into Kiran's attitude here a proof of his anglomania and his anti-Congress stance. Asnani concurs with him in this. Both obviously ignore the issue at stake here, *viz.*, the question of ends and means. See Kai Nicholson, *Social Problems in the Indo-Anglian and Anglo-Indian Novel* (Bombay : Jaico, 1972), 162 and Shyam M. Asnani, *Critical Response to Indian English Fiction* (Delhi : Mittal Publications, 1985), 43.

63. This summing up of Gandhi's views on mass-elite dynamics is based principally on J.D. Sethi, *Gandhi Today* (New Delhi : Vikas Publishing House, 1978), 20-24, 60-62, 120. A. Appadorai, *Indian Political Thinking in the Twentieth Century from Naoroji to Nehru* (Delhi : OUP, 1974), 90-92, and *Gandhi and the Contemporary World*, 13-30, 41-50.

64. Vide Suresht Renjen Bald, "Politics of the Revolutionary Elite : A Study of Mulk Raj Anand's Novels," in *Modern Asian Studies*, 8, No. 4 (1974), 473-89.

65. Rahoul resolves his dilemma by opting for social activism in preference to the pursuit of a specialized discipline. It is possible to find here a sort of wishfulfilment of the novelist's for he too had been faced with such a dilemma in the wake of the Dandi March in 1931 and he had opted for art, ostensibly under the impact of Gurudev Tagore. See Dorothy Blair Shimer, "Gandhian Influences on the Writings of Bhabani Bhattacharya," in *Perspectives on Bhabani Bhattacharya*, *op. cit.*, 23.

66. A sociologist, T.K. Oomen, does attempt to isolate two ingredients, *viz.*, cosmopolitanism and honesty at two constituents of what gives a leader 'charisma' in the Indian context. See "Charisma and not King-Emperor," *The Times of India*, January 22, 1987. However, the fact remains that charismatic leaders are endowed with the halo of King-Emperor by the people. See Girilal Jain, "The King-Emperor," *The Times of India*, January 7, 1987.

67. According to Max Weber, 'charismatic domination' evokes 'affective behaviour,' defined not with reference to a goal or a system of values, but by the emotional reaction of an actor placed in a given set of

circumstances. See Raymond Aron, *Main Currents in Sociological Thought*, trs. Richard Howard and Helen Weaver (Harmondsworth: Pelican, 1967) II, 229-30, 240-45. Carl J. Friedrich in *The New Image of the Common Man* (Boston : Beacon Press, 1950) clubs this notion of 'charisma' together with the Durkheimian notion of 'the sacred,' Pareto's concept of 'elites,' Carlyle's philosophy of the hero and Nietzche's vision of the superman. These were all 'offspring of a society, containing as yet many feudal elements.' All these doctrines represented so many different attempts 'to revive ancient ideas of social hierarchy and to erect obstacles to the spread of democratic notions.'

68. In an essay "Politics as a Vocation," Max Weber compared bureaucratization with capitalism, for both result from the concentration of powers — administrative and productive powers, respectively. Weber also saw the danger that "Socialism might result, not in the liberation of man, but in his enslavement to an all powerful bureaucracy." See T.B. Bottomore, *Sociology — A Guide to Problems and Literature* (Bombay : Blackie and Son Publishers Pvt. Ltd., 1978), 142.

69. Malgonkar's story "Bondage" in *Rumble Tumble* (New Delhi : Orient Paperbacks, 1977), 112-23, is a severe indictment of the Kafkasque functioning of such a polity. A Collector, corrupt to the core, close to retirement now and thus desperately trying to get an extension, hits upon a publicity gimmick. Under the Bonded Labourers' Freedom Act, he publicly supervises the 'liberation' of the son of an ex-tenant 'working' in the landlord's house. It is a different issue altogether that the boy was staying as practically a member of the former master's family while his father had been hospitalized and that after being 'liberated,' the boy had nowhere else to go. Back he came to his Baba, as he called the former master, and he got a warm reception.

70. Gandhi himself had objected to the manner in which the princely state of Junagarh was integrated into the Indian Union. Even if the end was noble, proper means should have been employed. Gandhi had advocated the desirability of mutual discussion and arbitration. See A. Appadorai, "Gandhi and the Settlement of Dispute," in *Gandhi and the Contemporary World*, 62.

71. *The Sword and the Sickle* (Bombay : Kutab-Popular, 1955), 207.

72. Cf. "Personally I dislike the praise of poverty and suffering. I do not think they are at all desirable and they ought to be abolished. Nor do I appreciate the ascetic life as social ideal, though it may suit individuals. I understand and appreciate simplicity, equality, self-control but not the mortification of the flesh." Jawaharlal Nehru, *Towards Freedom — The Autobiography of Jawaharlal Nehru* (New York : The John Day Co. 1942), 138.

□□□

6
The Way Out of the Labyrinth

HINDUISM IN its popularly practised form, with its glorification of status-quoism and otherworldly orientation, puts fetters on its adherents and inhibits their exercise of initiative.[1] Gandhism was a lion-hearted attempt to reinterpret and reinvigorate the stagnant faith. It awoke a whole subcontinent to purposive action, enabling the people to think of the immediate and endeavour to frame their own destiny.[2] However, there is an in-built Indian tendency to incorporate and take into fold all reformers — Buddha, Mahavir, Shankar, Ramanuja, the Bhakti-saints and Nanak would be obvious examples — thus rendering all their reforms redundant. This open-ended inclusivism has not left Gandhism unaffected. The deification of Gandhi and the making of Gandhism into a perfect, conclusive, closed chapter robbed its philosophy of its dynamism and made it into an outmoded creed.[3] With its spiritualizing and philosophizing bias, Gandhism was, even otherwise, vulnerable to the same inhibiting interpretations which had made Hinduism a fettering faith, especially in the post-Gandhi period when he himself was not there to put the priorities right. Only Gandhi could have resolved the seeming paradox whereby "the idea of activity and the idea of world- and life-negation could be brought into relationship in such a way that...activity in the world could be taken as the highest form of renunciation of the world."[4]

A fettering faith is a milestone round the neck, and a philosophy out of touch with the present context results in an impasse. The movement from the pre- to the post-Independence times has queered the pitch all the more. Idealism has given way to *realpolitik,* ideology has yielded to personal likes and dislikes, and fissiparous forces and destabilizing neighbours have pushed the nation to a blind alley.[5] It goes to the credit of Bhabani Bhattacharya, Manohar Malgonkar and Nayantara Sahgal that they have not been content with the mere depiction of helpless individuals caught in the political imbroglio. They go on to incorporate in their novels in a more or less subtle manner the values they deem essential for resolving the political impasse. We propose to take up here the differing ways out suggested by them.

The propensity in Bhattacharya, Malgonkar and Sahgal to take upon themselves the role of visionaries is but a continuation of the traditional Indian view of the poet as seer. This artistic tradition elevates creative writing to the stature of philosophy. Philosophy in Indian parlance is *darshan,* the vision of truth. In other words, the artist's commitment to aesthetics and his commitment to social values derive simultaneously from his higher and more comprehensive commitment to art as the vocation of the creator: *Kavi* is one attribute of God, the creator in *Yajurveda* (40, 8) and *Ishopanishad* (8). In Bhattacharya, Malgonkar and Sahgal, this awareness of their role as social and political visionaries is an integral part of their commitment to creativity and to the genre.

Bhabani Bhattacharya has dealt with the aesthetics of fiction somewhat systematically and in some detail. Both Nayantara Sahgal and Manohar Malgonkar (despite his protestations to the contrary)[6] are largely covered by what Bhattacharya has to say about the role of the novelist. Like Achebe,[7] Bhattacharya visualizes his role as a teacher. A novelist reveals, according to Bhattacharya, what he believes to be the truth, not dogmatically but dramatically. Bhattacharya sees the presentation of ideals as an integral part of the role of a novelist. Indeed, the artist's commitment is intensified by the modern imperatives of the situation.

> The stern realist is addicted to ideals. He wants to make life better. He dreams of a great destiny for humankind and not of its ignominious end under nuclear fission. And his pen is a powerful weapon for his fight.[8]

Bhattacharya would not like an artist to be afraid of being dubbed propagandist or tendentious if he has denounced injustice and oppression or has demanded freedom for his people or has pleaded for the universal. However, he is well aware that he is talking of ideas not *per se* but ideas in art :

> Art must teach but unobrusively, by its vivid interpretation of life. Art must preach but only by virtue of its being a vehicle of truth. If that is propaganda, there is no need to eschew the word.[9]

Bhattacharya's advice to the artistic fraternity is not to evade ethical values for fear "lest they contaminate the pure spirit of... creative endeavour."[10] What an artist has good reason to fear is "not the ethical values themselves but the wrong mode of their projection." It is proposed to explore here such values in the context of the political consciousness reflected in the novels of Bhabani Bhattacharya, Manohar Malgonkar and Nayantara Sahgal. What Bhattacharya terms the 'modes of projection' of such values would be taken up hereafter.

What is most obvious in the novels of Bhattacharya, Malgonkar and Sahgal is the forceful plea for a reinterpretation and reappraisal of Gandhism in the modern context. Then alone it can be a way out. They are convinced that what is needed is a creative outlook which would retain the innate vitality of the creed but discard the chaff. In pleading for a dynamic and creative perspective, these novelists are revealing another facet of their adherence to Gandhism.[11]

The Gandhian road towards an integrated view of life was neither linear nor pyramidical. Gandhi's concept of social progress was one of ever-expanding, unbroken, 'concentric' or 'oceanic circles.'[12] The Gandhian ideology is inherently dynamic, Gandhi himself having "grown from truth to truth."[13] It is in the light of the inherent dynamism of Gandhian ideology that the two characters of Satyajit and Bhaskar in *Ladakh* are to be interpreted. Satyajit is discovered posing to himself the hypothetical question : "What would Gandhiji have done?" (80) at every critical juncture in his life. The inescapable impression is that Satyajit has cast Gandhism in a mould and he denies it the freedom to grow. His friend Bireswar explains how by taking recourse to fasts whenever threatened by some physical temptation, Satyajit has only made himself more vulnerable (359). Rather than interpreting Gandhism dynamically to solve new problems in the Gandhian spirit, Satyajit seems to fumble robot-like, casting himself into a role determined *a priori*.

Whereas Satyajit smacks of intellectual sloth and moral debility in his application of Gandhism as a political ideology, Bhaskar has real application of both mind and heart. In the background of the incessant ticking of the clock of population (31) and the intermittent shells fired at the Sino-Indian border, Bhaskar rather than Satyajit appears to be the more authentic version of latter-day Gandhi, evolving Gandhism to forge new strategies to meet new challenges without betraying the true spirit of the creed. Precisely the same had been attempted by Gandhi all his life.

It is this dynamism which Bhattacharya, Malgonkar and Sahgal bring to the appraisal of the whole edifice of Gandhism, parts of which they discover to be obsolete and hence needless. The treatment meted out to Gandhi's prescription for men in public life merits attention in this context. Gandhi envisaged the highest goal to which man could aspire as the perfect observance of *brahmcharya,* which he defined as the "control of the senses in thought, word and deed."[14] Especially for men in public life, Gandhi was of the view that "Without the observance of *brahmcharya,* service of family would be inconsistent with service of the community. With *brahmacharya,* they would be perfectly consistent."[15] Gandhi obviously expected a man in public life to have no role with encumbrances in other realms of being. As an individual, Gandhi's advice to him is to "reduce oneself to zero." "It means," to quote Gandhi," to be the last in receiving good things, to serve everyone, not to expect gratitude and to be first in suffering. One who thus reduces himself to zero will always be absorbed in his work."[16]

It is significant to note that Indo-Anglian novelists in general have not responded favourably to the strict regimen Gandhi insisted on for social activists.[17] Bhattacharya, Malgonkar and Sahgal go farther than mere disapprobation. They explore the distortions such an exacting requirement is likely to cause in the private lives of those in politics.[18] Thus, they help make the case for a careful winnowing of Gandhism stronger.

Bhattacharya highlights the problems created by the Gandhian dictum on *brahmacharya* in *Music*. Unlike the idealistic formulations of *Hungers* where Rahoul, the husband and Rahoul the nationalist fighter for freedom co-existed in perfect amity, *Music* pits the individual in the protagonist against the social activist in him. Jayadev stubbornly clings to his role as a social reformer and refuses to assume the role of a husband in relation to his wife :

> Jayadev girded himself for a struggle. He could not afford to be distracted.... How could he pause and give himself to his private life at this great moment of history when India, proud with the freedom of which he had often dreamed, must reorient her national life on a new social basis? (150-51)

Jayadev, "who had no knowledge of the soul of a woman" (105), visualizes a "spiritual union" (106) with Mohini, whom he regards as 'Maitreyi,' whereas Mohini had "no ambition to be a 'Maitrayi'" (104). This incompatibility hampers Jayadev's work of rural-awakening and social uplift. This forestalls the possibility of Mihini's entering the same arena of social service. Bhattacharya does not focus on this aspect of their relationship in *Music*. But the conflict is played to the hilt in *Ladakh*.

Satyajit, the apostle of non-violence in *Ladakh*, has done grave violence to the sensibilities of his wife, Suruchi, by arbitrarily taking a vow of *akhand brahmacharya*. Suruchi fails to comprehend how "one's dedication to national service could gain strength from the state of celibacy" (19). Satyajit had been always tormented by a Harriet Green or a Stella Johnson in his system despite long fasts undertaken at Cambridge, for self-purification (186-87). Even in the post-*brahmacharya* phase, there were occasions "when the tormented stone god lost his iron restraint, and seized by something tempestuous, he drew Suruchi to him and made love" (20). However, ultimately, Satyajit does realize how Suruchi was "an urge for him to live, *relive*...and not on the Gandhian plane" (367) (emphasis in original). The new man in Satyajit, ready to accept every human need conditions the leader in him. The new Satyajit "would not have to step on each footprint of the Master's striding gait" (67), he would make his own footprints on the sand of time. The seemingly impregnable citadel of the Gandhian denial of life is breached when the woman in Sumita instinctively responds to the life in sculpture, when Satyajit himself realizes how, though the spirit is willing, the flesh is weak. Suruchi understands and appreciates Jhanak, the vivacious belle, who believed that "a woman's primal urge [is] to be nothing but a woman" (274). When Suruchi looks inwards at the stifled Jhanak within her, the wheel comes full circle.

In the same vein, *A Dream in Hawaii* is, at bottom, Swami Yogananda's dream which reveals the Neeloy in him. Really it was Debjani, who, through her insistence on seeing the Swami in Neeloy, had made him into one, leading him to deny the sensual aspect of life and acknowledging only the spiritual being in him (84). Ironically enough, it is only when he is at the pinnacle of his grandeur as a Swami that Yogananda realizes the truth of his inner being which continues to nurture Neeloy, resisting all outward impositions and control.

In Sahgal, too, we come across the same tone of censure of the strict regimen imposed in Gandhism. The distortion in Kunti Behn's perspective in *Happy* on account of the life of abstinence forced on her has already been commented upon.[19] The narrator in the same novel also provides occasion to indict the Gandhian dictum on the same ground. He is an unmarried crusader for freedom, committed to *brahmacharya.* But reading in between the lines one cannot help detecting in him secret longings for affluence, comfort and even female company.[20] However, this contrariness in the private and the public faces of the character remains merely on the implied level and is not made use of as an integral part of the design to criticize Gandhism. Other public men in Sahgal's novels, such as, Prakash Shukla, Abdul Rahman, Kalyan Sinha, Harpal Singh and others are presented as leading a normal sexual life, unencumbered with such puritanical prescriptions. In Devi, we even come across a public figure going in for self-fulfilment outside the marital bond.

Malgonkar, too, presents a forceful case for an enlightened appraisal of Gandhism in the modern context. He accomplishes this through the presentation of the present anomalous situation when Gandhian norms have become publicity gimmicks in the hands of the lumpen and the depraved.

In his novels, one comes across career-conscious military officers flaunting their faith in austerity and restraint just to catch the eye of their political mentors. Brigadier Behl in *Bandicoot* would not join the visiting Russian General for drinks. We later learn how this votary of Gandhism has had a young bison killed for a swagger-stick made of its prick (21). Kamal Kant in *Drum* considers the social mixing of men and women "woggish activities" (68). He even goes to the extent of holding *purdah* to be a good institution. He is rather sorry that it is no longer enforced (69).

Shantilal in *Drum* is another such 'Gandhian' Army officer. "He had always been known as the 'sadhu' — the holy man. He never drank, never smoked, never sang bawdy songs" (200). However, he had no compunctions about distorting the truth for personal advantage. He had been replaced by Kiran Garud in Colonel Watson's division simply because the Colonel had found Kiran better suited for the job. However, after Independence, Shantilal gave a purely ideological colour to the whole affair. Kiran was presented as a 'bootlicking wog' and he himself, by implication, as a nationalist. His progress in Independent India was quick enough.

Malgonkar discovers that mere outward show has become so much of a necessity in public life that the inner spirit of

Gandhism has been an inevitable casualty. Making prohibition a fad has successfully camouflaged the sordid reality of the daily denial of Gandhism in public life (*Bandicoot,* 60). In *Bandicoot,* Nadkar, notwithstanding his stature in and service of community, cannot be awarded *'Padamshree'* for he holds a 'Health Permit.' It is this again which stands in the way of his becoming a Congress candidate for the Parliamentary elections. It is a rare occurrence in the corridors of power to come across upright men in politics like Puran Das who "liked to live well and privately made fun of the austerity preached by the Congress" (142).

Bhattacharya concurs with Malgonkar and Sahgal in the desirability of examining Gandhism anew in the modern context. Still what stands out most conspicuously in his novels is the authenticity of his portrayal of *swarajya* (literally self-rule) as *Ramarajya*. *Ramarajya* can perhaps be seen as an outward manifestation of what is latent in the Indian racial consciousness as the *Satyuga* — the Golden Age of Right. Bhattacharya accepts *in toto* the major planks of Gandhi's political ideology in his presentation of, first the attainment of *swarajya,* and then the way in which it could be transformed into *Ramarajya.* Bhattacharya reposes absolute confidence in Gandhism[21] not merely as a strategy for unifying India and for going ahead to uproot the foreign rule, but also as a methodology to bring about a new social, political and economic order based on *Sarvodya* (the uplifting and prosperity of all).

Bhattacharya sees no short cuts to freedom and progress — neither violence nor miracles. Recourse to violence as a strategy is irresponsible, impulsive action. Rather than being a way to liberation, violence entails a burden of guilt. The villagers, in *Hungers,* who had set their *dak ghar* on fire, realised this to their chagrin (76). Meera's good-intentioned folly in banking on a *taveej* for making the lives of the villagers prosperous is exposed and freedom is presented as the *taveej* which can transform the lives of people if it is used in good faith (*Gold,* 30). Freedom is a means to the welfare of the people which, indeed, is the ultimate end.

Hungers presents political freedom as the *sine qua non* for self-realization of both the individual and the nation. In this holy *yagna* for freedom, it is incumbent as much on women as on men to offer themselves at the altar. Especially the intellectual elite are called upon to come out of their ivory towers and give their less enlightened but more enthusiastic brethren the lead even if it entails the sacrifice of their secure perch. Rahoul, an astrophysicist (*Hungers*), Jayadev, the highly cultured and scholarly scion of 'the Big House' and Harindra a doctor (both from *Music*), Biten a well-read Brahmin (*Tiger),* Satyajit, a Cambridge-trained economist (*Ladakh*) — all give up their sheltered ivory towers to join the struggle for making a new India. Perhaps the most significant in this context is the consent of the minstrel in *Gold* to contest the election in independent India. The minstrel had earlier been exhorting the people — from a distance — to safeguard their soon-to-be-won freedom. Now he involves himself with them in their endeavour to do that. Bhattacharya believes in social service as a preparation for politics, which in itself is a continuation of social service. One dimension of Satyajit's alienation from the masses in *Ladakh* is his aloofness from the political mainstream so much so that he fails to muster enough involvement of the people in his avowed mission to lead a *Shanti Sena* to Ladakh and he is easily dissuaded by a minister therefrom.

Music and *Ladakh* project another value Bhattacharya has faith in. They espouse a course of 'meditation' for attaining all-round prosperity and resolving all conflicts. *Music* pits orthodoxy and the new ways into a headlong clash. Mohini, her father, her grandmother, and Jayadev stand for change with continuity — no unquestioned acceptance of the past practices and mores — whereas Jayadev's mother stands for statis. The Big House, with its inhabitants split ideologically, is a picture of the whole nation in microcosm.

Music focuses on orthodoxy in matters of personal etiquette, social behaviour and religion. These include the practice of 'inspecting' the bride by the suitor's party, untouchability, aversion to modern medicines, prohibition against widow remarriage, vows and offerings to deities, belief in stars and in scores of superstitions. All these are presented as traits of the tradition-bound society which call for change. In contrast to observances or practices which hamper or lower the individual, the novel presents others having beneficial results, the institution of the professional match-maker, the itinerant story-teller, reciting stories from the *Puranas,* the practice of arranged marriages wherein women fulfil their ancient hunger to offer worship by worshipping their husbands (63).

Music has repeated references to the need for a synthesis of the old and the new, "the horoscope and the microscope" as Mohini's father puts it (52). But the synthesis remains merely on the conceptual level, with Jayadev, its chief theoretician. We are informed by the omniscient narrator how Jayadev had delved "back into India's remote past for a solution" (67) of her current problems. But Jayadev would use the past creatively: "Look back that you may look forward. Look to the roots of India in this fateful hour of flowering. Use the buried material of the past to write the new social charter" (68). "...the new man of his vision was not to be a hollow reincarnation, not a spiritless copy of ancient Hindu man" (68). Jayadev stands for a re-examination of the past in the light of the present and the likely future and thus for forging new strategies using past experience.

It is not inconsequential to see how *Music* closes on a note of triumph of the new ways of enlightenment. There are subtle whiffs to suggest which way the wind blows. Harindra and the other "young Turks" like him clean the pond poohpoohing the superstition that it is the abode of a crocodile who was a Brahmin in his previous birth and thus it would be sacrilegious to clean it (157-59). They oppose the marriage of an old widower with a young girl. While Jayadev's mother is forcing his wife, Mohini, to sprinkle blood from her bosom to appease the deity, his clear-cut exhortation is : "Do not bow down to such insult. You are the new India. The old orthodox ways have been our yoke, have enslaved us. Let us be free" (166). However, Mohini is discovered to be already pregnant and the *raison d'etre* of her mother-in-law's superstitious conduct is taken away. Still Mohini, in a mood of reconciliation and not opposition, lets the credit for the child go to the deity (188). So the spirit of faith is kept but the superstition is eliminated.

Whereas the rapprochement in *Music* is the genus, the same in *Ladakh* is a species thereof. The synthesis here is between the virtues of a narrow, isolationist Gandhism and open-ended industrialism. The realms wherein it is arrived at include the personal, the economic and the political. Both the spinning wheel and steel are shown to be complementary to each other, working as means to the same end of the betterment of the people. The Gandhian strategy of winning over your adversary in a non-violent manner is shown triumphing in personal and societal realms through the winning over of the Gandhigramians by Bhaskar. Even Sumita, more given to Satyajitism than Satyajit himself, is converted through exposure by Bhaskar to the vision from his side of the fence. The Mao-worshipping Chinese girls are won over through the exercise of soul-power and love (348). However, in the realm of national politics, the Gandhian gesture of a *Shanti sena* to ward off aggression fails to be efficacious for want of popular mandate. Satyajit's fast unto death undertaken for political-cum-ideological reasons does have the desired impact, for even the workers at Steeltown rally round in support of Gandhigram (368).

Action rather than idle abstraction is a value in Bhattacharya. The clamouring for action in Sumita (354) is perhaps another dimension of the synthesis of the contemplative renunciatory Satyajitism with fast-paced Bhaskarism. However, one more aspect of such insistence on action must not be lost sight of. The way Kalo in *Tiger* is brought round to face the lie, or rather as is put in the novel, to kill the tiger of the lie he was riding, is a testimony to the novelist's faith in the pristine dictum "*Satyameva Jayate*" (Truth alone triumphs). It is only from a platform of truthfulness that Kalo can make an impact on the masses and be a legend to arouse and inspire them. Thus to be a value, action has got to be positive and truthful.

What is significant to note is Bhattacharya's conviction that most of the strategies adopted in the struggle for freedom from an alien administration would be equally efficacious in the struggle against political and economic exploitation in post-Independence India. Though all his novels have been published in the post-Independence period, Bhattacharya in *Hungers* (1947), *Tiger* (1955) and *Gold* (1960) sets his stories in the pre-Independence period. People are shown opposing their tormentors in *Hungers* through non-violent assemblies and the show of solidarity among the downtrodden does make an impact. *Gold* shows womenfolk successfully using the same strategy in fighting against black-marketeers on the eve of Independence. Sohanlal, a positive character in the same novel, is apprehensive that the exploiting Seths in diverse guise would mushroom once the country is free. But Meera, the protagonist in the novel, feels sure of uprooting them all with strategies tested in the freedom struggle (124). The protagonist, Satyajit, in *Ladakh* (1966), set in the early 1960s, is depicted successfully arousing the conscience of the people through the exercise of soul power when he undertakes a fast-unto-death for safeguarding Gandhigram, the village run along Gandhian lines.

Here obviously Bhattacharya is repudiating the stand taken by eminent political thinkers like B.R. Ambedkar, C. Rajagopalachari and U.N. Dhebar, who held that recourse to Gandhian strategies of non-violent protests and fasts in a free democratic country was the grammar of anarchy.[22] Bhattacharya's position coincides with that of another group of political thinkers including M.P. Desai and J.B. Kripalani who were disinclined to surrender the individual's right of protest against the coercive power of the state even if it be a democracy.[23]

Bhattacharya's novels consistently espouse the perennial significance of Gandhism. In the pre-Independence context, in *Hungers, Gold* and even in *Tiger,* though in an oblique manner, the novelist validates Gandhian political ideology in an unalloyed way. However, coming to the post-Independence period, Bhattacharya would like Gandhism to be interpreted in an innovative, creative way. We have already seen how the Gandhian insistence on *brahmacharya* is objectively appraised in *Music, Ladakh* and *Hawaii* and the novelist finds it a needless encumbrance in the present context. What he presents is the need for synthesis between the old and the new in *Music* and the East and the West in *Hawaii*. The same is presented in *Ladakh* as the desirability of Gandhism to grow with time to be sharper and more efficacious for the present problems of a burgeoning population, the need for industrialization and national defence.[24] For Bhattacharya, then, an enlightened application of Gandhism in a creative manner, whereby the outer form may be modified but the inner vitality retained, is the only way out.

Nayantara Sahgal is a self-proclaimed votary of Gandhism. Her account of her childhood and youth is an account of the influence of Gandhian ideas on her.[25] A study of her novels shows that she shares most of Bhattacharya's Gandhian concerns and values. She takes her role as a social and political visionary most seriously. She has written not merely novels with political content but also incisive political columns in periodicals and papers which reinforce what the protagonists in her novels visualize as the way out.

Happy is the only novel by Sahgal which has the pre-Independence context as part of its background. Like Bhattacharya in *Hungers* and *Gold*, Sahgal, too, validates here the Gandhian strategies for the emancipation and growth of the people in all realms — sociological, economic, religious and political. The narrator and Sohanlal in *Happy* have a constructive programme of rural reconstruction which encompasses all these planes.

Sahgal's novels after *Happy* give a fairly accurate chronological account of the post-Independence political history[26] up to the imposition of the Emergency. Despite the changed context, the novelist doesn't give up hope and concludes that Gandhism has lost its efficacy in an India marked by calamities like the Partition and the subsequent violence, communal frenzy, caste and class-conflicts, regionalism, populism and the unscrupulous craze for power.

The Gandhian way to the multifaceted growth of the individual represents for Sahgal the acme of human civilization and, according to her, it would be wrong to expect that "this, the approach of love and peace, the formal stage of refining process could be arrived at suddenly."[27] It is important not to grow impatient and not to lose hope.

> The survival of India's people can matter only as long as her spirit survives — the spirit of Gandhi, and older than it is, the fathomless spiritual reservoir from which he drew his faith and inspiration.[28]

Sahgal visualizes in Gandhism a potent force, if used in an organized manner even today. It alone can involve the whole nation, cutting across barriers of class, caste or creed. Usman, in *Situation*, conveys the same idea when he tells Devi that non-violent protest against a dictatorial government is the only way out :

> There never was another way. Besides, do you realize, it's the only way most people in this country understand and will give their allegiance to? (116)

In each novel by Sahgal, there is a crusader for the cause of values cherished by Gandhi in the political field : openness, truth, non-violence, egalitarianism and the like. Even in the face of the daily denial of Gandhi in official circles, the torch is kept ablaze by Vishal (*Storm*), Raj (*Shadow*), Devi and Usman (*Situation*) and Sonali (*Rich*). Taking a bold stand unambiguously against evil, Vishal fights fissiparous forces single-handed with his firm conviction in the virtue of negotiation and faith in the innate dignity of man. The same is Raj's *modus operandi* in *Shadow*. Usman and Devi come out in the open after resigning their official posts to lead a popular movement against the unscrupulous leaders. Sonali also fights back her overpowering sense of helplessness in the face of the Emergency regime and comes to realize how "my own country stretched out before me, waiting to be lived" (234).

For Sahgal, Gandhism is not a mere political ideology, aimed at wresting power. It approximates to being a synonym for humanitarianism. It recognizes the fact that the "central consideration to any problem was the man who faced it" (*Morning*, 185). In her novels and journalistic writings, Sahgal has been unrelenting in her exposé of the shenanigans of lumpen politicians whose machinations amount to betrayal of the sacred trust the individual has reposed in the institution of the State. She exposes the hollowness of all ideological solutions where individuals are meant to serve the ends of ideology. Gyan's fiery populism (*Storm*), Kalyan's impatience for quick progress (*Morning*), Sumer's pseudo-radicalism (*Shadow*), the professed progressivism of 'the Cabinet Intellectuals' (*Situation*), Rishad's revolutionism (*Situation*) and the 'dynamic' policies of the Madam and her son in *Rich* — all are unambiguously indicted for these consider individuals to be merely "instruments of a process" (*Situation*, 125). In each novel, as we shall see below, Sahgal makes one character or the other her mouthpiece to denounce the unthinking and blind adherence to religion which saps individual endeavour and makes one subscribe to a pre-conceived notion of uniformity of response and behaviour.

Humanitarianism is much more than a mere 'undercurrent' in Sahgal's novels.[29] She believes that "a country battered into conformity or confined by ideological prejudices" can never have individuals living in it.[30] There is a crying need for change. We are urgently in need of revolution, both social and economic. It is of terrible and crucial significance what kind of human material leads this revolution and in what manner.[31] It becomes incumbent upon the intellectuals to involve themselves with the people and see that the 'human essence' is not abandoned. "To see that justice is done is not an optional task of the intellectual." Rather "it should be the essence of his functioning."[32] Steward D. McBride in his interview with Nayantara Sahgal for the *Christian Science Monitor* reported how much the novelist felt "frustrated with the failure of India's intelligentsia"[33] to resist the Emergency repression. Guarding freedom is a common cause, for freedom is not a gift. It is "an achievement" and every generation has to do its bit to "continue and preserve the tradition of freedom."[34]

The most crucial aspect of freedom Sahgal's protagonists valiantly strive for is freedom from an orthodox, outdated view of Hinduism. Sahgal relates the political ills the nation is afflicted with to a lop-sided interpretation of Hinduism.[35] The only way out is reappraisal of the ancient creed. Hinduism must adapt itself in response to the change in the environment of its adherents. All protagonists in Sahgal find themselves confined and held back by the beaten-track formulations of Hinduism. Whereas some outsiders like Mclvor (*Happy*), Raj (*Shadow*) and Usman (*Situation*) look at the creed critically as outsiders and seek to pinpoint its anchronisms, the novels abound in conscientious sceptics who give an inside critical view. The narrator and Sanad in *Happy*, Rakesh, Trivedi, Kalyan, Kailas (*Morning*), Vishal, Mara (*Storm*), Simrit, Ram Kishan (*Shadow*) and Sonali (*Rich*) fall in the latter category. The unambiguous conclusion is that popular Hinduism breeds attitudes which do not make a positive contribution to life. "What did it create but quietude? Did it toughen fibre to give emotional satisfaction? Did it help the soldier to fight better, the businessman to do his job better?" (*Storm*, 78). The answer that emerges is an emphatic 'no.'

A crying need is to re-examine the traditional tenets Hinduism consists of. "The enigma of Hinduism" (*Shadow*, 13), "the whole system of what a Hindu stands for has yet to be sorted out" (*Shadow*, 19). Sahgal realizes the need for "fresh air on Hinduism."[36] "The West has been in decay a long time...but the rot has a way of falling off and the rest renews itself because people are permitted to *think*" (emphasis added) (*Shadow*, 154). It is high time, some key attitudes, sanctified in Hinduism, are subjected to critical scrutiny. "Restraint is a fine thing but at this juncture in our history when we have to act and be responsible for our actions...passion and deeds would serve us better" (*Shadow*, 171). Renunciation, as such, is another noble virtue but there are times when it is wrong. "It makes a man drawback and do nothing in a situation when he should take more responsibility, face up to things and stand firm" (*Shadow*, 117).[37] Gobind Narain, Savitri Sahay, Prabha Mathur (*Happy*), Kalyan's parents (*Morning*), Harpal and Saroj (*Storm*), Simrit (*Shadow*), the peasants in *Situation* and the 'dumb driven majority' in *Rich* are obvious examples of restraint making people passive victims of exploitation. What is required is to emphasize the challenging aspects of the theory of *karma*, in its prospective aspects, along the lines provided by the narrator in *Happy* (165). It would present the belief in *karma* as the possibility of framing one's own future oneself.[38] It would involve people with what is here and now. It is indicated in the anagnorisis reached by Rishad and Usman in *Situation* that "revolution begins with oneself" (146). It is only through re-evaluation of what is the desirable virtue that a code of conduct can be framed for these critical times when "the world is at the threshold of immense changes" (*Shadow,* 43). "If the inert mass [of people] did not wake up to the fact that they were their own masters, the brutal and single-minded among them would" (*Shadow,* 43). Only action, responsible action, could see the people through. "Any Indian who had the capacity to think and act must use it in a big constructive way or a whole civilization would crumble under mould" (*Shadow,* 106).

Vishal and Trivedi, the Commissioner, in *Storm,* wish to use the Hindu tradition for meaningful, positive action. Vishal wishes to take out the "superb intellectual heritage" of Hinduism which has fallen into morass "supporting feeble issues like the preservation of cows." He wishes to take it "out of the stagnation," to provide the answers in ways that would best suit our temperament," using "tradition in a big enlightened way" (17). Trivedi turns to the *Bhagwad Gita,* which alone among the Hindu scriptures, he feels, tells us something 'specific,' something besides rituals. The *Gita* recommends action and the performance of duty unallied to reward. The way suggested not merely in *Storm* but also in the other novels by Sahgal is this message of *nishkam karma* especially the *karma, i.e.,* the dynamic aspect of action. Vishal in *Storm* has imbibed this lesson well, and faced by the 'storm in Chandigarh,' he turns to healthy, decisive action. He faces the problems of violence and communal disharmony, on the one side, and insensitivity, incommunicability and lack of 'the human touch' on the other. He advises Harpal, the Chief Minister of Haryana, not to submit passively to the threats of Gyan Singh, the Punjab Chief Minister. Vishal's stand against Inder, an insensitive husband, is made in the same spirit, motivated as it is by a desire to check the spread of violence.

With all her criticism of Hinduism, Sahgal is, in no way, irreligious or vituperative in her treatment of religion. If Hinduism is interpreted positively and purposively — as is done by Vishal, for example — far from putting fetters on the individual, it can show the way. Many characters in Sahgal refuse to be cowed down by a blind adherence to the ritualized faith. They interpret it in an enlightened way and involve themselves body and soul in the immediate lives of the masses. Sohanlal and the narrator in *Happy* throw themselves into the service of the people, believing in the Gandhian message of '*Vasudhaiva kutumbakam*,' the universal household of God. It is really the mesmeric mystique of Gandhi which weans them away from popular attitudes of running away from the present problems. In Kailas (*Morning*), we find again, such constructive interpretation, which makes him a political activist, committed to eradicate corruption.

Sahgal is unrelenting in her exposè of atheism, a corollary of pseudo-Radicalism. Atheism is the official creed in the rarefied circles of officialdom in *Situation*. Shivraj, the deceased Prime Minister, was a visionary. In spite of his impatience with fellow Hindus, he never became an atheist. It is not for nothing that, listening to Shivraj, Michael, an objective observer of the Indian scene, was reminded of the Sermon on the Mount (46). But in the new dispensation, being an atheist was the craze. Devi, Shivraj's sister, was the only minister who had "sworn by God at the oath-taking" (25).

Despite all its shortcomings, Sahgal would not like religion to be dispensed with for it provides an all-encompassed which no other ideology can ever dream of having :

> That awareness of good, of God, of the universe, whatever one called it, was pervasive and supreme. It descended to the dust of the village. It was everywhere. It had to be made to yield results, to become a song on one's lips, a great fighting strength...(*Shadow,* 201).

It is here that one comes across the inherent dynamism in Sahgal's view of religion. Her positive heroes are imbued with the same dynamism. Sahgal views religion as the 'awareness of the good.' Is the good positive, beneficial? Is it the ultimate value? God, universe or a defined good, all these are variations of the statement of that awareness. The import of using the words 'good,' 'God' and 'universe,' together is that this awareness is taken to be universal and dynamic. The universe is not static, it is dynamic. Yet the dynamism is self-controlled by an eternal law which can be abstracted from the concrete manifestation of it. The individual's action in the context of that law is his religion.

The great Indian leaders in the past had a dynamic view of religion. They used it in a positive and healthy way as a significant base for progress. They were religious "in spirit, if not in conventional observance."[39] It is only through such a dynamic Hinduism that a strategy could emerge to combat the evils plaguing the body politic. "Somewhere beneath it [Hinduism] a great vitality lay untapped waiting to be excavated by the living, if the living cared enough" (*Storm,* 92). Mahatma Gandhi had taken out non-violence from Hinduism and blown fresh breath into it, thus, using it as a weapon against the mightiest empire on earth. Usman, faced with the crumbling edifice of democratic institutions all around, comes to realize that "a Hindu remedy" has to be found to the political ills (*Situation,* 79).

The revitalization of one religion would obviously touch the truth of others as well. Rediscovering the pristine gospel of Hinduism would involve drawing on the best of other religions like Islam and Christianity. The enormity of the problem facing the modern man is such that "in India no single faith [in its extant form] has the answer" (*Shadow,* 186). The musings of Ram Kishan and Raj in *Shadow* are extremely relevant in this context. Coming from differing religious backgrounds — Hinduism and Christianity respectively — together they convey a message of give-and-take. The new message is an amalgam of the timeless universality of Hinduism and concern for the temporal welfare in Christianity — both believing in God as the source of all value and as a symbol of all good. This synthesis can provide a formidable challenge "to combat the genius of Marx" (201). In its new form, Hinduism will "become a source of strength and hope in the hut and the factory" (195). The need is to find a sustaining idea from out of Hinduism "to move it out of the universal into the particular" (234). This will "provide the stamina, the sticking point we need to resist what we don't believe in and give us the will to act" (234). So far as the immediate needs are concerned, non-violence in a reinvigorated form can give the lead. It needs to be shorn off its philosophizing and imbued with an action-oriented thrust "so that it could be passed on like an inheritance" (*Situation*, 177). Such non-violence would be an idea concretized, rendered into a shape people would rally round, for "what sustains the people is an idea that people believe in and are willing to work for" (*Shadow,* 235).

Non-violence redefined would be the "Hindu remedy," a way of protest against repression and atrocities, "the only way most people in the country understand and will give their allegiance to" (*Situation,* 116). Such a strategy is shown immediately yielding positive results in *Situation.* Usman, the V.C. of Delhi University, involves the whole student community in soul-searching not by philosophizing or dilating upon abstractions but by jumping himself into the cauldron of action and exhorting others too to involve themselves in constructive action. He resigns his official post and launches a non-violent struggle against the authorities' apathy and craze for power. He succeeds in inculcating a sense of responsibility and concern for the long-term perspective in the students.

It is obvious that Sahgal visualizes the only way out to be through the transmutation of abstractions into a credo of positive, decisive, responsible action. "There have been enough words. We have to act [now]" (*Situation*, 66). Raj's suggestion to Simrit in *Shadow* is to live life in full, with "refusal to bend the knee, bow the head." Ram Krishan appropriately terms it as "non-violence in action" (181). Such a solution-seeking does not remain merely theoretical. Sahgal's protagonists are not merely given to theorizing about Hinduism, they also practise what they preach. The narrator in *Happy,* Rakesh, Vishal, Kailas, Raj, Devi, Rishad and Sonali have already been seen in their capacities as both thinkers and doers.

In all her novels, Sahgal reveals her protagonists fighting valiantly against repressive political forces, inspired by their action-oriented creed. What is much more remarkable, the novelist creates an unmistakable impression that other characters also, though cowed down by the circumstances at the moment, can better their lot, if they redefine their faith. The political danger of unscrupulous change conspired by Sumer Singh in *Shadow* can be easily met with purposive, and forthright action. Hinduism, rendered in specific terms, can help settle all temporal problems. Raghubir and Prabha Mathur (*Happy*), Kalyan's parents, Nita and Sir Arjun Mitra (*Morning*), Saroj (*Storm*), Simrit (*Shadow*) and the hapless, impotent multitude in *Situation* and *Rich* — all these with a revitalized and reinvigorated Hinduism will feel involved in the here and now and assert themselves against exploitation. Such a shuffling of priorities will also embolden the morally upright persons like Kailas (*Morning*), Vishal, Harpal (*Storm*), Raj (*Shadow*), Usman, Devi (*Situation*) and Sonali (*Rich*).

Sahgal obviously sees in a rejuvenated and positively interpreted Hinduism the only way out. In a recent letter to the writer, she had this to say :

> I have...seen it [Hinduism] as fettering as far as emotional and spiritual and intellectual growth are concerned, but only because people had misinterpreted it and its

> messages. I think we still have to define what Hinduism means, what its scope and limits are, and only then will we draw strength from it in the way that a Christian, Muslim or Sikh draws strength from his religious heritage.[40]

Sahgal's espousal of Gandhism is also motivated by her realization that it has been a remarkable endeavour, to blow new life into the centuries' old faith. However, she would like Gandhism to be subjected to the same objective appraisal which she would like to apply to Hinduism, so that the chaff is removed and the real spirit comes to its own. The way out as Sahgal sees it is action-oriented and dynamic Hinduism and Gandhism, without the confusing abstraction-mongering or the paralysing otherworldly orientation.

Malgonkar, too, is acutely aware of the political plight of persons caught in the trap of redundant ideology and defeatist attitudes. The tea-estate workers in *Combat* are fettered by their version of faith. They acquiesce as spinelessly in the machinations of a demagogue (Jugal Kishor) as they had acquiesced in the exploitation of an insensitive master (Winton). The subjects of the princely state, Begwad, in *Princes,* are similarly mere playthings not merely in the hands of their regal masters but also their fire-spitting leaders. Both Gian and Debi in *Ganges* feel on their pulse the crucial want in the ideologies they were living by.

Even though Malgonkar shares with Bhattacharya and Sahgal the realization of the dangers of a stagnant ideology, he is different from them as regards his suggestion of the way out. While Bhattacharya and Sahgal stand for specific ideas or strategies, Malgonkar stands for the human definitions of these. It is in men rather than in abstract institutions or values that he sees the ray of hope.

Malgonkar's novels are replete with unabashed eulogy of Englishmen in general for their sense of duty, devotion and commitment to principles in handling difficult situations in India — values which he clubs together to form a code his protagonists live by. Even if Malgonkar views Englishmen not as rulers primarily but as men who exemplify the values he cherishes, his attitude is in striking contrast with that of Bhattacharya and Sahgal who present Englishmen as a mixed lot, some good, some bad, like any other people.

Malgonkar's positive heroes hold the English as their ideal. Kiran Garud in *Drum,* illustrates this propensity to deify the English as the picture of perfect commitment and devotion to a valued cause. "Whenever Kiran was confronted with a tricky situation, he always tried to think what a British C.O. would have done in his place" (59). The English tea-estate managers in *Combat* have gone "half-native" (8) in their concern and consideration for the natives. The principal at the Princes' College in *Princes* is extremely punctilious, unawed by his privileged pupils. Gian and his brother, Hari, in *Ganges,* look up to the "crop of honest, selfless English officers at the top" (124) to give them justice.[41] This expectation is fulfilled in ample measure. An English principal ignores Gian's petty politicking and issues him a character-certificate even though Gian is being tried for murder. An English judge, unswayed by all the pressure brought on him, awards Gian only life-imprisonment and not capital punishment. Earlier another English judge had delivered a scrupulously fair and impartial judgment, giving back to Gian and Hari their ancestral land. The English Superintendent of the Jail where Gian is kept is a strict disciplinarian, but thoroughly fair. Gian believes that the very system of administration of justice is a gift of Englishmen. Whereas earlier the law of the jungle — an eye for an eye and a tooth for a tooth — prevailed, now even murderers are being rehabilitated (137-38). In *Princes,* Abhay holds the Englishmen in the same high esteem. He is relieved when he finds an Englishman intervening during his duel of honour with his mother's paramour. Only an Englishman could fully understand such conduct on Abhay's part and ensure that the rules of the game were adhered to. During the negotiations for the signing of the Instrument of Accession, Abhay comes into contact with Indian politicians and bureaucrats and the encounter makes him miss their predecessors, the English. "The British, I feel, would have been civil even as they were putting us on the block — civil as well as punctual" (310).

The 'heroic hero,'[42] of *Ganges,* Debi, has "a grudging admiration for their [*i.e.,* the Englishmen's] tradition of fairness" (266). They are depicted as understanding the spirit which motivates terrorists like Debi, even if they themselves are the targets. It is this innate fair-mindedness and uprightness of the Englishmen which makes Debi feel shocked at their inglorious running away from Burma in the wake of the Japanese attack (265-66).

Whereas the commitment, devotion and scrupulousness of Englishmen is taken as axiomatic, the corruptibility, inefficiency, irresponsibility and self-seeking of Indians are taken so much for granted that an honest politician like Puran Das in *Bandicoot* has specifically to be distanced from the rest of the tribe. In *Ganges,* Gian believes that an average Indian is "mixed up, shallow and weak" (128) and the novel shows it to be so. Debi is revolted by the sight of the INA Brigadier, for he finds in him "all that was rotten and degrading in the country : its softness, its corruption, its dishonesty" (264). Gian doubts "whether India could ever do without the British. It was they who were so scrupulous about the ends of justice" (129). The doubt is writ large in Malgonkar's corpus for the Indian politicians are presented as thoroughly unscrupulous in their naked lust for power. Lala Vishnu Saran Dev (*Drum*), Jugal Kishor (*Combat*), Kanak Chand (*Princes*) and Krishna Manikam (*Bandicoot*) represent fully what their creator thinks of their calling.[43]

The values the Englishmen exhibit in abundance and the average Indian woefully lacks form a code. Adherence to this code, Malgonkar feels, is essential for protecting individual and community interests. The values comprising the code are all listed in the estimate of Tony Sykes, the apotheosis of the manly code of Malgonkar's : "Disdain for danger, a capacity for coolness under stress, an unfailing readiness to take responsibility and, over all, a stubborn, almost stupid refusal to bend under pressure" (*Princes,* 209). One can add to these, loyalty, courage, strength, skill, grace, steadfastness, gentlemanliness, sense of duty and so on.[44] All these attributes are obviously traditional and conservative. They are also a somewhat overworked version of the do's and don'ts hammered home in generations of pupils in public schools, inculcating in their wards a queer amalgam of "muscular christianity" (the reverse of piety) with Roman stoicism and the stiff-lipped ideals coldly asserted in the poetry of Virgil and Horace.[45]

Himself a retired Army officer, Malgonkar specifically refers to these values as having emanated from the Army code after it had "shed away its unethical overtones and become refined into a standard of behaviour *for men who had to enforce discipline without appearing to do so*" (*Bandicoot,* 48) (emphasis added). *Drum* is explicitly stated to be "the story of the success or failure of the efforts of one of the officers of the [Satpura] Regiment to live up to its code" (10). Besides the Army, the Malgonkar code finds fertile ground in the true-to-the-soil world of the peasantry (which has its vital code of justice/vangeance) and the princely order (which had its own unwritten code of honour).

The single most-prized value of the code is loyalty — loyalty to a friend and to the group one belongs to. All the positive characters in Malgonkar represent loyalty and camaraderie irrespective of caste, creed, colour or community — Kiran Garud, Abdul Jamal, Bertie Howard, Ropey Booker (*Drum*), Jamadar Dongre, Tony Sykes, Abhayraj (*Princes*), Kiran Garud, his subordinate, Ranoji, Gilchrist (*Bandicoot*). This keeping in touch, this willingness to help, is termed '*hikmat mali*' by Nadkar in *Bandicoot*:

> If one can help, one helps. But the point...is that one never talks about it afterwards (16).

The values in the Malgonkar code forge a human bond which transgresses the pragmatic norms of political or rational behaviour. Malgonkar insists on his protagonists' adherence to these values in their roles as individuals and as publicmen. Malgonkar's men, rather, have their public lives governed by this set of private values. Abdul Jamal in *Drum* lies to save his friend, Kiran, in the official enquiry into their officer's suicide. Kiran had been having an adulterous relationship with the deceased's wife. Kiran, an officer of the Indian Army on the Indo-Pakistan border, flouts all barriers to go to and share drinks with Abdul Jamal, now an officer in the Pakistan Army, even though the two countries are at war with each other. 'Spike' Ballur, Kiran's officer, 'understands' Kiran's gesture and thus he saves Kiran from the repercussions of his action. Politicians, thoroughly innocent of the code and the values therein, could have been depended on to raise hell.

Winton's failure in *Combat* is to be attributed to his betrayal of the code. He is loyal to none, not even to his own feelings. His treatment of Gauri and Ruby brings that out. He catches Gauri stealing tea-leaves. But he does not act "in tune with the recognized behaviour-pattern of his calling in the East" (5). Winton attributes it to "an absurd, purely impulsive weakness of mind" (5). But he is only deceiving himself. As his later show of unprovoked aggression against her reveals, a latent lust for her motivates him. His betrayal of Ruby — the half-caste mistress in whom he had found sexual and emotional release and fulfilment — is much more palpable. What perverts his response to her is the fear lest his career should take a nosedive if he marries her (277).

Another distinguishing attribute of Malgonkar's men is courage in the pursuit of a desirable goal. It is a rare brand of valour contemptuous of rational, practical and other such considerations. The value is well-illustrated by 'Bull' Hampton in *Drum.* Despite a 'game leg,' he hates to be sent back home from the war-front. Even though the orders to his unit are to withdraw, he deliberately engages a column of Japanese Army in action at Twin Pagoda Hill and dies in harness. Kiran, the controlling voice in *Drum,* is full of approbation :

> That was the sort of thing that created Regimental legends; not a dozen cold and beautifully planned actions backed by tacital logic (137).

The valour of Jamadar Dongre and Tony Sykes evokes the same praise in Abhay, the narrator in *Princes*. The purposeful dare-devilry executed by Debi and other fire brand terrorists in *Ganges* is also presented in a manner which would earn the appreciation of the readers. Gian, in going back to Duriabad to save Sundari, even though he very well anticipates the communal holocaust there, displays the same courage.[46]

Winton, in *Combat,* again proves the rule by default. He fails, for he does not measure up to the exacting standards set for his men by Malgonkar. That is the impression the novel creates, even though one could make a case for exculpating Winton from the charge of cowardice. Winton goes after a rogue elephant along with Kistulal, the tracker. The elephant is traced successfully but Winton fails to nab it for the rifle does not fire. Winton runs in desperation, leaving his tracker to be trampled by the angry elephant. In the company of men like 'Bull' Hampton, Tony Sykes, Abhay and others, Winton would stand out as one who displays rank failure of nerve at a critical juncture.

Another value highlighted in Malgonkar's novels is justice, in a Sophoclean sense of the term, a purely amoral balancing of the scales with the issues seen in a fairly straightforward manner, uncomplicated by rational, legal or other niceties. The only way Abhay can obliterate the shame of his mother's having eloped with Abdulla Jan, a palace functionary, is by having a man-to-man duel with him, even if it happens to be a busy restaurant where he confronts him. In *Princes,* Abhay attributes the humiliation of his father, the King of Begwad, to the political activities of Kanak who was spearheading a people's movement for the princely state's accession to India. Abhay is motivated by his sense of 'justice' when he publicly horsewhips Kanakchand, even if Kanak happens to be a minister. For others the whipping may be an act of madness but for Abhay, it brings a fulfilment of personality. Against the background of the feudal atmosphere of Konkshet, reeking in corruption, Gian discovers, in *Ganges,* that honest violence is the only dignified way of self-fulfilment.

His murder of his brother's assassin sounds "justifiable according to the code of family honour."[47]

Winton again proves to be the black sheep in Malgonkar's herd. He comes to know of the adulterous relationship between his wife, Jean, and Eddie, an Anglo-Indian subordinate of his. The way he conducts himself after this discovery is in striking contrast to the conduct of Tony Sykes in *Princes* who, also, had discovered that Abhay was his rival for Minnie's love. But whereas Tony never allowed this knowledge to spoil their 'clean, clearly professional relationship,' Winton chooses a most dastardly way to seek vangeance. Actually his case for 'vangeance' is much weaker. His wife is doing to him what he had done to her through Ruby. Moreover, his revenge is taken in a cold, calculating and sinister way rather than in a bold, brash and manly manner. He sends Eddie to kill the one-tusker with his and cartridges. Such revenge-seeking, far from being self-fulfilling, culminates in degeneration and disintegration.

Belief in justice implies, as a corollary, subjecting one's own self to justice according to one's deserts or the role one is to play. The motto of the school run by Ludlow in *Princes* is illuminating in this respect. It runs thus : "The way a man takes a loss is a measure of his manliness" (107). Abhay's father defines this article of the code to his son thus :

> It is most important not to squeal, to show hurt. Be a man, my son.... It is a great thing to be a man...a true man. Tears are the refuge of the weak (33-34).

Keeping a poker-face when confronted with unbearable problems is a cardinal principle for leaders of men in Malgonkar. Cockburn's advice to Winton in *Combat* underscores the same quality of mind :

> Let's put on our old school ties and pretend we're Kipling boys running the Empire. Don't let's speak of unpleasant things about the last war or the horrors of the coming war. Let's forget all the messes we're heading for... (48).

This is not a rehash of Fitzgerald's *Omar Khayyam* but, as Abhay terms it, "a glimpse of the proverbial British phlegm, a show of business as usual under stress" (*Princes*, 134). Kiran in *Drum* invokes such stoicism to defend the exacting schedule in the Army and the seemingly insensitive and callous mess rituals.

> All this was a part of the process...of putting you through your paces, a process of hardening your resistance to stress; it was all an essential part of your grooming as an officer and a gentleman, fit to command the King's men (79).

Kiran himself manfully receives the 'dressing down' his senior subaltern, Bertie Howard and 'Bull' Hampton, the Adjutant, give him as a 'Bum Wart.' Kiran is of the firm conviction that "to take a dressing down in what was called the right spirit was an attribute of strength" (*Drum,* 133). It is put more bluntly in *Princes* for Abhay's benefit : "The sooner we learn to take it [a whipping] without flinching, without showing that we are hurt, the better" (33). The way Abhay's father reacts to the signing of the Instrument of Accession illustrates this well. The extinction of the princely state means the crumbling of whatever the Maharajah valued. However, the valiant man chooses brave and eventful death in preference to a dull and drab existence of servility in a colourless world. His choice shows a certain dignity, defiance and valour which Abhay, both as a son and as a Malgonkar persona cherishes. Abhay himself has imbibed the value. While at Ludlow's school, he had voluntarily subjected himself to the taxing schedule. Later he had followed the much more rigorous routine in Army with the same élan, claiming no princely privileges. Here it is that Kanakchand is found wanting. He sneaks up from behind and hooks Charudutt's leg with his foot while playing mango-seed football. He submits as his, an essay written by his classmate, Abhay, in a competition. When he is found out and flogged, instead of taking his punishment manfully, he cowers and whines. Abhay can hardly conceal his contempt for this lack in Kanak. "No one could have told him [Kanak] about lions and lambs and how important it was to take one's punishment without squealing" (76).

Malgonkar's obviously, is a plea for action to protect values which are, in essence, traditional. Bhattacharya and Sahgal, in one sense, can be taken as novelists of ideas, even though as novelists they are committed to concretization of themes and problems in terms of felt life. Malgonkar, however, is a believer in men rather than philosophic values or institutions. The values he cherishes are more elemental and earthly. Another Indo-Anglian novelist who resembles him in this respect is Khushwant Singh.[48] Singh and Malgonkar are essentially writers of adventure tales of charismatic heroes and daring outcasts who are in the very thick of epoch-making events — World War, rebellious movements, freedom struggle, Partition. In such crucial times, the need of the hour is action, valorous action and not empty words. Malgonkar pokes fun at pacifist soldiers and fire-spitting demagogues mouthing abstractions. They are always shown to have some personal axe to grind behind such façade.

We have seen that both Bhattacharya and Sahgal see a way out in action rather than in idle speculation. Malgonkar's espousal of values like courage, loyalty, justice, revenge, etc. seems to make a plea for a muscular Hinduism, which is comparable to the rejuvenated and reinvigorated faith, the need for which emerges in Bhattacharya and Sahgal. However, this is not to lose sight of the difference in their perceptions. In both Bhattacharya and Sahgal, there had been a plea for the synthesis of the old and the new. Malgonkar is quite different in this respect. His is an advocacy of the old-fashioned, traditional values.

Not merely are the values comprising the Malgonkar code conservative and traditional, they also have an elementary simplicity and fascination, rather a tribal air about them. Malgonkar's men are faced with a choice between loyalty and betrayal, courage and cowardice, honour and dishonour, whereas the choice for both Bhattacharya and Sahgal had been between truth and deceit, proper and improper, moral and immoral, human and ahuman. That accounts for Malgonkar touching some intimate human strings in his readers, even in those whom the philosophic, high-sounding edifice of Bhattacharya and Sahgal would leave cold. This despite the fact that all three are committed to realization and concretization of these values in terms of human experience.

The way Malgonkar presents his protagonists acting single-mindedly in pursuit of the values they cherish, the impression is gathered that he would have no extraneous or peripheral issue cloud their perspective. His men are prompted primarily by being true to themselves and winning the love and respect of their colleagues and subordinates. They display manifest indifference to the political, scientific and the metaphysical problems of the day. Kiran, Abdul, 'Bull' Hampton (*Drum*), Hiroji, Abhayraj, Tony Sykes (*Princes*), Debi, Gian (*Ganges*), Nadkar and Reddy (*Bandicoot*) — all adhere to the code with persistence in a straightforward manner unencumbered with pragmatic considerations. Winton in *Combat* proves the rule by negative analogy. It is his lack of candour with himself which vitiates his responses and ultimately drives him to the wall.

Concentrating on simple values, Malgonkar's protagonists reject tangential concerns as distracting and irrelevant. They have, especially, a bias against the Establishment.[49] A typical Malgonkar man is "wrought in the Clark Gable Hollywood tradition — cynical, grinning, a lady's man, cocking an outrageous snook at the Indian Establishment whether armchair generals or Congress politicians or hypocritical preachers of *ahimsa* in a country at war, forging its soul in the smithy of blood and fire."[50]

The inherent anti-Establishmentarianism makes Malgonkar's positive heroes validate intra-group ties and associations even as they debunk and decry the impersonal, routine apparatus of the state. Politicians in the fictional universe of Malgonkar, on the contrary, strut about as charlatans, conspicuous for their lack of anything decent or uplifting. We discern in his novels an unambiguous indictment of political ideology as something divisive of amity and togetherness. Especially democracy in its philosophic and institutional dimensions comes off poorly in his presentation. Despite an emphatic assertion of the relevance of the human factor in politics, interspersed in his novels, a much larger scope and a much sharper focus is given to the unsavoury concomitants of democracy, which are seen as stifling of all individual aspirations. Along with debunking of ideology as such, goes a counterbalancing emphasis on personal and public realms.

From a close observation of the modern political scene, Bhattacharya, Malgonkar and Sahgal derive differing conclusions. Bhattacharya's is a strong plea for rediscovering the true essence of ways rooted in our tradition and employing them in a constructive manner, moulding the method, if need be, to sharpen its efficacy. A genuine application of the all-encompassing political philosophy of Gandhi would seem the most suitable in the present times as much as it had been in the past. Sahgal would readily agree with Bhattacharya here. She rather finds Gandhism a revivified facet of the otherwise stagnant Hinduism, a point of view which makes Gandhism very much relevant to the present context. Sahgal is of the conviction that only a vitalized version of Hinduism can infuse life in the passive masses and make them active participants in the political process. Malgonkar, on the other hand, has no patience with vague abstractions and philosophic and theoretical speculations. What matters for him is the bustle of action rather than the pale cast of thought. Action could even be impulsive, seemingly irrational. Whereas Bhattacharya and Sahgal present a view largely shared by many other novelists,[51] Malgonkar with his "fundamental subversion of the accepted values of post-Independence India, its virtual (perverse?) ignoring of the pacifist tradition and its deliberate refusal to compromise with the modern world,"[52] becomes one of the most original novelists in his field in this respect.

REFERENCES

1. See Chapter 4, "The Contours of A Crippling Creed."
2. See Chapter 5, "The Ossifying of the Gandhian Panacea," 105-7, 121-23.

3. Dr. Vincent Smith in Bhattacharya's *Hawaii* puts in thus : "Mahatma Gandhi in his homeland has been turned on a high pedestal, a dead image with flowers on its stone feet" (116). The result has been the making of places associated with Gandhi 'the places of ritualized pilgrimage' while "the new institutions in India dedicated to Gandhism" are "a world apart" (119).
4. Albert Schweitzer, *Indian Thought and Its Development* (Boston : Beacon Press, 1957), 237-38.
5. See Chapter 3, "Chronicling the Political Web," 53-57.
6. "I do strive deliberately and hard, to tell a story well : and I revel in incident, in improbabilities, in unexpected twists. I feel a special allegiance to the particular subcaste among those whose caste-mark I have affected, the entertainers...." Manohar Malgonkar in *The Times Literary Supplement*, June 4, 1964, 491.
7. See Chinua Achebe, "The Novelist as Teacher," in *New Statesman*, January 29, 1965.
8. "Literature and Social Reality," *Perspectives on Bhabani Bhattacharya*, ed. Ramesh Srivastava (Ghaziabad : Vimal Prakashan, 1982), 5.
9. *Ibid.*, 4.
10. "Literature and Social Reality," *Perspectives on Bhabani Bhattacharya*, ed. R.K. Srivastava, 4.
11. There is another not-so-obvious aspect of these novelists' adherence to Gandhism which can well be seen as part of the treatment of Gandhism in their novels taken up here in Chapter V. By choosing to write in English, though they had fully developed literature in their native languages, Bhattacharya, Malgonkar and Sahgal follow Gandhi, who had defended the English edition of *Harijan* by asserting that "the superior role of the English language cannot go." See Bhabani Bhattacharya, *Mahatma Gandhi — As a Writer* (New Delhi : Arnold Heinemann, 1982), 171. When Mulk Raj Anand asked Gandhi whether it was wrong to write in English, Gandhi assured him that it wasn't. See Mulk Raj Anand, "Pigeon-Indian : Some Notes on Indian English Writing," in *Studies in Australian and Indian Literature*, eds. C.D. Narsimhaiah and S. Nagarajan (New Delhi : I.C.C.R., 1972), 247.
12. *Harijan*, December 30, 1939.
13. *Harijan*, September 19, 1939.
14. Quoted by K.P.Saksena in "Gandhi and International Concern with Human Rights," in *Gandhi and the Contemporary World*, eds. K.P. Misra and S.C. Gangal (Delhi : Chanakya Publications, 1981), 157.
15. M.K. Gandhi, *The Story of My Experiments with Truth* (Ahmedabad : Navjivan Publishing House, 1976), 237.

16. *The Message of Mahatma Gandhi*, ed. U.S. Mohan Rao (New Delhi : Publications Division, Ministry of Information and Broadcasting, 1968), 115.
17. R.K. Narayan in *The Painter of Signs* (Mysore : Indian Thought Publications, 1977) makes the hero, Raman, realize that a pair of coloured glasses with uneven, defective lenses, which make the beautiful Daisy appear grotesque, are "better than Gandhi's plan to keep one's mind pure" (40). Kirillov in Raja Rao's *Comrade Kirillov* (New Delhi : Orient Paperbacks, 1978) regards Gandhi as 'a kleptomaniac' and 'an ungrown adult' who should have read Freud. Kirillov's wife, Irene, wonders if only sex is meant to make or break men. P., in the same novel, remarks that "Gandhism is bad for moral health. All ascetics smell the spermatozoa" 104.
18. The position taken by the novelists coincides with the one Nehru had taken on this subject. This is what he said : "I think Gandhi is absolutely wrong on this matter. His advice...as a general policy can only lead to frustration, inhibition, neurosis, and all manner of nervous and physical ills." Quoted in Tariq Ali, *The Nehrus and the Gandhis* (London : Picador, 1985), 75.
19. See Chapter 5, "The Ossifying of the Gandhian Panacea," 119-20.
20. In his rationalization about his giving up smoking and remaining unmarried (*Happy*, 24) is discernible a note of wistfulness and longing. Time and again we find him either referring to "the other realm" or actually losing himself, even though for a short time, in that world. In Gobind Narain's drawing room, the narrator's life and work at Sharanpur "had little reality" (24). The way he lets himself go impulsively carried over by Maya's beauty and her loneliness and grief, the way he offers a lame excuse therefor and the confession that Maya's image "had lain buried in the depths" (89) of his consciousness tell their own tale. See M.K. Bhatnagar, "The Individual as Politician — One Facet of Nayantara Sahgal as a Political Novelist," *MDU Research Journal*, 1 (April 1986), 99-100.
21. Cf. the ironic, sceptic treatment meted out to Gandhism in novels by some other novelists. The protagonist, Dr. Mohindra, in Mulk Raj Anand's *Gauri* (New Delhi : Arnold-Heinemann, 1976), poses the rhetorical query : "And now many have become the shareholders of the *Ramrajya*, earning dividends for once following Gandhi and going to jail?" (208). For Zahid in Attia Hosain's *Sunlight on a Broken Column* (New Delhi : Arnold-Heinemann, 1979), non-violence is "against human nature" (163). Kirillov in Raja Rao's *Comrade Kirillov* (New Delhi : Orient Paperbacks, 1978), terms it "a biological life" (34). For Irene, his wife *Satyagraha* is "a piece of gross childishness" (99). Ram Chander in D.F. Karaka's *We Never Die* (Bombay : Thacker & Co., 1944), finds

the strategy 'feeble,' 'futile,' appealing to one's emotions alone, not to judgment (95). For Malgonkar's skepticism, see Chapter V, "The Treatment of Gandhism as a Political Ideology, 202-15.

22. See C. Rajagopalachari, *Rajaji's Speeches* (Bombay : Vidya Bhavan, 1958), I, 182-91.
23. See *Harijan*, February 6, 1954.
24. See Chapter 5, "The Ossifying of the Gandhian Panacea, 110-13. Also see above, 155-56.
25. Cf. "I grew up during the national movement. My parents went to jail repeatedly during our fight for freedom.... I was born and brought up within the atmosphere and hopes and ideals of the Congress party. Its leaders were familiar to me. Our home was their meeting place and many decisions momentous to India were taken in it. I became a novelist and political journalist, and all my writing, fiction and non-fiction, has been about contemporary India."

    From the address to colloquim at Radcliffe Institute, Novemebr 4, 1976, included in Nayantara Sahgal, *Voice for Freedom* (Delhi : Hind Pocket Books, 1977), 55-66.
26. See Chapter 3, "Chronicling the Political Web," 53-57.
27. Nayantara Sahgal, *From Fear Set Free* (Delhi : Orient Paperbacks, n.d.), 41.
28. *Ibid.*, p. 6.
29. M.N. Sharma, "Nayantara Sahgal's Novels," *Journal of Indian Writing in English*, 4 (January 1976), 43. For a detailed consideration of the place accorded to the individual in Nayantara Sahgal's novels, see Manmohan Bhatnagar, "The Indo-Anglian Political Novel — A Study of Nayantara Sahgal," Distt. Panjab University Chandigarh, 1981, 70-93.
30. Nayantara Sahgal, "The face in the Crowd," *Indian Express*, January 23, 1973.
31. Nayantara Sahgal, "Struggle for Power in the Congress," *Indian Express*, September 18, 1969.
32. Nayantara Sahgal, "Injustice and the Intellectual," *Indian Express*, October 29, 1977.
33. Reported in Nayantara Sahgal, *Voice for Freedom*, 101.
34. Nayantara Sahgal, *Freedom Movement in India* (New Delhi : NCERT, 1970), 135.
35. For a detailed presentation, see Chapter 4, "The Contours of A Crippling Creed," 82-84, *et passim*.
36. Nayantara Sahgal, "Fresh Air on Hinduism," *The Sunday Standard*, December 1, 1968.

37. Cf. Shivaji's way of valuing this virtue of renunciation as reported by Malgonkar, "Saffron is the colour of renunciation, and holy men in India who have renounced all worldly attachments wear saffron garments. It is said that Shivaji, after he had established his kingdom, invoked the blessings of Ramdas, the saint gave Shivaji a strip of his saffron robe which Shivaji began to fly as the flag of his kingdom." *The Sea Hawk* (New Delhi : Vision Books, n.d.), 111.
38. Sahgal thinks that it is wrong to relate one's birth in a particular caste to one's *karma*. Such an attitude invests stratification along caste lines — a temporal dispensation — with moral significance, which is quite unwarranted. She takes the theory of *karma* to be one of aspiration. For her it is "the very heart of the Hindu view of evolutionary development, with the good life, constructively lived as its central purpose." Nayantara Sahgal, "Majorities and Minorities," *The Sunday Standard*, November 12, 1972.
39. "Conscience and the Hindu," *The Sunday Standard,* December 14, 1973.
40. Letter dated April 5, 1987.
41. Cf. "The far-too-familiar picture of the clean-limbed empire-building Englishman who lived by a code and was just as ready to die for it was, God knows, largely true to life. But it belonged to a later period of history. The early Englishmen were a race of smaller men without stature; a collection of greedy ledger-clerks and grocery salesmen; and their code, if they had a code, had no relationship with the playing fields of Eton.

    It was not until the late eighteenth century that England began to send out to India some of the men from her ruling classes. A surprsingly large proportion of them rules well and wisely with a sense of responsibility for the land and its people that was second to none. A few of them even came to love India and the Indians and devoted their lives to the service of the country. When they left, they left behind lifelong friends and tradition of service such as future administrators have found it well-nigh impossible to live up to." Manohar Malgonkar, *The Sea Hawk,* 97.
42. The term is G.S. Amur's, Gian is called 'the unheroic hero.' *Manohar Malgonkar* (New Delhi : Arnold-Heinemann, 1973), 105.
43. To call it the viewpoint of Kiran. Winton, Abhay and Nadkar respectively would only be a half-truth. It is no coincidence that not only his novels but also stories like "Pull-Push, "A Pinch of Snuff," "The Fixer" present the same impression. All these stories figure in *Rumble Tumble* (Delhi : Orient Paperback, 1977).
44. At another place, Malgonkar explains, "those rare and undefinable attributes that go to make a leader : a philosophy of life that was a combination of Omar Khayyam and Kipling's 'If,' with strong overtones of religious discipline." He also has the following observation from

Norsell's *Greek and Roman Mythology,* quoted : "Whoever possessed size, strength, wildness and fierceness was called the son of a Possiden." Manohar Malgonkar, *The Sea Hawk, op. cit.*, 120.

45. Haydn Moore Williams, "The Doomed Hero in the Fiction of Khushwant Singh and Manohar Malgonkar," *Explorations in Modern Indo-English Fiction,* ed. R.K. Dhawan (New Delhi : Bahri Publications, 1982), 193-94.
46. Another very good illustration of both courage and loyalty one comes across in the story "Bachcha Lieutenant" in *Modern Indian Short Stories*, eds., Saros Cowasjee and Shiv. K. Kumar (Delhi : O.U.P. 1985), 79-85. Both Jamadar Tukaram Shindey and his British officer, Lieutenant Wilson die in an exhibition of courage and loyalty for each other. An instance of courage and consideration for others is to be had in "To Hold a Tiger" in *A Toast in Warm Wine* (New Delhi : Orient Paperbacks, 1974), 127-35.
47. Haydn Moore Williams, "The Doomed Hero in the Fiction of Khushwant Singh and Manohar Malgonkar," *Explorations in Modern Indo-English Fiction*, 196.
48. Khushwant Singh's protagonist, Jugga in *Train to Pakistan* (1956) has many attributes of Malgonkar's men. A Sikh *budmash,* Jugga is a passionate man of action. The various key-characters miserably fail to cope with the appalling tragedy of the Partition. The magistrate is thoroughly corrupt and lecherous. The Congress politicians are universally despised and derided. The communist ideologue is "a milquetoast intellectual" — a mere theorizer. It is Jugga whose act of self-sacrificing heroism saves the Muslim refugees from being massacred. Jugga performs each role he finds himself in with élan, whether it is passionate fornication in the fields or being subjected to savage torture in a police-cell. What earns his contempt is cowardice and hypocrisy.
49. This anti-Establishmentarianism is the direct outcome of Malgonkar's perception of the putrid political scene and not that of nostalgia for English rule. Kai Nicholson's interpretation of this aspect of *Drum* misses the point completely. Kiran's refusal to lend the Army tent for a Congress meeting does not mean that "officers like Garud who had fought for the British and for the defence of India have neither forgotten nor forgiven the Congress party's attitude towards the INA officers...." Nor is it the result of Kiran Garud's ignorance of the political change in India. See Kai Nicholson, *Social Problems in the Indo-Anglian and Anglo-Indian Novel* (Bombay : Jaico, 1972), 162.
50. Haydn Moore Williams, "The Doomed Hero in the Fiction of Khushwant Singh and Manohar Malgonkar," *Explorations in Modern Indo-English Fiction*, *op. cit.*, 195.

51. Chapter 2, "Political Underpinigs in the Early Phase" discusses many novels, espousing Gandhism. Among some others, dealing with Gandhism and some aspects of Hinduism, could be cited : Mulk Raj Anand's *The Sword and the Sickle* (1942), Balachandra Rajan's *The Dark Dancer* (1958), Kamala Markandaya's *Nectar in a Sieve* (1954) and Padmini Sengupta's *Red Hibiscus* (1962).
52. Haydn Moore Williams, "The Doomed Hero in the Fiction of Khushwant Singh and Manohar Malgonkar," *Explorations in Modern Indo-English Fiction, op. cit.*, 194-95.

7

Artistic Alchemy

LITERATURE CANNOT remain unaffected by the social and the political, for political awareness forms an integral part of the artist's consciousness as a human being. But the artist's dialogue with the social and the political forces must be subsumed within the creative process which "transcends the horizons of society only when integrating the hell and paradise of human life into the symbols of the whole."[1] The primacy of the imaginative experience is characterized by immediacy and closeness. Ideology, on the other hand, is general and though intellectually it may be inclusive, it is not easily reconcilable with individual, authentic, imaginative experience. For that reason, it may be so much extraneous matter for the novelist. With an overload of ideology, a novelist is so much more vulnerable but when he succeeds, he reaps far richer dividends. At its best, artistic alchemy generates such intense heat[2] that the ideas it appropriates are melted into human gestures and fused with the emotions of its characters. However, for that, ideas have to come to life and be endowed with the capability for moving characters. Rather than being, in Stendhal's phrase, "a pistol shot in the middle of a concert,"[3] politics in the novel has to be integrated with the patterns of life traced, and has to function as the germinal nucleus fermenting the human story. Politics, thus, is to be presented in art through the medium of living men and women and their actions. When the fundamental urges and interests of people are thwarted by a repressive set-up, they get involved in the institutional parameters of their immediate environment. They are motivated, primarily, by their search for fulfilment, and ideology, thus, gets coalesced with and adds immeasurably to the human content. What follows is a study of this coalescing of the 'claims'[4] of art and life inclusive of politics, in Indian English "fiction" with special focus on the novels of Bhattacharya, Malgonkar and Sahgal.

Bhattacharya is concerned with the modes of projection of the artist's convictions about life.[5] But he scrupulously refrains from an obtrusive presentation of his political vision. Nor does he, the creator of his fictional universe, comment upon the scene or on the doers and their deeds. Nowhere do we come across an impression or statement thrust on the readers or a view presented which goes against the current of action. He does comment in a neutral voice occasionally but the comment does not stand out, it springs effortlessly from the action which occasioned it. One example would suffice. In *Hungers,* Bhattacharya presents starving destitutes who see lots of delicious eatables in the market but far from attacking or grabbing them, they forcibly turn their gaze away.

> The peasants' hands were manacled with their antique moral tradition. The rice robbers were safe from peril because of the peasants' tradition (111).

Bhattacharya's terse comment as an omniscient narrator causes no eyebrows to be raised. It is a comment which is natural and spontaneous in the political/ideological framework (worked out earlier) which is perceptible and as such is acceptable because in that the novel is conceived.[6]

Bhattacharya's denunciation of exploitation — political, caste-based or economic — is rendered in human terms and not ideological terms. *Hungers* presents a moving spectacle of persons reeling under economic and political depredation. The political message that self-rule is a must even for individual self-fulfilment is presented not through ideological debate but through Rahoul, the protagonist, who comes to realize it on his pulse. Again, the nexus between black-marketeers and the alien rulers is made all too patent not through rhetorical argument but by making men like Samarendra Basu and Sir Abalabandhu kowtow to the British. The strategy used here is of making human agents act in a manner which leads to the ideological as an inescapable conclusion. In *Tiger,* there is an ominous alliance between Mangal Adhikari, the priest, Motichand, the speculator and Sir Ablabandhu, the anglophile toady, which reflects the ganging up of the upper classes and the business magnets to perpetuate their hegemony — religious, economic and political — over the masses.

In *Tiger* and *Hungers,* the novelist renders in active human terms what the sensitive man in him had himself seen.

> My creative writing had its true genesis in the hunger-hit streets of Calcutta where the great famine raged. I had an intense need of release from the agony of the traumatic experience.[7]

However, there remain some minor blemishes from the artistic viewpoint where the novelist seems to be passionately carried over. We may refer to a few instances. In *Tiger,* Kalo is thrown behind the bars for three excruciating months just because he had stolen a few bananas from a carriage (30). A famished person is subjected to unspeakable atrocities simply because he could not take his eyes off the food staked in an eating house. The bully of a magistrate asks the convict, "Why did you have to live?" (30). However, these only underscore the relative ease with which ideology is humanized and harmonized within a non-ideological framework elsewhere in Bhattacharya's corpus.

In *Music,* Bhattacharya handles the old vs new debate like an artist. His fairness is manifest in ridiculing both the over crazy modernists and the blinkered traditionalists by subjecting the practitioners of these to comical situations. The ideological current is carried covertly through gentle irony and humour rather than passionate denunciatory outbursts. Old Mother and Mohini's mother-in-law stand for the old time-tested values, while Mohini's father and her husband, Jayadev, stand for change. However, Bhattacharya is chary of neat, mutually exclusive categories. The old Mother is not absolutely allergic to modern ways,[8] while both Jayadev and Mohini's father stand for change — change with continuity. The ideological point, *viz*., the desirability of a synthesis of the old and the new ways, is made in a subtle manner. The bizarre practice of dedicating some part of one's body or some other essential of life[9] is exposed as ridiculous not after the fashion of an ideologue or a doctrinaire but through the impromptu invention of such a dedication by the protagonist, Mohini. Her mother-in-law is determined to have the young bride's nose bored — for a bride without a nose-ring is unbecoming. Mohini shudders at the very idea. This is how she wriggles out of the difficult situation.

> "You see, Mother," she spoke with quick invention, "this nose is dedicated to Kali. As a child I used to catch cold so often and had breathing trouble, so old Mother vowed away my nose to the goddess to win her protection..." (145).

In a similar vein of light-hearted ridicule are indicted the 'modern' practices such as the meticulous inspection, in physical details, of a would-be bride by the groom's party (42), smoking regardless of the presence of elders (44) and so on.

Gold presents most artistically the message that freedom must be used as a means to egalitarian ends. The 'axes' here are "hardly visible and the grinding is not very audible."[10] Meera's grandfather, the minstrel, gives her a *taveej* which will turn copper into gold if she performs distinterested acts of kindness. The village Seth, in partnership with her, contrives various acts of 'kindness' : a poor man is forcibly evicted so that Meera could rehabilitate him later; a body is reported to have tumbled into a well so that Meera could volunteer to go into the well to save him; a compulsive drunkard and a habitual prostitute are to be joined in wedlock by Meera. All these endeavours obviously fail to produce the desired result and thereby is conveyed the novelist's message.[11] Freedom will fail just as the *taveej* has failed if genuine kindness is missing.

Bhattacharya is for the incidental and the parenthetical in both *Music* and *Gold*. Witness the childish pranks of Mohini with her brother Heeralal in exchanging funny-sounding English names (5-8), Mohini's early crushes (9-10), the play of her youthful fancy (19-24), the affair of the snake-charmer with Bindu, the maid's daughter (23-26). Similarly by limiting ourselves to the first few chapters only of *Gold,* for example, we discover the drowning of Nago, the Seth's son (16-21), the village women's non-violent movement (27-32), the reaction of Hosiar Singh, the village constable (24-25), and the attempts of the village *halwai* to woo Meera. Bhattacharya's is obviously a manner farthest from a theoretician's. Though lacking in the taut and relentless thrust of an ideologue, these bits cohere because of being the imaginative comprehension of life. It is in such instances that one discovers the novelist of ideas and 'the cogenital novelist' in Bhattacharya joining hands and collaborating with each other.

Ladakh X-rays Gandhism in humanistic terms to detect chinks in its armour. But this too is accomplished situationally: pitting Satyajit against Roopa (171-73) and the haunting reminiscences of Harriet Green and Stella Johnson (176-77), pitting Sumita against a sculpture in an amorous posture (127), and by presenting Suruchi, left alone to mourn the grievous loss of Ajoy and Sanjoy stifled within her (20-21). The novel succeeds in exposing Gandhism as contrary to life. Gandhian non-violence is presented as partly irrelevant and anachronistic, not in cerebral verbiage but through Satyajit's failure to evoke popular response to his *Shanti* march to Ladakh. It is in a similar vein that the underlying discontent in Bhaskar and Roopa precipitates the awareness of the inadequacy of a purely consumeristic, modernist way of life.

Hawaii, too, is an artistic success, characterized by an in-depth analysis of the inadequacies in a Yoganand and Walt who may stand in the reader's mind for the Eastern and the Western modes of living respectively but they are presented as mortals in the first instance.

Bhattacharya's fairness in his presentation of different conflicts is his remarkable artistic achievement. He never loads the dice consciously against any combatant value or institution. Whether it is the Englishmen as a class (*Hungers*), the rich as a stratum of society (*Hungers, Gold*), the old and the 'modern' values (*Music, Hawaii*), the low and the 'high' born (*Tiger*), Gandhism and 'hi-tech' values (*Ladakh*), his brush spreads evenly black and white. And the black and white emerge from within, they are not imposed from the outside. Despite his obvious bias for the poor, the downtrodden, the 'new' values and Gandhism, Bhattacharya is loath to generalize and thereby oversimplify matters. What saves the novelist from being merely a proletarian writer is his ability to see good and evil on a scale other than purely an economic or ideological one. The limelight in the novels of Bhattacharya is evenly shared. Those who receive it include not merely the poor Kajoli and her family but also the rich Rahoul; not only the 'low' born Kalo but also the 'high' born Biten; not merely the traditional old Mother but also the 'modern' Jayadev; not merely the Gandhian Satyajit but also the modern Bhaskar; not merely the austere Sumita but also the permissive Roopa; not merely the Eastern Yoganand but also the Western-seekers.

Nayantara Sahgal portrays the political scenario in eminently human rather than in ideological terms in novels like *Happy, Morning, Storm, Shadow, Situation* and even *Rich*. The long drawn out fight for freedom, the high hopes at the attainment of Independence, the mushrooming of opportunists and ideologues soon thereafter; the rise of fissiparous forces tearing at the national fabric, the rise of pseudo-Radicalism, apathy, unconcern and rank self-seeking, pushing the nation to a point of extremity; the edifice of egalitarian democracy reeling under the unscrupulous Emergency-regime[12] — the tortuous course taken by the country in recent years comes alive in essentially human terms. The political commentator in her toes the trail blazed by the delineator of the human drama in her.

What is most noteworthy about Sahgal's authorial strategy is her scrupulous objectivity. By permitting the readers a peep into her characters' tortuous process of thinking, she gives her creations autonomy independent of her and ensures that their inner reality is not subjected to an external or superimposed viewpoint. Though the narrator, himself a character in the novel, does the filling in job regarding other characters in *Happy,* it is based on either his long association with most major characters or on their confiding in him. This keeps intact their inner vitality. In *Morning* and *Storm,* too, there are Rakesh and Vishal respectively who approximate the role performed by the narrator with matching finesse. Sahgal painstakingly portrays the environmental influences which shape her characters such as Kalyan, Kailas, Hari Mohan, Neeta, Rashmi and others. *Storm* relies on a shuffling of perspective, enabling the reader to share the differing points of view of characters such as Harpal Singh, Gyan Singh, Vishal and Inder. The result in both *Morning* and *Storm* is the same — the successful creation of a set of characters moving in an actual three-dimensional context. *Shadow* is characterized by greater sophistication insofar as it relies more on the readers' capability to infer from what is presented by her in bald detail. Simrit's relationship with Raj and Som comes out by implication through the presentation of Som's relationship with Lalli, his business-partner, and his British employer. Som's actions in themselves are a commentary on his values. *Situation* takes the presentation further through highly suggestive and meaningful juxtapositions of persons and situations : Shivraj's humanistic idealism, the cabinet intellectuals' ahuman pseudo-Radicalism, Devi's bewildering helplessness, Rishad's honest violence.

Another noticeable feature of the novelist's suggestive presentation of ideological posture is her use of commonplace symbols. These symbols, far from standing out intrusively, merge imperceptibly in the message they are charged with. The Sharanpur club, with its mixed clientele in *Happy* symbolizes the changed reality in post-Independence India. The mutilation of the wall painting in Inder's office in *Storm* signals the vulnerabilities of the finer values of life in the face of brute violence. The window in Sumer Singh's office in *Shadow,* devoid of an outside view, tells its own tale. It is a fair picture of the mind of Sumer. The forgotten picture of the late Prime Minister — the idealist visionary, Shivraj — in *Situation,* falling down and being trampled over is a fair indication of the rejection of his cherished values in the changed scenario. The oppressive weather in the same novel is another politically pertinent symbol, a nagging reminder of the oppressive regime. The rain when it finally comes, signals a cessation of one phase as well as the commencement of another. *Rich* has its truncated beggar — a symbol of the ravaged body politic.

Malgonkar's *Drum, Combat, Princes, Ganges* and *Bandicoot* present the novelist's perspective in eminently human (and thus specific) rather than philosophic terms. The Malgonkar code is expressed in diverse particular situations and it is through the particular that the general is expressed at times tacitly, at times not so tacitly. The political message in Malgonkar's novels is rendered in human terms. While Jugal Kishor represents the pre-Independence Congress politician, intoxicated with power, Kanak, Lala Vishnu Saran Dev and Krishna Manikam present the spectre of authoritarianism masquerading under a façade of democracy. Kiran, Abhay, Nadkar and Reddy represent the dedicated ones fighting valiantly to stem the rot. Gian's early infatuation with Gandhism is the concretization of an average Indian's affair with the philosophy that had taken the whole country by storm, as Malgonkar sees it. In a similar vein are Debi and Shafi, human actors embodying another historical force — militant nationalism.

Combat is presented through the point of view of an interested party — Winton himself. It is the tale of the failure and death of a man who finds that his public school values and his 'middle-class rectitude,' imbibed in England, fail him in his confrontation with the Indian scene. However, by trusting the tale rather than the teller, one could reasonably reconstruct the situation and arrive at a fair appraisal of Winton's character *vis-a-vis* his antagonists. Reading in between the lines, one discovers how selfish, dishonest, cowardly and mean Winton is.[13] Despite the sleight of hand Malgonkar displays in the arrangement of his narrative, *Combat* has an effortlessness, a certain inevitability about it. The way in which Winton, lacking in the values comprising the Malgonkar code, goes down, has the inevitability of the denouement of a Greek tragedy. This, by implication, facilitates the impression how indispensable these values are for men in offices of importance.

Malgonkar does present his code through characters but the hand of their creator is all too visible in their movements. *Drum* begins with Malgonkar's artistic protestations in a rather hesitant epilogue-like section entitled "Some years Earlier" (9-10). Therein he claims to render his vision in human, experimental terms :

> This book is largely the story of the success or failure of the efforts of one of the officers of the Regiment to live up to its code (10).

However, the celebration of the Army code in *Drum* involves the bestowing of stock responses upon the protagonist even in potentially gripping situations. This makes the Malgonkar hero a mannequin with doctored reactions rather than a figure in flesh and blood. One does not notice this want of life as much in Kiran's encounter with Colonel Manners or with Lala Vishnu Saran Dev as one does in Kiran's intimate scene with Bina, the woman he thinks he is "terribly in love with." The way Kiran plays the pucca sahib with her — by knowingly ignoring the secret message her whole being flashes to him[14] — does signal the triumph of the subscriber to the Malgonkar code but the stifling of the individual in him.

In *Princes,* the controlling voice is that of Abhayraj, the Crown Prince of Begwad, and it is through his blinkered view that the outside world is presented. What is of primary concern for us here is the incalculable damage such a jaundiced perspective inflicts on the socio-political reality without the pale of the princely domain. Kanakchand is the chief victim. He is presented at the outset as a 'sound coin' despite his being a cobbler's son. He is also presented as sincere, high-spirited and genuinely under the influence of the reformist political movement which had entered the princely states from British

India. There are unmistakable signs of condescension in Abhay's appraisal of Kanak but the later presentation of him as a 'demented demagogue,' solely motivated by personal prejudices seems absolutely out of place. Abhay confronts Kanak as the latter sits with a half-filled bottle of whisky under the table. The prejudice in Abhay's reporting of his encounter with Kanak-chand is all too patent.

> 'What is it that you want, Kanakchand?' I asked. 'I want nothing, nothing for myself. I stand for the people, the downtrodden people of this state, for their birthright....'
> 'That is all nonsense, and you know it,' I said. He was quiet for a while but his eyes smouldered.
> 'Yes, I suppose I do want something for myself. I want revenge. I want to wash away the insult of poverty...the shame of untouchability' (288).

The encounter culminates in Kanakchand left spluttering and foaming at the mouth, struggling for words. A similar bias had marked Kiran's presentation of Lala Vishnu Saran Dev (*Drum*) and Winton's impression of Jugal Kishor (*Combat*).[15] However, whereas in the former, the person concerned was not so integral to the scene, in the latter, the possibility of one's seeing beyond the blinkered perspective of the narrator wasn't so effectively precluded as is the case in Abhay's view of Kanak.

What militates against a fair presentation of the issues in *Ganges* and renders the conclusions suspect is the distribution of the mantle of non-violence and violence to men of unequal merit. Malgonkar loads the dice against non-violence by making Gian, its exponent, a weak, wavering individual, using *ahimsa* as a mask to cover his want of manliness. On the other hand, Debi, the votary of violence, is idealized.[16] This makes the progression of the narrative sound rather too neat and pat. It is this purposive oversimplification which one comes across again in the portrayal of the Englishmen in general and the Indians in public offices in particular. Whereas Malgonkar paints the former in blemishless white, the latter make him go for the darkest shades. It is this alchemy of contrasting simplistic hues, the artistic grey conspicuous by its absence, which marks Malgonkar's figures in general. As has been made out in the foregoing analysis, characters like Lala Vishnu Saran Dev, Kanakchand and Jugal Kishor have been painted in unrealistically gloomy shades. While the positive protagonists are reflected in sparkling white, the few dark spots therein are glossed over and have to be spotted only after scratching the surface. A few such spots would appear from the analysis given below.

Malgonkar's glorified protagonists have some rather unedifying and unpalatable aspects about them. They are egotistical, unconcerned, blinkered and even male chauvinists. Kiran believes, he is in love with Bina but he brusquely boasts to her father, "My career is more important to me than anything else — more important than your daughter" (*Drum,* 196). Winton and Abhay, both owe a lot to the first women in their lives, namely Ruby and Minnie respectively, who lead them to emotional and physical maturity. Yet both display remarkable insensitivity and shallowness in their appreciation and treatment of them. In comparison with Winton who lets the Anglo-Indian Ruby fade out of his life for fear of failure (198), Abhay appears somewhat considerate. After the first bit of romantic euphoria is over, Abhay coolly assesses Minnie's value and enters into a business deal with her. However, both Abhay and Winton are so self-centred that they woefully fail to comprehend their women. Winton offers a pair of sapphire and gold ear clips to Ruby as a gift. But he is at his wits' end as he fails to discover why it should make her cry. Similar is the predicament of Abhay who finds Minnie in tears when he offers to marry her. These lacunae represent obvious blemishes in presentation, for all these protagonists are presented as the yardstick against which lesser mortals are measured. These paragons of the Malgonkar code are presented as embodiments of values which would take one to the light beyond the tunnel. This is sought to be accomplished by brushing something under the carpet, slurring over or being even unmindful of the unedifying attributes of the positive heroes in Malgonkar's fictional universe.

Malgonkar does present his political message through 'men in action' rather than in abstract arguments. Nevertheless the fact remains that the ideology rests rather uneasily on the artistic edifice. The one-sidedness of the tale breeds suspicion against the teller. By turning to the tale rather than to the teller, one finds a number of disquieting queries raising their heads. *Hikmat mali* is presented as part of the much-vaunted virtue of loyalty. But how is it qualitatively different from the sort of arrangement Lala Vishnu Saran Dev desires of Kiran in *Drum*? How is Kanak's revenge regarded as that of a sheep while Abhay's is that of a lion? What of Jugal Kishor's plan to force Winton to go after the rogue-elephant? Such posers go against the ideological current of Malgonkar's novels and point to the author's inability to carry his readers fully with him.

Bhattacharya's characters mark the triumph of the artist in their creator. They are not bundles of ideological platitudes, grinding their maker's axe, but mortals who have psychological compulsions to adopt a particular course of action. They feel the ideological battles on their pulse. They are psychologically convincing and it is their credible conduct from which we draw ideological conclusions. With the objectivity, of an artist Bhattacharya creates both positive and negative heroes, giving them all private motivations for their public deeds.[17] Samarendra (*Hungers*), Kalo, Biten (both from *Tiger*), and Seth Shamsunder (*Gold*) are obvious examples.

Bhattacharya goes farther. He makes the ideological rhetoric of his protagonists consistent and convincing. Jayadev (*Music*), Satyajit, Sumita, and Bhaskar (all from *Ladakh*) pursue the same ideals in both their private and public lives. A person like Rahoul (*Hungers*) veering away from sheltered academics to the fret and fury of national politics, is humanized, and the change in him is presented as the inevitable outcome of his search for self-fulfilment as an individual.[18] What is most creditworthy is the pains taken by Bhattacharya in rounding off to perfection the personality of a minor character like Roopa in *Ladakh* by linking her permissive ways with the unhappy childhood (136) and the later experience with a colleague, Wakefield. Her movement to the discovery of the 'Indianness' in her — when she realizes that she would not be content to be a mere moment in the life of Bhaskar (334) — is parallelled by Bhaskar's movement towards Satyajitism. The synthesis of the two erstwhile contrary ideologies, Satyajitism and Bhaskarism[19], is accomplished successfully for it is rendered not in doctrinal but in essentially human terms of experience and enlightenment. Roopa and Suruchi, with their instinctive attachment to life, learn to hold on to something 'metaphysical,' Sumita, tied to abstractions to the detriment of the woman in her, learns to acknowledge the claims of herself in totality. A similar movement towards each other is made by Satyajit (who lived by *a priori* notions) and Bhaskar (who lived from moment to moment).

Bhattacharya agrees with Robert Scholes that great characters are the result of a powerful combination of two impulses : "the impulse to individualize and the impulse to typify."[20] The same is the case with his memorable characters. As types, they become symbols of the time and as individuals they become timeless. S.K. Desai finds Bhattacharya relying on the strategy of symbolization or as he terms it, *sadharanikaran.*[21] An obvious example is the birth of Rahoul's daughter after the agony and suffering of Monju which parallels the birth of a new national mood after the trials and tribulations of war and a protracted struggle for freedom. It is easy to link the two, for Rahoul, while all ears to the radio-news about the Second World War, is really thinking of the child (*Hungers,* 1-7). In a similar vein, we can detect in Rahoul an emissary of the urban, the educated and the Westernized, in Kajoli, a symbol of the rural, the traditional and the innocent, in Jayadev and Harindra (*Music*), spokesmen of modernism and so on. However, to dub them like that only, losing sight of the simultaneous operation of the process of individuation would be to read Bhattacharya only superficially. 'The novelist of ideas' and 'the congenital novelist' working in a spirit of give-and-take make the characters a happy blend, in varying degrees, of the typical and the individual.

Bhattacharya creates no author-surrogates in larger-than-life dimensions to dominate the scene and render covertly what their creator eschews overtly. Bhattacharya is well aware of the requirement of fictional characters being flesh-and-blood creations :

> ...literary art is not black and white. The most heroic character must have his feet on common earth and the dastardly villain, even more difficult to create, needs to be redeemed by the 'human touch.' Otherwise credibility is lost. The willing suspension of disbelief on the reader's part is withdrawn.[22]

This is what he has to say about the manner in which his characters take birth and develop :

> I start with a broad idea of what the people are going to be like. In the process of writing, they often become new persons.[23]

Walt Gregson (*Hawaii*)[24] and Roopa (*Ladakh*)[25] are the ones depicting such autonomous growth, going by the creator's own testimony. However, we do have some minor characters who betray the conscious hand of their creator rather than the shaping power of imagination forming them. In *Hungers,* the man who surrenders his food ticket and the woman who bares her bosom for the sake of others fall into this category.

It can safely be said that Bhattacharya does not force any character to embody certain principles or ideals at the cost of his flesh-and-blood existence. Even the seeming colossuses are given feet of clay. Devata in *Hungers* has a greedy son in Samarendra; the minstrel in *Gold* has a wife who nags; Satyajit and Swami Yogananda in *Ladakh* and *Hawaii* respectively have repressed physical desires; Kajoli in *Hungers* has a weakness for fancy-coloured ribbons (87) and the old Mother in *Music* has a fascination for English pictures (30).

So far as the creation of characters capable of ideological baggage is concerned, Malgonkar succeeds eminently with Winton in *Combat.* Once the internal contours of his character are understood, Winton's career rushes onwards of its own volition without the manipulating hand of the creator.[26] Gian's pubic posture, too, is rendered inevitable, given his internal mechanics. In a similar vein, the ideological predilection of Debi is made the outcome of the trauma he underwent in his adolescence.[27]

There are other characters in Malgonkar whose political postures will seem but extensions of their personal selves, if one goes strictly by the testimony of the controlling voice. It is obvious that Winton in *Combat* sees in the politics of Jugal covert endeavours to settle personal scores. Abhay in *Princes* interprets Kanak, the politician, in a similar vein. It is obvious that this simplistic view of their public activities would deprive them of the complexity of being which they potentially have. Jugal and Kanak have a mesmeric hold over the people they lead. The possibility of their having genuine ideological predilections which make them arouse the people against their exploiters — Winton (*Combat*) and Hiroji (*Princes*) — cannot be easily brushed under the carpet. The inescapable inference is that Malgonkar presents only a blinkered view of Jugal and Kanak here. The events themselves carry an impression which seems at odds with the 'official' view. Herein lies the novelist's inability to capture the inherent complexity of his own creations.

The failure in characters like Lala Vishnu Saran Dev and Kiran in *Drum*[28] is even more palpable. These figures belong to a separate category altogether insofar as they are one-dimensional, cardboard mannequins sans the depth a personal self would have accorded them. The case of Shafi in *Ganges* is unique in that he is made abruptly to catapult from angelic grandeur to demoniacal depths. As the brain behind the Ram-Rahim Club, whose members in their devout patriotism spurn narrow obscurantism, Shafi gets converted one fine morning into a rabid communalist. There is only one encounter between Shafi and Hafiz — where the latter brainwashes the former — on which the metamorphosis of Shafi is based. This one encounter is insufficient to reconcile the two diametrically opposed selves of Shafi. The unmistakable impression is that Malgonkar handles his characters here like dumb, driven cattle. Far from breathing life into a character and then letting him create a role for himself in the story, as we have seen Bhattacharya doing to a large extent, Malgonkar tailors his recalcitrant figures to fit the particular design he would like his tale to carry.

Sahgal makes her fictional universe throb with beings of flesh-and-blood rather than abstracted ideologues. She suggests the general through the particular. The narrator, Sohanlal, Sanad (from *Happy*), Kailas Vrind, Prakash Shukla, Abdul Rahman, the President (from *Morning*), Vishal Dubey, Trivedi, Harpal Singh (from *Storm*), Raj (*Shadow*), Usman, Devi Rishad (from *Situation*) and Sonali (*Rich*) — all present their constructive political ideology in an essentially human idiom. Sahgal goes farther in her commitment to the humanization of political rhetoric. She presents her characters in lifelike grey as blends of virtues and vices. She succeeds most in those characters where she penetrates deeply into their psychology to discover the instincts which propel them to action, whether it be worthy of approbation or not. In Kalyan Sinha in *Morning*, we have a character viewed in entirety. The novelist notes his concern for the exploited, the weak and the helpless as well as his recourse to exploitation and whatever other means he deems fit for quick progress. In *Storm,* Harpal is presented in the wholeness of his personality with his successes and failures, idealism and frustrations. Gyan Singh is both the down-to-earth charmer and the demagogue. Rishad in *Situation* gets a similarly thorough treatment with both the ahuman terrorist and the humanist reformer rolled in one.[29]

Another aspect of Sahgal's delineation of her characters, unencumbered with the dictates of ideology, is her even-handed portrayal of people subscribing to different creeds. This is all the more remarkable if we consider the fact that her primary occupation is with the theme of the antiqueness of Hinduism *vis-a-vis* other faiths which, she feels, are more in tune with the requirements of the present critical times.[30] Sahgal does not let her impression of Hinduism cloud her perception of life and people as an artist. Liberalism and obscurantism are not exclusive to any one religion in her novels. McIvor in *Happy* and Raj in *Shadow* are liberal Christians. Saleem and Saira in *Morning* and Usman in *Situation* are humanist Muslims. On the other hand, the Granges in *Happy* and Nadira *in Situation* represent the pull of fundamentalism. However, the fairness or the ability to catch the grey areas rather than being conditioned by the few streaks of black or white in one's personality is sadly lacking in other characters like Hari Mohan (*Morning*), Gian Singh (*Storm*) and Sumer Singh (*Shadow*). Nevertheless they are not reduced to one-dimensional cardboard figures because their outward actions are inextricably intertwined with their internal mechanics. As we have seen earlier,[31] it is the internal psychology of Kunti Behn, Harilal Mathur, Sohanlal (all from *Happy*), Kalyan Sinha, Hari Mohan (both from *Morning*), and Sumer Singh (*Shadow*), that makes these characters credible and thus carry the ideological weight the novelist puts on them. The manner they conduct themselves under this 'handicap'[32] helps the novelist present her interpretation of the political situation in thoroughly human terms.

In spite of Sahgal's general success in making her characters credible, one cannot simply wish away abstractions like the Cabinet Intellectuals and the minister of Minerals and Metals in *Situation* and the ogre-like Madam and her son in *Rich,* where the political columnist in the novelist seems to have taken over. *Rich,* especially, is interspersed with vague apprehensions, unsubstantiated allegations and wild fantasy — all undigested in art — which could perhaps go well with journalism of a particular hue but do not with serious literature. *Rich* leaves one with the impression that political consciousness is rendered here in political rhetoric without being fully integrated with the gamut of life presented; it remains extraneous to art.

Sonali, the novelist's persona in the novel, uses terms and situations reminiscent of the political reality without the novel. They do not seem to emanate from the fictional experience incorporated. At one juncture, she thus expresses herself about the Emergency-dispensation : "You know perfectly well, everything is controlled by one and a half people" (32). This computation of the ruling coterie had been earlier made famous in the novelist's political columns.[33] This is how the 'Son' is described to have started, by

> vasectomizing the lower classes, blowing up tenements and scattering slum-dwellers to beautify Delhi, setting up youth camps with drop-outs in command, loafers and ruffians who would otherwise have been no more than loafers and ruffians.... Look at the way he'd sprung full-blown, up and doing, into the power structure, while grandpa had to spend years in jail and mummy had doll processions before making it to the executive suite (83).

There are other references in a similar vein. K.L., another voice given the mantle of narration, ruminates thus : "...suppose Madam's son had stayed a hijacker of cars and not become leader of cultural revolution" (188). This is how K.L. reacts to the news of J.P.'s being in hospital :

> After they've finished with him, he'll be ready for his grave. Hospital's where they'd keep him, wouldn't they? It is more convenient for bumping him off, with all that hospital care around him. They'll say he was old and ill... (76).

Rose, another character, who is presented sympathetically in the novel, presents farther reaches of such conjectures. She imagines :

> She was listening to a doctor-butcher prescribe an appallingly simple prescription for death behind bars, to be followed by two days' national mourning for an old and misguided freedom fighter, who had regrettably, died of old age in prison... (46).

Rich obviously has politics not fully subsumed in art. While politics can certainly form a legitimate subject-matter of art, it should be fully integrated with the human narrative. That is where the rub lies in *Rich.* The novel is so much interspered with political rhetoric out of harmony with the experience of the characters and unwarranted by the fictional context that one cannot help seeing beyond the curtain. What one discovers is the unedifying spectacle of the novelist pulling her mannequins by strings and guiding their responses. Sahgal had succeeded in legitimizing her indictment of the pseudo-radicalism and the dictatorial propensities in the post-Independence set of leaders in her earlier novels because it had sprung in human terms from out of the fictional context painstakingly created within these novels. The expose of the machinations of the Madam and her son in *Rich* is so much excrescence, for the intensity of the artistic process here has not fused it with the human action delineated.

Rich seems to be more a lyric of political experience than a slice of life captured dispassionately. It signals the defeat of the congenital novelist in Sahgal even if it has facilitated a personal catharsis, as she herself confesses :

> With *Rich Like Us,* I have reached the end of the road. It exorcised that whole shame-making national experience from my system.[34]

Like Bhattacharya seeking emotional release from the trauma of famine-stricken Calcutta in novels like *Hungers* and *Tiger,*[35] Sahgal, in *Rich,* seems to seek release from the nightmare of Emergency. And the release gets the better of the artist here.

The way a novelist draws the curtain suggests the tenuous agreement between the artist and the ideologue. Hence an examen of the manner wherein a finale is brought about would be an index of the success attained in the artistic rendering of the vision. The ending of Bhattacharya's novels go to reveal where the novelist's priorities lie. A neat philosophic denouement is not what Bhattacharya is after. The denouements in his novels are psychologically conditioned rather than ideologically directed. *Hungers* leads to the completion of Rahoul's search for self-fulfilment which had been suggested at the outset.[36] *Music* heralds the triumph of the modernist, reformist inclination in the face of stiff resistance from an unthinking reverence for old ways — a denouement very much on the cards. In *Tiger,* Kalo's eventual change of heart and confession of his fraud appears anything but contrived, placed as it is at the end of a long series of agonizing moments for Mangal Adhikari when he himself has gnawing doubts and when his own dear Chandralekha gets ready to sacrifice herself to keep the pretence. *Gold* concludes with the coming forth of the minstrel to espouse overtly what the action therein had covertly suggested. In *Ladakh,* however neat and pat the conclusion may sound in isolation, a little consideration would reveal how the novelist by infecting Bhaskar's modernism with discontent and making Satyajit's Gandhism propped on an edifice of repression, had cleared the decks for a synthesis of the two. Sumita's metamorphosis from a pale shadow of the austere Satyajit to a woman feeling passion on her pulse, "the wave that sweeps you away on its crest" (373) is also eminently prepared for.

Except for Sahgal's political lyric in *Rich,* the endings of her novels are dictated by the inner alchemy of the characters rather than by the ideological directions of the novelist. Sanad's coming round to self-realization under the influence of his wife, Veena (*Happy*); Kailas's taking to activist politics to stem the rot (*Morning*); Vishal's cool-headed appraisal of the deteriorating situation in Chandigarh and his resolve to face it boldly (*Storm*); Raj's concern for the vanishing 'tribe of India-lovers' (*Shadow*); Usman's coming to the streets to lead a popular movement against the government (*Situation*); Sonali's resolve not to be cowed down but work for the future of her country (*Rich*) — the endings are psychologically motivated rather than ideologically conditioned. Rather than being superimposed on mannequins, the final responses grow imperceptibly from the innermost being of the characters. Consequently, ideological penaceas, if any, appear to be inevitable products of an intensely human, dynamic situation.

The endings of Malgonkar's novels reveal the artistic and the ideological strains in the novelist, in differing degrees of cohesion. The disintegration and death of Winton, with which *Combat* concludes, has an artistic inevitability about it which is highly commendable.[37] Even though *Ganges* presents the two protagonists — Gian and Debi — in colours of glaring contrast at the outset,[38] the anagnorises they reach towards the end are thoroughly prepared for. The validation of love through both Gian and Debi is most convincing[39] and thus the ideological impression of the primacy of personal bonds over political theorizing is reached inevitably in a human idiom. In a similar vein, *Princes* has a denouement in perfect accord with its one-sided perspective. The novel closes with Abhay's father courting death like a hero by conscious choice in preference to life in 'colourless' India after Independence. On the other hand, there is Kanakchand who whines and groans as Abhay administers to him the horsewhipping he 'deserved.' The ending, however, causes few eyebrows to be raised for the narrative had taken such a one-sided turn ahead of the finale.[40] However, *Drum* betrays the guiding hand of the ideologue in Malgonkar. The novelist acknowledges the contribution of Duggie Sawhney, "who cut out two chapters from the book" (5), of Pattie Somdutt, "who thinned out the remainder" (5) and of Pat Totterdell, "who made me change the ending" (5). Nevertheless, it is Malgonkar alone who is to be blamed for the contrived finale wherein the protagonist survives all obstacles — personal, social, professional and political. The 'they-lived-happily-thereafter' ending of the novel signals more the wishful thinking of an ideologue than faithful depiction of the probable situation by a novelist. Thus while the human narrative in Bhattacharya and Sahgal generally leads the reader imperceptibly to a particular ideological conviction, in the fictional universe of Malgonkar, one has the impression, at times, of being led by the nose.

Bhattacharya, Sahgal, and even Malgonkar in patches, weave their narratives so deftly that the human and the political appear but parts of one artistic patina. One significant component of this interlocking is the psychological motivation given to the characters in their political causes. The black-marketeer in Samarendra in *Hungers* is presented as an unfortunate growth of the poor adolescent in him (216). Seth Shamsunder in *Gold* has the same bare and austere background to egg him on in his political ambitions. The rebel in Kalo was born when the proud father in him had to sell, because of rapacious exploitation, the medal his daughter had won (*Tiger*, 168). Behind the reformist in Biten, fighting against the hegemony of the upper classes, is a repentant brother who failed to save his sister from putrid orthodoxy and senseless ethnocentricism in caste-stratification (*Tiger*, 169). In *Ladakh*, the ideological is reached in a most artistic manner through the particular. The realization of the inadequacy of an exclusive, self-abnegating creed in personal life — as Satyajit awakes to the traces of passion in him — precedes the inadequacy of such exclusivism in the domains of economy and politics. Likewise, it is the woman in Sumita who wakes up before the theoretician in her succumbs. In Bhaskar, too, it is a personal discontentment with the high-paced technology-propped life which pushes him to Satyajitism, ideologically.

Sahgal also makes the political self of her characters but an extension of their individual beings. In *Happy*, Nootan's public posture is but a means to seek the fulfilment of his inner craving for fame (85). Sir Harilal Mathur's anglomania is a public manifestation of his gratitude to the English who had released him from a compulsive inferiority complex (*Happy*, 155). Kunti Behn's professed Gandhism is a sublimation of her repressed desires (*Happy*, 60). Kalyan's penchant for quick results as a minister is related, along with his manifest contempt for Gandhism, to his early orphaned life (*Morning* 77). Vishal's political constructivism is built on a broken marriage (*Storm*, 29). Gyan Singh's populist rhetoric is to be seen in the context of his turbulent childhood (*Storm*, 120). So is Harpal's humanitarianism to be appreciated against the background of a guilt-complex (*Storm*, 48). Sumer Singh, in *Shadow*, is smarting under a desperate need to prove himself. That makes him 'hell-bent' in whatever he does, whether in politics or in bed. In *Rich,* Nishi's support for the Emergency-regime is but a ploy to buy peace for her father incarcerated under Emergency provisions.

In Malgonkar's novels also we discern an attempt to make political platitudes spring from personal predicaments. Winton's desperate urge to succeed, itself the result of the unmitigated failure of his life in England, conditions his public responses as the tea-estate manager *vis-à-vis* the workers (*Combat*, 122) and their leader Jugal. Jugal, too, as a trade union leader and then as a minister, settles personal scores with Winton. In *Ganges*, the fiery terrorism of Debi and Shafi and the philosophic Gandhism of Gian are presented as the outgrowth of their personal circumstances. Kanakchand's popular movement against the royal order in the princely state of Begwad is presented in *Princes* as but a devious means to avenge his humiliation, suffered years ago. Likewise, the political postures flaunted by 'chocolate-cream soldiers' in the fictional universe of Malgonkar such as K.K. (*Drum*, 67-68), Shantilal (*Drum*, 200) and Behl (*Bandicoot*, 18) are but ploys to curry favour with the authorities and fulfil their personal ambition of career-advancement. That makes them go, as Kiran puts it, 'pinch-hitting' (*Drum*, 92) for their political bosses.[41]

In the novels of Bhattacharya, Malgonkar and Sahgal, not merely does the personal prompt the political, the latter too affects the former. Ideological commitments or political convictions, far from remaining merely external postures, enter the life-blood of the protagonists and condition their very being. Satyajit's adherence to one version of Gandhism is reflected within his family too. Sumita, his daughter and alter ego, toes the line of his ideology in her life. It is the ideological confrontation between Bhaskar and Satyajit which shapes their personal relationship with each other. Countering "Satyajitism, working at several levels" (128) becomes crucial for Bhaskar. In Kiran Garud, in *Drum*, one comes across the Regimental code circumscribing his personal relationships. Kiran dishes out predictable responses like a robot programmed with the Malgonkar code. He behaves in the same deadpan manner, whether he is dealing with Bina, the girl he says he loves, Mr. Sonal, her father or Ropey Booker, his former officer and present friend. To all, he dished out general axioms encompassing the code. *Princes*, however, exemplifies an artistic synthesis of the personal and the political. It is the political threat faced by Begawad which prompts Abhay to shed his alienation from his father's world and side with him. Thenceforth the personal and the political merge and become one for Abhay.[42]

Another significant aspect of the coalescing of the personal and the political is the presentation of characters who are aware of the duality inherent in their existence in the two realms. Public-men are viewed not merely as public-men but also as individuals. This double role-playing may pose problems of adjustment but issuing forth from a single consciousness, it makes the psychological and the political converge. There is also to be discerned in some characters a full blossoming of this creative strategy for ideological purposes, when the twin roles are lived simultaneously in a spirit of harmony, not in an either-this-or-that mood. We have already seen how because of this reason the Gandhian insistence on '*brahmacharya*' for men in public life had been rejected.[43]

It is the dual awareness of being both Jayadev's wife and the young mistress of the Big House which makes Mohini share her food with the cartman during her first journey to her husband's place (*Music*, 78). Jayadev (*Music*, 179), Kalo (*Tiger*, 114), Devi (*Situation* 21) and Abhay's father (*Princes*, 180) too reveal similar awareness of dual existence which entitles them to privileges but also delimits their freedom as individuals. Even a thoroughly personal event such as a marriage ceases to be exclusively personal for such a being (*Princes*, 175). Meera's grandmother knows that when her husband sings in the streets, he is the minstrel and "belongs to the people. When he is under this roof, he is ours" (*Gold*, 58). The duality of awareness does not militate against the integrity of the character.

But sometimes the individuals wilt under the burden of playing the double role simultaneously. In *Tiger*, Kalo's public role as a priest makes greater and greater inroads into his personal self as the mask eats into his spirit (126). His daughter, Chandralekha's role as Mother of the Sevenfold Bliss, does not even sanction sympathy for the diseased and the afflicted who flock to seek her blessings (220). Never, of course, can she express any passion for Biten, the man she loves. Like Meera, who finally has to throw away the *taveej* and with it her role as the means of Sonamitti's transmutation in *Gold*, Chandralekha has to kill the Mother in her to let the women in her live (*Tiger*, 225).

However, the reconciliation of such 'role-conflict' is not drastic. Jayadev's mother who had obdurately been living principally as the mistress of the Big House rather than as a mother, throws off decorum to the winds as she runs to her son when he is bitten by a snake (119). Jayadev's insistence on being a social reformer alone and not a husband to his newly-wed wife, Mohini, would perhaps give way to a mature understanding *a la* Satyajit in *Ladakh* when Jayadev is "closer to life, more attuned to reality" (*Music*, 124). Devi and Rishad do get beyond the stage where they hated "this side of...life to be cluttered with other" (*Situation*, 60). They rise to an awareness of the complementary nature of these two selves which is exemplified best by Shivraj. Shivraj was "unique" as a leader. His individuality added to rather than hampered his public life. Despite being a political himself, Shivraj aroused in his countrymen, "so very unpolitical [a] bond of trust" (61). Michael rightly realizes that the public personality of Shivraj, "swaying the crowd" on the platform and his individual personality, "the light he had left among his friends" (161), cannot be separated. Indeed, one completes the other. Shivraj lived as an individual and as a public man in a manner wherein "public and private issues met and became one" (161). This is how political ideology and human psychology are integrated into the vision of imagination.

Bhattacharya, Malgonkar and Sahgal highlight the umbilical link between the political and the personal in another way, too. In their novels, the political and the personal are brought together by the device of juxtaposition. During Harpal's public meeting at Pinjore in *Storm*, the "slack indifference," "the paralysis" in the air, remind Vishal "incongruously [?] of the long brooding silences during his marriage, the hours when he had felt trapped in hopelessness" (41). The situation at Saroj's place with children paying scant attention to their mother reminds Vishal of "the situation the Centre faced…its appeal falling on deaf ears" (50). The fascination for gadgetry in Brij, Simrit's young son, gets connected in Raj's mind with Sumer Singh's desire to sever all links with the past (*Shadow*, 129). Earlier, the question "How had such a future arisen from such a past?" (125) had engaged the attention of both Raj in relation to Brij, Simrit's son, and Sardar Sahib in relation to Sumer and other unscrupulous politicians. The heartless terms of the consent her husband made Simrit sign had precipitated in her the realization how her husband and Sumer were alike : "There is no human difference between them" (222). Simrit's distaste for what her husband stands for is magnified to include whatever is distasteful about the age in general (34-35). Even for an outsider like Raj, the consent terms "were a sort of Hiroshima" (138). Ram Krishan "thought of his country beginning to look distorted like this room" (176). The "battle in the Exchange between bulls and bears" in the consciousness of Samarendra is linked with the Second World War (*Hungers*, 29). Sumita is found inattentive like "an Hon'ble member of the House" (*Lakadh*, 239). For Winton in *Combat*, Jugal Kishor is his "private Hitler" (*Combat*, 107). Basu in *Ganges* juxtaposes his acid-burnt wife and the riot-afflicted country to highlight the causal link between the personal and the public. "That is what has happened to the face of India — the mutilation of a race conflict" (289). Obviously, the novelists are using here political images like archetypal images, making the political and the personal coalesce imperceptibly.

Far from running parallel, the political and the human narratives converge on some basic issues of equally vital concern in the two realms. And these basic issues are the real and universally human issues. These are survival, security, freedom, the choice of values, etc. As the speech by Nehru at Gorakhpur explains (*Hungers*, 42), it is the fundamental urge for food and security which makes the hunger-marchers and the political agitationists make common cause with each other.[44] The Big House at Behula in *Music* becomes a picture of India in microcosm. On the one hand are the individuals — Mohini, her father, her grandmother, Jayadev and his mother — faced with a choice between old and new values. On the other is the country herself, "not yet truly free" (181) and "like a prisoner held too long in a dark cell" (181) faced with such a choice. In *Ladakh,* the forging of an amalgam of Satyajitism and Bhaskarism is as urgent for the nation as it is for Jhanak and Sumita, Suruchi and Roopa, Bhaskar and Satyajit.

Morning not only presents freedom on the political plane but also extends it into the subterranean springs of human action. It is of as much importance to politicians — Kailas, Kalyan, Hari Mohan, Prakash, Shukla, the President — as it is to the individual human beings like Nita, Rakesh, Mira, Uma, Leela, Celia and Barbara. *Storm* depicts violence making inroads not merely into the body politic but also into the personal lives of the people. Inder, with his "ancient tribal, male roots" (102), feeling 'squeamish' about the expression and comprehension of human emotions, is made the prototype of the rabble-rousing, demagogue, Gyan Singh, on the personal level. Vishal, the central observer of the scene of political violence and the individual observer of violence in human relationship, sympathizes with the victims of both, equating explicitly Harpal Singh, the Haryana CM with Saroj — both victims of violence in the public and the personal realms respectively (222). In *Shadow*, too, the explicit linking of Sumer Singh, with his penchant for quick progress, and Som, with his fascination for gadgetry, comes long after the two have been linked through implied situations and undertones. Like the world of Sumer, engrafted with "other people's solutions" (155), the world of Som and Vetter revalues round an alien axis. Both Sumer and Som, in the political and the personal realms respectively, stand for "a clean up, a break away" (192) with "the whole Indian post" (129). The lament about the conspicuous absence of the breed of "India lovers" (20) can apply, with equal validity, to the representatives of the two domains. *Rich* again highlights the same issues — unscrupulous greed, rampant corruption and heartless misuse of authority — which are afflicting the nation, as well as the individual people like Sonali, Rose and others. *Ganges* begins with the unearthing of the idol of Shiva from the Piploda land and the conversion of Gian's grandfather from a worshipper of Vishnu (the god of protection) to that of Shiva (the god of destruction). It ends with *tandav nritya* of Shiva, literally and logically. *Ganges* encompasses a whole epical theme, both personal and political, which is a sweeping wave of destruction and disintegration.

The personal and the political are so intertwined that they suggest the same solution to the afflictions. *Hungers* presents freedom as one common solution to the personal and the economic-political problems.[45] Even for self-fulfilment as an individual, a self-dependent polity is presented as a prerequisite.[46] In a similar vein in *Music,* a 'conscious amalgam' of the old and the new, the traditional and the modern, is offered as a panacea for the conflicts, whether at the personal or the political levels. Vishal in *Storm* crusades for the inculcation of the same values — persuasion, understanding and compassion — whether he is with Gyan and Harpal, the Chief Ministers of Punjab and Haryana respectively, or with Saroj, a 'wronged' wife. Vishal's advice to Saroj and Harpal to be frank and bold is reminiscent of his nostalgic craving for "the open politics" of the good old days (245). Raj in *Shadow* thinks that the individual has to come out in the open and assert himself thereby seeking to influence the personal and the political forces.

Situation interlocks the personal and the political selves of its major characters in a very artistic way.[47] Devi finds her public self impinging on her private aspirations. Her son Rishad finds his parasitic personal existence meaningless. However, both are depicted as growing from a "clandestine" life, private and public respectively, to a stage of anagnorisis where the duality is harmonized. It is through his personal relationship with Suvarnpriya Jaipal that Rishad achieves political maturity. And it is Devi's personal commitment to her brother, the deceased PM, Shivraj, that decides for her the political course she is to take. Joining forces with Usman, who is leading a mass-movement for the restoration of the values Shivraj cherished, Devi finds she is coming home. The personal tragedy of the gang-raped Madhu is symbolic of the plight of the nation where the individual is deemed to be 'only an instrument of the process' (125). Usman realizes that such private disasters can be checked only through political means, by arousing the youth to a feeling of individual responsibility.

One most creative contribution of these novelists is their integration of the personal, the political and the religious into the psychological reality of man's mind and its ways of working. They find in the response mechanism of popular Hinduism the root cause of most forms of exploitation at the personal and the political level.[48] The evil nexus between 'the cultural elite' and 'the governing elite' is revealed through Seth Sham Sunder, in *Gold*, who spreads the legend of Atmaram to help his commercial and political designs. Sir Abalabandhu's paper in the same vein spreads the legend of the mother of Seven-fold Bliss for much the same ends in *Tiger*. *Princes* presents the people of princely states as superstitious, ritual-ridden and servile even though their political outlook is not presented there as the inevitable outcome of their religious beliefs. Malgonkar's *Ganges* presents Gian having the realization — as he shed his 'sacred thread' with a heavy heart — "You could not have both orthodoxy and freedom" (73). What is termed Aji's 'equanimity' in the face for gross injustice and exploitation[49] is really passivity and servility to circumstances, which she shares with the INA Brigadier Debi meets in the Andamans. It is this which makes them see "an *avatar* of Vishnu" in Hitler to deliver them from misery (147). *Storm* reveals how smug, acquiescent, inactive and fatalistic, the Indians are and how they accept blindly whatever is meted out to them be that the insensitivity of a spouse or the unscrupulousness of a Chief Minister. Usman in *Situation* realizes how violence on the national scene and in the personal lives of people is born of their stagnant faith in the *avatars*. They see a god in "the man in the loin-cloth" (*Rich*, 157) and "the young idol on his white horse…on a river bank in Lahore" (*Rich*, 157). It is the same defying instinct which makes them term the PM a "many-armed goddess" (*Rich*, 155). Hinduism, with its glorification of mystification, and mystification of evil (*Rich*, 136), its conversion of the real into a tiny dot in a continuum, frustrates an individual's attempts to find out if he has got his deserts right here and now. Hinduism, thus interpreted, brings together the personal and the political in *Rich* like nothing else does.

It can safely be averred on the basis of the foregoing study that Indian English fiction represented at its best by novelists like Bhattacharya, Malgonkar and Sahgal, with stray aberrations here and there, has succeeded in rendering artistically a consciousness of politics and political actions. Works like *Ladakh*, *Princes*, *Ganges*, *Storm* and *Shadow* accomplish the grounding of action and character so firmly on politics that they "come alive only through politics."[50] Taken together, Indian English fiction in general presents a fairly representative as well as authentic example of the transmutation of the political consciousness into art through the medium of the imagination which integrates individual as well as social psychology and reflects its working in both personal and public action.

REFERENCES

1. Albert Salomon, "Sociology and the Literary Artist," *Spiritual Problems in Contemporary Literature,* ed. Stanley Romaine Hopper (New York : Doubleday, 1952), 24.
2. Cf. "[It is] the intensity of the artistic process, the pressure...under which the fusion takes place, that counts." T.S. Eliot, "Tradition and the Individual Talent" in *English Critical Texts,* eds. D.J. Enright and Ernst De Chickera (Delhi : OUP, 1962), 298.
3. Quoted in Irving Howe, *Politics and the Novel* (New York : Horizon Press, 1957), vii.
4. "How is the novelist to reconcile these two claims, how keep the delicate balance between the demands of life and art. This is his central problem as a craftsman." David Cecil, "The Forms of English Fiction," *The Fine Art of Reading* (New York : The Bobbs-Merril Co., 1957), 128.

5. "What he [the novelist] has good reason to fear is not the ethical values themselves but the wrong modes of their projection." Bhattacharya, "Literature and Social Reality," *Perspectives on Bhabani Bhattacharya,* ed. Ramesh K. Srivastava (Ghaziabad : Vimal Prakashan, 1982), 4.
6. This cohabitation of 'normative objectivity' and 'subjective creativity' in the novel impressed M.K. Naik, who considers the novel to be one of Bhattacharya's "better efforts." See his *A History of Indian English Literature* (New Delhi : Sahitya Akademi, 1982), 216.
7. Bhattacharya in an interview with Ramesh Srivastava, *Perspectives on Bhabani Bhattacharya,* 220. In another interview included in *Contemporary Novelists in the English Language* (New York : St. Martin's Press, 1972), Bhattacharya explains that the famine in Bengal caused "emotional stirrings" which were "a sheer compulsion to creativity." The result was *So Many Hungers*! (71).
8. She has a weakness for English pictures (30). Moreover, she "had compromised with modernity and her struggle to uphold the orthodox way was without passion." But Mohini's mother-in-law was "stern, adamant like iron"; she had "nothing in her nature that would allow change" (130).
9. Heeralal's hair (38) and the right hand of Jayadev's mother (85) have been dedicated to propitiate gods. A widow in Calcutta had dedicated her evening meals (85).
10. K.R. Srinivasa Iyengar, *Indian Writing in English* (Bombay : Asia Publishing House, 1973), 418.
11. Harish Raizada believes that all of Bhattacharya's novels convey their message in such an allegorical mode. See his "Fiction as Allegory : Novels of Bhabani Bhattacharya," *Perspectives on Bhabani Bhattacharya,* 83-100. Narsingh Srivastava finds in *Gold* a rich profusion of symbolic and allegoric meaning. See his article "Symbol and Allegory in *A Goddess Named Gold,"* in *Perspectives on Bhabani Bhattacharya,* 149-65. For praise along similar lines, see H.M. Williams, *Indo-Anglian Literature 1800-1970 : A Survey* (Bombay : Orient Longmans, 1976), 92 and K.R. Chandrashekharan, *Bhabani Bhattacharya* (New Delhi : Arnold-Heinemann, 1974), 86-87.
12. For a detailed presentation, see Chapter 3, "Chronicing the Political Web," 53-62.
13. For an unfolding of Winton's character, lacking in the values the Malgonkar code comprises, see Chapter VI, "The Way Out of the Labyrinth," 176-84.
14. He drew her close to him and brushed her hair back with his hand and her face rose up to him like a lifting flower.

    "Please don't cry," he said.

"Darling, why did we have to meet, ever? Why did I have to fall in love with you...why, why did you have to be what you are?"

She pushed him away from her and turned her face. Then, still keeping her face away from him, she said :

"I want to go home, please."

"Yes of course," Kiran said (192).

15. For details, see Chapter 5, "The Ossifying of the Gandhian Panacea," 138-39.
16. See Chapter 5, "The Ossifying of the Gandhian Panacea," 133-35.
17. See for details Chapter 5, "The Ossifying of the Gandhian Panacea," 117-18.
18. Vide Jasbir Jain, "The Human Dimensions of Statis and Growth," *Perspectives on Bhabani Bahttacharya,* 52-54.
19. For what these two 'isms' stand for and how they are presented as 'complementary' to each other, see Chapter 5, "The Ossifying of the Gandhian Panacea," 111-13.
20. Quoted in an interview with Bhattacharya, *Perspectives on Bhabani Bhattacharya, op. cit.*, 226.
21. "Bhabani Bhattacharya : The Writer Who Rides a Tiger," *Perspectives on Indian Fiction in English,* ed. M.K. Naik (New Delhi : Abhinav Publications, 1985), 125.
22. "Literature and Social Reality," *Perspectives on Bhabani Bahttacharya, op. cit.,* 5.
23. "Bhattacharya at Work : An Interview," *ibid.,* 225.
24. *Ibid.*
25. An interview in *Mahfil,* 5, Nos. 1 and 2 (1968-69), 45.
26. Cf. "The ending of "*Combat of Shadows* has the perfect symmetry of a Greek nemesis...." G.S. Amur, *Manohar Malgonkar* (New Delhi : Arnold-Heinemann, 1973), 75.
27. For details, see Chapter 5, "The Ossifying of the Gandhian Panacea," 131-32.
28. For details of the only dimension the character of Lala Vishnu Saran Dev has, see Chapter 5, "The Ossifying of the Gandhian Panacea," 138. For Kiran, see above, 199.
29. Rishad is shown developing from an idealist anarchist who believed that "revolution was made by circumstances, not men" (58) to the Gandhian humanist who knows that "revolution begins with oneself, is not a lesson given to others" (146). See below, 218-19.
30. See for details Chapter 4, "The Contours of a Crippling Creed," 98-101 and Chapter 6, "The Way Out of the Labyrinth," 171-72.
31. See Chapter 5, "The Ossifying of the Gandhian Panacea," 118-20.
32. See above, 191.

33. See her collection of interviews and speeches, *Voice for Freedom* (Delhi : Hind Pocket Books, 1977), 14.
34. Quoted by R.P. Chadda in "A Rich Tribute," *The Sunday Tribune,* January 4, 1987.
35. See above, 193.
36. See Chapter 5, "The Ossifying of the Gandhian Panacea," 113-15.
37. For a detailed presentation of Winton's character and the manner wherein he 'deserves' such an ending, see Chapter 6, "The Way Out of the Labyrinth," 176-83.
38. See Chapter 5, "The Ossifying of the Gandhian Panacea,"128-35.
39. For the credible manner wherein such a 'volte-face' is managed by the novelist, see Chapter 5, "The Ossifying of the Gandhian Panacea," 130-35.
40. See above, 199-201.
41. For a detailed presentation of the manner wherein the political is made the consequence of the personal in all these characters, see Chapter 5, "The Ossifying of the Gandhian Panacea," 117-22.
42. G.S. Amur presents the view most clearly—in graphic form. See his *Manohar Malgonkar, op. cit.*, 81.
43. See Chapter 6, "The Way Out of the Labyrinth," 157-60.
44. Cf. "The two stories of the time — The hungers and the Quit India Movement — were intrinsically one." Bhattacharya, in an interview with Ramesh Srivastava, *Perspectives on Bhabani Bhattacharya*, 229.
45. See Chapter 5, "The Ossifying of the Gandhian Panacea," 113-14.
46. Vide Dorothy Blair Shimer, *Bhabani Bhattacharya* (Boston: Twayne Publishers, 1975), 29.
47. For a detailed treatment of this aspect in the novels of Nayantara Sahgal, see M.K. Bhatnagar, "The Individual as Politician — One Facet of Nayantara Sahgal as a Political Novelist," *MDU Research Journal*, 1 (April 1986), 98-104.
48. See Chapter 4, "The Contours of a Crippling Creed," 82-85, *et passim.*
49. She is dispossessed of her land, her grandson is murdered and the assassin allowed to go scot-free.
50. Walter Allen, *The English Novel* (London : Penguin, 1971), 205.

❑❑❑

8

Conclusion

THE FOREGOING examen of the rendering of political consciousness in Indian English fiction shows how politics has been a favourite theme with the novelists. We have also seen why it has been like that. Looking round, going deep into the self and the tradition and catering to a heterogeneous audience, the Indian English novelist invoked the shared national experience and thus succeeded in attracting a pan-India readership, cutting across linguistic, geographic and communal barriers. The crystallization of this conscientious, imaginative and active concern with politics in a purposive and pointed direction coincided with the impetus given to the national movement for freedom by leaders like Bal Gangadhar Tilak, Mahatma Gandhi and the militant nationalists. This preoccupation with the condition of man, here in this world, in relation to his immediate environment and its institutional infrastructure heralded an epoch-making change. For the first time in recent Indian history, it focused on man, both as an individual and as a social being. This is vitally reflected in the novels taken up for study here.

The novels under close study are essentially and characteristically different from the novels of the earlier age. The novels of the late nineteenth and early twentieth century had presented but a partial account of the human situation. They lacked interest "in the events of ordinary life as lived by man on this earth."[1] Man was not viewed as essentially a social entity in these novels, which were in tone and treatment, generally romantic. Bankim Chandra Chatterjee (*Rajmohun's Wife*, 1864) and Romesh Chunder Dutt (*The Slave Girl of Agra*, 1909) represent this tendency of domesticizing the picture or throwing a veil of romance over it so as to distance it from wider relevance.[2]

The nineteenth century Renaissance influenced the novelists to make them "descend to the humble walks of life, to sympathize with a common citizen or even a common peasant,"[3] as one early Indian English novelist himself put it. It was the nascent consciousness of national identity which accounted for the sea-change the novels underwent in the 1930s.[4]

The 1930s, aptly termed 'the Gandhian Age' in Indian history,[5] marked an important change in national life. Gandhi himself was responsible for this, for it was he who more than anyone else "tied together the personal and the national, the ethical and the political, the emotional and the spiritual."[6] This enabled the individual "to connect his personal anxieties with national hope."[7] This bringing down of the frame of reference from a romantic utopia or a mythical heaven to this world of fret and fury influenced the writers to look for real India not in holy Varanasi but in the inconspicuous Indian villages, faced with issues of more immediate concern. Consequently, the artists delved deep into the political problems of man and literature was "identified with and [deemed] essential to the nation."[8]

We have already seen how this concern with political questions became a dominant emotion in the novels of Bhattacharya, Malgonkar and Sahgal. They render political consciousness not as passive reflectors. Their novels are imbued to the core with an awareness of the political happenings and the manner wherein these circumscribe the potential of the individual for self-fulfilment. They also probe deeper and come out with a diagnosis of the afflictions of the body politic as well as with a suggestive prescription to cure these distortions. The diagnosis delineated in their novels is precisely the same — fake religiosity rendering the individual vulnerable to exploitation by making a virtue of passivity. As regards the remedy, Bhattacharya, Malgonkar and Sahgal are one in their advocacy of a dynamic and more forthright faith. They accord due recognition to Gandhism as one significant endeavour to put the stagnant

Hinduism on a new and proper keel, even though they would like to interpret the Gandhian ideology, too, anew, keeping in mind the extended modern context. While Bhattacharya and Sahgal espouse democratic and egalitarian values, in Malgonkar we have traditional, conservative values of yore presented as desirable, being the values of a permanent nature, like discipline, courage and the dignity of human responsibility.

Irving Howe has defined the political novel as one in which "political ideas play a dominant role or in which the political milieu is the dominant setting."[9] By this definition, the novels discussed here in the preceding chapters can also be taken as political novels, for political consciousness is not there in the background, to be deduced painstakingly by a discerning critic, it has become the basic constituent of the novels. What is of much more importance is that the human and the ideological are woven criss-cross into a single patina. In this respect, too, the novels of Bhattacharya, Malgonkar and Sahgal blaze a new trail.

Ideology or political concerns are not easy to coalesce with immediate human experience. We have seen that a large number of novels, right from the advent of Indian English fiction, have set their narratives in an explicitly delineated political milieu, some to give their tales a local habitation and name, others perhaps for more compelling reasons. But the search for the emergence of a genuine political novel seemed doomed to failure for the attempts by different hands failed again and again. Excessive romanticization and sentimentality marred the narrative in novels like *Kandan the Patriot, Inquilab*, *Sunlight on a Broken Column* and *The Death of a Hero*. The total lack of perspective in the maze of accruing details proved to be the undoing of novels like *Some Inner Fury*, *The Sword and the Sickle* and *Inquilab*. Politics remained just one strand in the complicated pattern in *Zohra*, *Waiting for the Mahatma* and *Some Inner Fury*. There was another category of novels which discarded depth in favour of the width of coverage. Examples would be *Conflict* and *Train to Pakistan*. Even overdoing the political bit to the detriment of the human leaves the reader dissatisfied as is proved by a novel like *Dusk before Dawn*.

The novels of a number of writers in the modern, post-Independence context, most notably those of Bhattacharya, Malgonkar and Sahgal obviously mark an advance upon the work of their predecessors as far as the artistic rendering of political consciousness is concerned. Bhattacharya and Sahgal generally do not allow their personal predilections to intrude upon the scene. The political and the ideological in them spring from the human. The artists, role in the spinning of their yarns is reminiscent of the Keatsian concept of negative capability or rather of T.S. Eliot's concept of impersonality. So fairly do they allow combatant values to interact and speak for themselves. The more frequent strategy in Malgonkar is that of presenting a more simplified picture with the central controlling voice guiding the responses of the readers at almost every social and political juncture.

In their best novels, Indian English novelists make the ideological coalesce perfectly with the individual. This they accomplish in a number of ways. They observe the politicians and ideologues not merely in the glare of their public lives but also in the soft shades of their existence as individuals. These dual planes on which such characters function do not remain islands unto themselves. Rather the two meet and we see not merely the individual aspirations seeking fulfilment through political means but also political ideals casting their shadows into the personal lives of public men. In the inextricable manner wherein the personal and the political are entwined, quite often political remedies get suggested for personal predicaments. In a similar vein, experience in the personal realm of an individual is shown to contribute to the precipitation of political commitments. The stylistic juxtaposition of the personal with the political is thus a subtle way to highlight the political as but an extension of the personal.

Perhaps the most significant contribution of these novelists — both as discerning observers of the political scene and as political novelists — is that they relate exploitation in both the personal and the political realms to the lackadaisical interpretation of Hinduism by which people live. Not merely is the diagnosis for personal and political discomfiture the same, the remedy for that also is the same. An action-based, this-worldly orientation, the novelists believe, would go a long way to establishing interpersonal and political affairs on a basis of equality and dignity. Political consciousness, thus, in a large chunk of post-Independence Indian English fiction, especially in the novels of Bhabani Bhattacharya, Manohar Malgonkar and Nayantara Sahgal, far from being mere window-dressing, becomes an index of the litterateurs' concern with the questions of utmost significance for man in the present-day Indian context. Without overburdening the novels or distracting the readers, political consciousness in their novels is rendered artistically as an essential part of the total awareness and ambition of man as a rational, imaginative and social being, thinking, feeling, living and creating as part of an organized political structure.

REFERENCES

1. Dorothy M. Spencer, *Indian Fiction in English : An Annotated Bibliography* (Philadelphia : Univ. of Pennsylvania Press, 1960), 9.
2. Vide T.W. Clark, ed., *The Novel in India : Its Birth and Development* (London : George Allen & Unwin Ltd., 1970), 62-64.
3. Romesh Chunder Dutt, quoted by Krishna Kripalani in "Modern Literature," *A Cultural History of India*, ed. A.L. Basham (Oxford : Clarendon Press, 1975), 415.
4. Mulk Raj Anand, "Cultural Self-Comprehension of Nations," an 'Afterword' to G.P. Sarma's *Nationalism in Indo-Anglian Fiction* (Delhi : Sterling Publishers Pvt. Ltd., 1978), 415.
5. K.R. Srinivasa Iyengar, *Indian Writing in English* (New York : Asia Publishing House, 1962), 248.
6. Francis G. Hutchins, *India's Revolution* (Cambridge, Massachusetts : Harvard Univ. Press, 1973), 113.
7. *Ibid.*
8. M.E. Derret, *The Modern Indian Novel in English — A Comparative Approach* (Brussels : Editions de L' Institute de Sociologie, Universite Libre de Bruxelles, 1966), 22.
9. *Politics and the Novel* (New York : Horizon Press, 1957), 17.

❑❑❑

A Selected Bibliography

I. GENERAL LITERARY CRITICISM INCLUDING BOOKS ON INDO-ANGLIAN FICTION

Achebe, Chinua. "The Novelist as Teacher," *New Statesman*, January 29, 1965.

Alvarez, A. *Hungarian Short Stories*. London : Oxford Univ. Publication, 1967.

Anand, Mulk Raj. "Pigeon-Indian : Some Notes on Indian English Writing," *Studies in Australian and Indian Literature*, eds. C.D. Narsimhaiah and S. Nagarajan. New Delhi : I.C.C.R., 1972.

Asnani, Shyam. *Critical Response to Indian English Fiction*. Delhi : Mittal Publications, 1985.

Badal, R.K. *Indo-Anglian Literature*. Bareilly : Prakash Book Depot, 1975.

Bakhtiyar Iqbal, ed. *The Novel in Modern India*. Bombay : The P.E.N. All India Centre, 1964.

Bald, Suresht Renjen. *Novelists and Political Consciousness : Literary Expressions of Indian Nationalism 1919-1947*. Delhi : Chanakya Publications, 1982.

——. "Politics of the Revolutionary Elite : A Study of Mulk Raj Anand's Novels," *Modern Asian Studies*, 8, No. 4 (1974).

Barbash, Yuri. *Aesthetics and Politics*. Moscow : Progress Publishers, 1977.

Basu, Amalendu. "Bengali Writing in English in the Nineteenth Century," *Bulletin of the Department of English of the Calcutta University,* N.S., 3, No. 2 (1967-68).

Blake, Nelson Manfred. *Novelist's America : Fiction as History*. New York : Syracuse University Press, 1969.

Cecil, David. *The Fine Art of Reading*. New York : The Bobbs-Merril Co., 1957.

Clark, T.W. *The Novel in India — Its Birth and Development*. London : George Allen and Unwin Ltd., 1970.

Coppola, Carlo. "Politics and the Novel in India — A Perspective," *Politics and the Novel in India*, ed. Yogendra K. Malik. New Delhi : Orient Longman, 1975.

Dhawan, R.K., ed. *Explorations in Modern Indo-English Fiction*. New Delhi : Bahri Publications Pvt. Ltd., 1982.

Derret, M.E. *The Modern Indian Novel in English — A Comparative Approach*. Brussels : Editions de L'Institut de Sociologie, Universite Libre de Bruxelles, 1966.

Enright, D.J. and Ernst De Chickera, eds. *English Critical Texts*. Delhi : O.U.P., 1962.

Fleishman, Avron. *The English Historical Novel*. London : The John Hopkins Press, 1971.

Gupta, Rameshwar, ed. *The Banasthali Patrika* (*Special Mahatma Gandhi Number*). Banasthali Vidyapith, 1969.

Hollander, Paul. "Models of Behaviour in Stalinist Literature : A Case Study of Totalitarian Values and Controls," *American Sociological Review*, 31 (1966).

Howe, Irving. *Politics and the Novel*. New York : Horizon Press, 1957.

Iyengar, K.R. Srinivasa. *Indian Writing in English*. Bombay : Asia Publishing House, 1973.

Jain, Jasbir. "The Changing Image of Gandhi in Indo-Anglian Fiction," *Indian Literature*, 22 (July-August 1979), 182-90.

Jha, Rama. *Gandhian Thought and Indo-Anglian Novelists*. Delhi : Chanakya Publications, 1983.

Jotwani, Motilal, ed. *Contemporary Indian Literature and Society*. New Delhi : Heritage Publishers, 1979.

Leavis, F.R. *Lectures in America*. New York : Doubleday, 1969.

Lenin, V.I. *Collected Works*. Moscow : Progress Publishers, 1967.

Ludington, Townsend. "The Idea of the Political Novel," *The American Political Novel — Critical Essays*, ed. Harish Trivedi. New Delhi : Allied Publishers Pvt. Ltd., 1984.

Machwe, Prabhakar. *Modernity and Contemporary Indian Literature*. New Delhi : Chetna Publications, 1978.

Malik, Yogendra K., ed. *Politics and the Novel in India*. New Delhi : Orient Longman, 1975.

Mehta, P.P. *Indo-Anglian Fiction — An Assessment*. Bareilly : Prakash Book Depot, 1969.

Melwani, Murli Das. *Themes in Indo-Anglian Literature*. Bareilly : Prakash Book Depot, 1976.

Mukherjee, Meenakshi. "Awareness of Audience in Indo-Anglian Fiction." *Quest*, 52 (Winter 1967).

——. "Beyond the Village," *Critical Essays on Indian Writing in English*, eds. M.K. Naik, S.K. Desai and G.S. Amur. Dharwar : Karnataka University Press, 1968.

——. *The Twice-Born Fiction*. New Delhi : Arnold-Heinemann, 1971.

Nahal, Chaman. "Telling of Time Past," *The Hindustan Times Weekly,* March 15, 1981.

Naik, M.K., S.K. Desai and G.S. Amur, ed. *Critical Essays on Indian Writers in English*. Dharwar : Karnataka Univ. Press, 1968.

——. *A History of Indian English Literature*. New Delhi : Sahitya Akademi, 1982.

——. *Mulk Raj Anand*. New Delhi : Arnold-Heinemann, 1973.

——. ed. *Perspectives on Indian Fiction in English*. New Delhi : Abhinav Publications, 1985.

——. "The Political Novel in Indian Writing in English," *Politics and the Novel in India,* ed. Yogendra K Malik. New Delhi : Orient Longman, 1975.

——. *Raja Rao*. New York : Twayne, 1972.

——. *The Writer's Gandhi*. Patiala : Punjabi University, 1967.

Narsimhaiah, C.D., ed. *Fiction and the Reading Public in India*. Mysore : University of Mysore, 1977.

Narsimhan, Raji. *Sensibility Under Stress : Aspects of Indo-English Fiction*. New Delhi : Ashajanak Prakashan, 1976.

Nayak, H.M., ed. *Gandhiji in Indian Literature : Proceedings of a National Seminar on Gandhiji in Indian Literature*. Mysore : Institute of Kannada Studies, University of Mysore, 1971.

Nicholson, Kai. *A Representation of Social Problems in the Indo-Anglian and the Anglo-Indian Novel*. Bombay : Jaico, 1972.

Parmeshwaran, Uma. *A Study of Representative Indo-English Novelists*. New Delhi : Vikas Publishing House, 1975.

Rockwell, Joan. *Fact in Fiction : The Use of Literature in the Systematic Study of Society*. London : Routledge & Kegan Paul, 1974.

Salomon, Albert. "Sociology and the Literary Artists," *Spiritual Problems in Contemporary Literature*, ed. Stanley Romaine Hopper. New York : Doubleday, 1952.

Sarma, G.P. *Nationalism in Indo-Anglian Fiction*. New Delhi : Sterling Publishers Pvt. Ltd., 1978.

Sartre, Jean Paul. *What is Literature*? New York : Washington Square Press, 1966.

Shamota, N. *On Artistic Freedom*. Moscow : Progress Publishers, 1966.

Sharma, K.K., ed. *Indo-English Literature : A Collection of Critical Essays*. Ghaziabad : Vimal Prakashan, 1977.

Sharma, Sudarshan. *The Influence of Gandhian Ideology on Indo-English Fiction*. New Delhi : Soni Book Agency, 1982.

Singh, R.S. *Indian Novel in English — A Critical Study*. New Delhi : Arnold-Heinemann, 1977.

Speare, Morris Edmund. *The Political Novel*. New York : Russel and Russel, 1966.

Spencer, Dorothy M. *Indian Fiction in English — An Annotated Bibliography*. Philadelphia : University of Pennsylvania Press, 1960.

Spender, Stephen. *The Destructive Element*. London : Jonathan Cape, 1935.

Taine, Hippolyte-Adolphe. "From the Introduction to the History of English Literature," in *Twentieth Century Criticism — Major Statements*, eds. William J. Handy and Max Westbrook. New Delhi : Light & Life Publishers, 1974.

Trivedi, Harish. "Defining the Political Novel," *The American Political Novel — Critical Essays*, ed. Harish Trivedi. New Delhi : Allied Publishers Pvt. Ltd., 1984.

Verghese, C. Paul. *Essays on Indian Writing in English*. New Delhi : N.V. Publications, 1975.

——. "Indian English and Man in Indo-Anglian Fiction," *Indian Literature*, 13 (March 1970), 6-26.

——. *Problems of the Indian Creative Writer in English*. Bombay : Somaiya Publications, 1971.

Wilding, Michael. *Political Fictions*. London : Routledge & Kegan Paul, 1980.

Williams, Haydn Moore. *Studies in Modern Indian Fiction in English*. Calcutta : Writers' Workshop, 1973.

——. *Indo-Anglian Literature 1800-1970 : A Survey*. New Delhi : Orient Longman, 1976.

II. BOOKS ON RELIGION, HISTORY, POLITICS, SOCIOLOGY, GANDHISM AND OTHER ALLIED TOPICS

Akbar, M.J. *India : The Siege Within*. London : Penguin, 1985.

Ali, Tariq. *The Nehrus and the Gandhis — An Indian Dynasty*. London : Picador, 1985.

Appadorai, A. *Indian Political Thinking in the Twentieth Century from Naoroji to Nehru — An Introductory Survey*. Delhi : O.U.P., 1971.

Aron, Raymond. *Main Currents in Sociological Thought*, trs. Richard Howard and Helen Weaver. Harmondsworth : Pelican, 1967.

Bhambhri, C.P. *Bureaucracy and Politics in India*. Delhi : Vikas Publications, 1971.

Bhargava, G.S. *After Nehru*. New Delhi : Allied Publishers, 1966.

Bhatia, B.M. *Famines in India*. New York : Asia Publishing House, 1963.

Bose, N.K. and P.H. Patwardhan. *Gandhi in Indian Politics*. Bombay : Lalvani Publishing House, 1967.

Bottomore, T.B. *Elites and Society*. Harmondsworth : Penguin Books, 1964.

——. *Sociology — A Guide to Problems and Literature*. Bombay : Blackie and Son Publishers Pvt. Ltd., 1978.

Caldarola, Carlo, ed. *Religion and Societies : Asia and the Middle East*. Berlin : Monton Publishers, 1982.

Carras, Mary C. *Indira Gandhi — In the Crucible of Leadership*. Bombay : Jaico, 1976.

Chandra, Bipan, Amales Tripathi and Barun De. *Freedom Struggle*. New Delhi : National Book Trust, 1980.

Chandra, Pratap. "Two Religious Traditions," *The Times of India*, January 6 and 7, 1987.

Coppola, Carlo, ed. *Journal of South Asian Literature* (Mohan Rakesh Number), 9 (Fall-Winter, 1973).

Dalvi, Brigadier J.P. *Himalayan Blunder*. Bombay : Thacker and Co. Ltd., 1969.

Deussen, Paul. *Sixty Upnishads of the Veda*, tr. V.M. Bedekar and G.B. Palsule. Delhi : Motilal Banarsidas, 1980.

Dube, S.C. *Indian Village*. Ithaca, New York : Cornell Univ. Press, 1955.

Eisentadt, S.N. *The Protestant Ethic and Modernization*. New York : Basic Books, 1968.

Elder, J.W. "Fatalism in India : A Comparison between Hindus and Muslims," *Anthropological Quarterly*, 39, 227-43.

Embree, Ainslie T. *India's Search for National Identity*. Delhi : Chanakya Publications, 1980.

Fischer, Louis. *The Life of Mahatma Gandhi*. New York : Harper and Brothers, 1950.

Flaherty, Wendy O. *Asceticism and Eroticism in the Mythology of Shiva*. London : O.U.P., 1973.

Fliegel, F.C. *et al. Innovation in India — The Success or Failure of Agricultural Development Programmes in 108 Villages*. Hyderabad : n.p., 1967.

Friedrich, Carl J. *The New Image of the Common Man*. Boston : Beacon Press, 1950.

Gajendragadakar, P.B., ed. *Research on Gandhian Thought : A Round Table*. Bombay : K.V.I.C., 1970.

Gandhi, M.K. *An Autobiography or The Story of My Experiments with Truth*, tr. Mahadev Desai. Ahmedabad : Navjivan Publishing House, 1928.

——. *Economics of Khadi*. Ahemdabad : Navjivan Publishing House, 1950.

——. *The Gospel of Selfless Action or the Gita*. Ahmedabad : Navjivan Publishing House, 1946.

——. ed. *Harijan* (1933-1948). Ahmedabad.

——. *Hind Swaraj or the Indian Home Rule*. Ahmedabad : Navjivan Publishing House, 1938.

——. *Hindu Dharma*. Ahmedabad : Navjivan Publishing House, 1950.

——. *Man vs Machine*. Ahmedabad : Navjivan Publishing House, 1966.

——. *The Message of Mahatma Gandhi*, ed. U.S. Mohan Rao. New Delhi : Publications Division, Ministry of Information and Broadcasting, 1968.

——. *Sarvodya*. Ahmedabad : Navjivan Publishing House, 1958.

Gandhi, M.K. *Speeches and Writings of M.K. Gandhi*. Madras : G.A. Natesan and Co., n.d.

——. *Village Industries*. Ahmedabad : Navjivan Publishing House, 1960.

——. *Yarvada Mandir*. Ahmedabad : Navjivan Publishing House, 1945.

——. *Young India* (1919-1932), Ahmedabad.

Hutchins, Francis G. *India's Revolution*. Cambridge, Massachussets : Harvard Univ. Press, 1973.

Iyer, Raghavan N. *The Moral and Political Thought of Mahatma Gandhi*. New Delhi : O.U.P., 1973.

Jain, Girilal. "King-Emperor," *The Times of India*, January 7, 1987.

Kapp, K.W. *Hindu Culture, Economic Development and Economic Planning in India*. Bombay : Asia Publishing House, 1963.

Kaul, B.M. *Untold Story*. Delhi : Allied Publishers, 1967.

Khera, S.S. *India's Defence Problem*. New Delhi : Orient Longman, 1968.

Kriplani, J.B. *Gandhi : His Life and Thought*. New Delhi : Publications Division, Government of India, 1970.

Majumdar, R.C., R.C. Raychaudhary and Kalinkar Dutta. *An Advanced History of India*. London : O.U.P., 1960.

Mannheim, Karl. *Ideology and Utopia*. London : Kegan Paul, 1936.

Massoles, Jim. *Nationalism on the Indian Subcontinent : An Introductory History*. Melbourne : Thomas Nelson, 1972.

Misra, K.P. and S.C. Gangal, eds. *Gandhi and the Contemporary World : Studies in Peace and War*. Delhi : Chanakya Publications, 1981.

Morris-Jones, W.H. *The Government and Politics of India*. Bombay : B.I. Publications, 1979.

Nag, Kalidas. *Tolstoy and Gandhi*. Patna : Pustak Bhandar, 1950.

Naipaul, V.S. *India : A Wounded Civilization*. New Delhi : Vikas Publishing House Pvt. Ltd., 1977.

Nair, Kusum. *Blossoms in the Dust*. New York : Frederick A. Praeger, 1962.

Nayar, Kuldip. *India After Nehru*. Delhi : Vikas Publishing House Pvt. Ltd., 1975.

Nehru, Jawaharlal. *Towards Freedom — The Autobiography of Jawaharlal Nehru*. New York : The John Day Co., 1942.

Oomen, T.K. "Charisma and Not King Emperor," *The Times of India*, January 22, 1987.

Owen, H.F. "The Nationalist Movement," *A Cultural History of India*, ed. A.L. Basham. Oxford : Clarendon Press, 1975.

Pandit, Vijay Lakshmi. *The Scope of Happiness*. Delhi : Orient Paperbacks, 1981.

Prasad, Durga. *Light of Truth — An English Translation of "Satyarth Prakash."* New Delhi : Jan Gyan Prakashan, 1970.

Pyarelal. *Mahatma Gandhi : The Early Phase*. Ahmedabad : Navjivan Publishing House, 1965.

——. *Mahatma Gandhi : The Last Phase*. Ahmedabad : Navjivan Publishing Hosue, 1958.

——. *Mahatma Gandhi : The Discovery of Satyagraha on the Threshold*. Bombay : Sevak Prakashan, 1980.

Rao, M.C. Ramalingeswara. *Sreemad Bhagwad Geeta — Translation and Commentary*. Meerut : Annu Prakashan, n.d.

Saran, A.K. *Hinduism and Economic Development in India*. Archives de Sociologie des Religions, 15, 87-94.

Sarkar, Sumit. *Modern India 1885-1947*. New Delhi : Macmillan, 1983.

Schweitzer, Albert. *Indian Thought and Its Development*. Boston : Beacon Press, 1957.

Sethi, J.D. *Gandhi Today*. New Delhi : Vikas Publishing House, 1978.

Shankhdhar, M.M. "The Relevance of Gandhism : A Point of View," *Gandhi Marg*, June 1981.

Singer, Milton. *When a Great Civilization Modernizes : An Anthropological Approach to Indian Civilization*. New York : Praeger Publishers, 1972.

Singh, Darbara. *Indian Politics*. Delhi : Sundeep Prakashan, 1978.

Singh, Khushwant. *Khushwant Singh's India*, ed. Rahul Singh. Bombay : IBH Publishing Co., 1969.

——. *Khushwant Singh's View of India*, ed. Rahul Singh. Bombay : IBH Publishing Co., 1982.

——. *We Indians*. New Delhi : Orient Paperbacks, 1982.

Spear, Percival. *India : A Modern History*. Ann Arbor : The Univ. of Michigan Press, 1961.

Tagore, Rabindranath. *Nationalism*. London : Macmillan, 1950.

Tendulkar, D.G. *Mahatma*. New Delhi : Publications Division, Government of India, 1960.

Thoreau, Henry David. *Civil Disobedience*. New York : Twayne Publishers, 1967.

Vivekanand. *Lectures from Colombo to Almora*. Almora : Advaita Ashram, 1933.

Weber, Max. *Religions of India : The Sociology of Hinduism and Buddhism*. Glencoe : Free Press, n.d.

III. THE THREE SELECTED INDO-ANGLIAN NOVELISTS, THEIR WORKS AND CRITICAL STUDIES ON THEM

(1) Bhabani Bhattacharya

(a) Novels

So Many Hungers! 1947; rpt. Bombay : Jaico Publishing House, 1964.

Music for Mohini. 1952; rpt. Delhi : Orient Paperbacks, 1984.

He Who Rides a Tiger. 1954; rpt. New Delhi : Arnold-Heinemann, 1977.

A Goddess Named Gold. Delton : Orient Paperbacks, 1960.

Shadow from Ladakh. 1966; rpt. London : W.H. Allen, 1967.

A Dream in Hawaii. 1978; rpt. Delhi : Vision Books, 1983.

(b) Other Works

"Indo-Anglian," *The Novel in Modern India*, ed. Iqbal Bakhtiyar. Bombay : P.E.N. All India Centre, 1964.

"Literature and Social Reality," *Perspectives on Bhabani Bhattacharya*, ed. R.K. Srivastava. Ghaziabad : Vimal Prakashan, 1982.

Mahatma Gandhi as a Writer. New Delhi : Arnold-Heinemann, 1982.

Steel Hawk and Other Stories. Delhi : Hind Pocket Books (P) Ltd., 1968.

(c) Critical Studies on Bhabani Bhattacharya

Chandrashekharan, K.R. *Bhabani Bhattacharya*. New Delhi : Arnold-Heinemann, 1974.

Sharma, K.K. *Bhabani Bhattacharya : His Vision and Themes*. New Delhi : Abhinav Publications, 1979.

Shimer, Dorothy Blair. *Bhabani Bhattacharya*. New York : Twayne Publishers, 1975.

Srivastava, R.K., ed. *Perspectives on Bhabani Bhattacharya*. Ghaziabad : Vimal Prakashan, 1982.

(d) Articles in Periodicals and Essays in Books on Bhabani Bhattacharya

Badal, R.K. "Bhabani Bhattacharya and His Novels," *The Literary Half Yearly*, 12 (July 1971), 77-85.

Boparai, Harcharan Singh. "The Achievement of Bhabani Bhattacharya," *Perspectives on Bhabani Bhattacharya*, ed. Ramesh K. Srivastava. Ghaziabad : Vimal Prakashan, 1982.

Crawford, Cromwell. "Bhabani Bhattacharya : A Mediating Man," *Perspectives on Bhabani Bhattacharya*, ed. Ramesh K. Srivastava. Ghaziabad : Vimal Prakashan, 1982.

Desai, S.K. "Bhabani Bhattacharya : The Writer Who Rides a Tiger," *Perspectives on Indian Fiction in English*, ed. M.K. Naik. New Delhi : Abhinav Publications, 1985.

Dhawan, R.K. "Bhattacharya's Narrative Techniques," *Perspectives on Bhabani Bhattacharya*, ed. Ramesh K. Srivastava. Ghaziabad : Vimal Prakashan, 1982.

Fisher, Marlene. "Personal and Social Change in Bhattacharya's Novels," *World Literature Written in English*, 12 (Nov. 1973), 288-300.

——. "Women in Bhattacharya's Novels," *Perspectives on Bhabani Bhattacharya*, ed. Ramesh K. Srivastava. Ghaziabad : Vimal Prakashan, 1982, 66-82.

Goyal, Bhagwat S. "The Sensuous and the Sublime : Bhabani Bhattacharya's *A Dream in Hawaii*," *Perspectives on Bhabani Bhattacharya*, ed. Ramesh K. Srivastava. Ghaziabad : Vimal Prakashan, 1982, 179-84.

Jain, Jasbir. "Coming to Terms with Gandhi : *Shadow from Ladakh,*" *Journal of Indian Writing in English,* 3, No. 2 (1975), 20-23.

——. "The Human Dimensions of Statis and Growth," *Perspectives on Bhabani Bhattacharya*, ed. Ramesh K. Srivastava. Ghaziabad : Vimal Prakashan, 1982, 52-65.

Joshi, Sudhakar. "An Evening with Bhabani Bhattacharya," *The Sunday Standard,* April 27, 1969.

Kaliwnikova, Elena. "The Problems of Bhabani Bhattacharya's Novels," *Perspectives on Bhabani Bhattacharya*, ed. Ramesh K. Srivastava. Ghaziabad : Vimal Prakashan, 1982, 101-10.

Lal, P. "*Shadow from Ladakh* — A Note," *Explorations in Modern Indo-English Fiction,* ed. R.K. Dhawan. New Delhi : Bahri Publications Pvt. Ltd., 1982, 169-71.

Raizada, Harish. "Bhabani Bhattacharya : Novelist of Social Ferment," *Explorations in Modern Indo-English Fiction*, ed. R.K. Dhawan. New Delhi : Bahri Publications Pvt. Ltd., 1982, 157-68.

——. "Fiction as Allegory : Novels of Bhabani Bhattacharya," *Perspectives on Bhabani Bhattacharya*, ed. Ramesh K. Srivastava. Ghaziabad : Vimal Prakashan, 1982, 83-100.

Rao, A.V. Krishna. "*He Who Rides a Tiger* — A Study," *Perspectives on Bhabani Bhattacharya*, ed. Ramesh K. Srivastava. Ghaziabad : Vimal Prakashan, 1982, 141-48.

Sharma, K.K. "Bhabani Bhattacharya's *So Many Hungers!* — An Affirmative Vision of Life," *Indo-English Literature : A Collection of Critical Essays*, ed. K.K. Sharma. Ghaziabad : Vimal Prakashan, 1977.

Sharma, P.P. "Bhabani Bhattacharya : Artist/Propagandist?," *Perspectives on Bhabani Bhattacharya*, ed. Ramesh K. Srivastava. Ghaziabad : Vimal Prakashan, 1982, 41-51.

Shimer, Dorothy Blair. "Bhabani Bhattacharya — Gandhi Biographer," *The Journal of Indian Writing in English*, 2 (July 1984).

——. "Gandhian Influence on Bhabani Bhattacharya," *Perspectives on Bhabani Bhattacharya*, ed. Ramesh K. Srivastava. Ghaziabad : Vimal Prakashan, 1982.

Singh, R.S. "Bhabani Bhattacharya : A Novelist of Dreamy Wisdom," *The Banasthali Patrika*, No. 13, 1984.

Srivastava, Narsingh. "Symbol and Allegory in *A Goddess Named Gold,*" *Perspectives on Bhabani Bhattacharya*, ed. Ramesh K. Srivastava. Ghaziabad : Vimal Prakashan, 1982.

Srivastava, Ramesh K. "Bhattacharya at Work : An Interview," *Perspectives on Bhabani Bhattacharya*, ed. R.K. Srivastava. Ghaziabad : Vimal Prakashan, 1982.

——. "Introduction," *Perspectives on Bhabani Bhattacharya*, ed. R.K. Srivastava. Ghaziabad : Vimal Prakashan, 1982.

——. "The Theme of Hunger in Bhattacharya and Markandaya," *Explorations in Modern Indo-English Fiction*, ed. R.K. Dhawan. New Delhi : Bahri Publications Pvt. Ltd., 1982, 172-83.

(2) Manohar Malgonkar

(a) Novels

Distant Drum. Delhi : Orient Paperbacks, 1960.

Combat of Shadows. London : Hamish Hamilton, 1962.

The Princes. London : Hamish Hamilton, 1963.

A Bend in the Ganges. Delhi : Orient Paperbacks, 1964.

Spy in Amber. New Delhi : Orient Paperbacks, 1971.

The Devil's Wind. New York : Viking Press, 1972.

Open Season. New Delhi : Orient Paperbacks, 1978.

Shalimar. New Delhi : Vikas Publishing House Pvt. Ltd., 1978.

Bandicoot Run. Delhi : Orient Paperbacks, 1982.

(b) Other Works

"Bachcha Lieutenant," *Modern Indian Short Stories*, eds. Saros Cowasjee and Shiv K. Kumar. Delhi : OUP, 1985.

Bombay Beware. New Delhi : Orient Paperbacks, 1975.

Line of Mars. Delhi : Hind Pocket Books, 1978.

The Men who Murdered Gandhi. Delhi : Orient Paperbacks, 1981.

Rumble Tumble. Delhi : Orient Paperbacks, 1977.

The Sea Hawk : Life and Battles of Kanhhoji Angrey. Delhi : Vision Books, n.d.

A Toast in Warm Wine. Delhi : Orient Paperbacks, 1974.

(c) Critical Study on Manohar Malgonkar

Amur, G.S. *Manohar Malgonkar*. New Delhi : Arnold-Heinemann, 1973.

(d) Articles in Periodicals and Essays in Books on Manohar Malgonkar

Asnani, Shyam. "A Study of the Novels of Manohar Malgonkar," *Critical Response to Indian English Fiction*. Delhi : Mittal Publications, 1985.

——. "The Indian Princes : Their Portrayal in the Indo-English Novel," *Critical Response to Indian English Fiction*. Delhi : Mittal Publications, 1985.

The Baltimore Sunday Sun. "Review of *A Bend in the Ganges*," April 4, 1965.

Chaddah, R.P. "Partition in Indo-Anglian Fiction," *Journal of Indian Writing in English*, 5 (July 1977).

Chinneswararao, G.J. "Anand's *Private Life* and Malgonkar's *Princes*," *The Journal of Indian Writing in English*, 4 (January 1976).

Cowasjee, Saros. "The Partition in Indo-English Fiction," *Explorations in Modern Indo-English Fiction*, ed. R.K. Dhawan. New Delhi : Bahri Publications Pvt. Ltd., 1982.

Dwivedi, A.N. "The Historian as Novelist : Manohar Malgonkar," *Perspectives on Indian Fiction in English*, ed. M.K. Naik. New Delhi : Abhinav Publications, 1985.

Edinburgh Magazine, "Review of *Distant Drum*," June 1961.

Jain, Jasbir. "Vishnu and Shiva : Symbols of Duality in *A Bend in the Ganges*," *The Journal of Indian Writing in English*, 3, No. 1 (1975), 21-23.

Jha, Mohan. "The Theme of Communalism in Indo-Anglian Fiction," *Indian Journal of English Studies*, 21 (1981-82).

Jones, Jill Hugh. "Review of *The Princes*," *Quest*, 44 (January/March 1965).

Robertson, R.T. "Review of *A Bend in the Ganges*," *Richmond News Leader*, February 7, 1965.

Sharma, K.K. "The 1947 Upheaval and the Indian-English Novel," *Explorations in Modern Indo-English Fiction*, ed. R.K. Dhawan. New Delhi : Bahri Publications Pvt. Ltd., 1982.

Singh, Ram Sewak. "Manohar Malgonkar, the Novelist," *Indian Literature*, 13, No.1 (1970), 113-21.

TLS Review of Manohar Malgonkar's *A Bend in the Ganges* in *Essays and Reviews from TLS*, III (1964). London : O.U.P., 1965.

TLS. Review of *Distant Drum*, May 12, 1961.

TLS. Review of *The Princes*, June 21, 1963.

White, Robin. "*A Bend in The Ganges*," *New York Times Book Review*, February 14, 1965.

Williams, Haydn Moore. "The Doomed Hero in the Fiction of Khushwant Singh and Manohar Malgonkar," *Explorations in Modern Indo-English Fiction*, ed. R.K. Dhawan. New Delhi : Bahri Publications Pvt. Ltd., 1982.

——. "Manohar Malgonkar : The Captains and the Kings," *Journal of Indian Writing in English*, 8 (January-July 1980).

(3) Nayantara Sahgal

(a) Novels

A Time to be Happy. 1958; rpt. New Delhi : Sterling Paperbacks, 1975.

This Time of Morning. New York : W.W. Norton & Co. Inc., 1965.

Storm in Chandigarh. London : Chatto & Windus, 1969.

The Day in Shadow. Delhi : Vikas Publishing House, 1969.

A Situation in New Delhi. Delhi : Himalaya Books, 1977.

Rich Like Us. London : Heinemann, 1985.

Plans for Departure — A Novel. London : Heinemann, 1986.

(b) Other Works

Freedom Movement in India. New Delhi : N.C.E.R.T., 1970.

From Fear Set Free. New York : W.W. Norton & Co. Inc., 1968.

Indira Gandhi's Emergence and Style. New Delhi : Vikas Publishing House, 1978.

Prison and Chocolate Cake. London : Victor Gollancz, 1963.

A Voice for Freedom. Delhi : Hind Pocket Books, 1977.

(c) Articles

"The Book I Enjoyed Writing Most," *Bhavan's Journal,* 20 (January 6, 1974), 41-44.

"Challenge to Our Thinking, *Tattler,* 2 (August 1974).

"Change...but to what?," *The Sunday Standard*, May 28, 1972.

"Conscience and the Hindu," *The Sunday Standard*, December 21, 1975.

"The End of an Era of Tolerance," *The Sunday Standard,* August 17, 1969.

"The Face in the Crowd," *The Sunday Standard*, January 23, 1972.

"Failure of the Educated," *The Sunday Standard,* July 22, 1973.

"Fresh Air on Hinduism," *The Sunday Standard,* December 1, 1968.

"An India Beyond Politics," *The Sunday Standard*, January 28, 1970.

"Injustice and the Intellectual," *The Indian Express*, October 29, 1977.

"Majorities and Minorities," *The Sunday Standard*, November 12, 1972.

"The Making of Mrs. Gandhi," *South Asian Review*, 8 (April 1966), 189-210.

"Mrs. Gandhi's Political Style," *The Indian Express*, June 6 and 7, 1977.

"Murder of Gandhiji Continues," *The Sunday Standard*, November 23, 1969.

"Nehruism in Retreat," *The Sunday Standard*, May 27, 1973.

"Religion and its Travesty," *The Sunday Standard*, March 6, 1975.

"Should We Follow the Leader," *The Sunday Standard*, February 21, 1971.

"The System — Not the Leader," *The Sunday Standard*, January 17, 1971.

"The Turning Point in Indian Politics," *The Sunday Standard*, November 8, 1970.

"The Vanished Art of Government," *The Sunday Standard*, October 6, 1974.

"What does Hinduism Stand for Today," *The Sunday Standard*, November 10, 1968.

(d) Critical Studies on Nayantara Sahgal

Bhatnagar, Manmohan. "The Indo-Anglian Political Novel — A Study of Nayantara Sahgal," Diss. Panjab University, Chandigarh, 1981.

Jain, Jasbir. *Nayantara Sahgal*. New Delhi : Arnold-Heinemann.

Rao, A.V. Krishna. *Nayantara Sahgal — A Study of Her Fiction*. Madras : M. Seshachalam and Co., 1976.

(e) Articles in Periodicals/Newspapers and Essays in Books on Nayantara Sahgal

Anklesaria, Zerin. "Unsoured Idealism," *The Sunday Standard*, April 6, 1986.

Asnani, Shyam M. "Contemporary Politics : Its Portrayal in the Novels of Nayantara Sahgal," *Critical Response to Indian English Fiction*. Delhi : Mittal Publications, 1985.

——. "The Novels of Nayantara Sahgal," *Indian Literature*, 16, Nos. 1-2, 1979, 36-69.

——. "Portrayal of Man-Woman Relationships in the Novels of Nayantara Sahgal," *Critical Response to Indian English Fiction*. Delhi : Mittal Publications, 1985.

Bhatnagar, M.K. "The Individual as Politician : One Facet of Nayantara Sahgal's Achievement as a Political Novelist," *M.D.U. Research Journal*, 1 (April 1986), 98-104.

Choudhary, Neerja and Kalpana Sharma. "Interview : Nayantara Sahgal," *Himmat*, 9 (May, 1975).

Derrett, Margaret E. "*The Day in Shadow* : Review," *Journal of Asian Studies*, 22 (August 1973), 727.

Jain, Jasbir. "The Aesthetics of Morality : Sexual Relations in the Novels of Nayantara Sahgal," *Journal of Indian Writing in English*, 6, No. 1 (1978), 41-48.

"The Politics of Hinduism in the Novels of Nayantara Sahgal," *Littcrit*, 2 (December 1976), 45-47.

Jussawala, Feroza. "Of Cabbages and Kings : *This Time of Morning* and *Storm in Chandigarh*," *Journal of Indian Writing in English*, 5, No. 1, 43-50.

Kumar, Shiv K. "*The Day in Shadow*," *Books Abroad*, 48 (Winter 1974).

Mukherjee, Meenakshi. "Review of *The Day in Shadow*," *Quest*, July-August 1972, 92-94.

Patnaik, Bibudhendra Narayan. "Nayantara Sahgal's Novels," *Sambalpur University Journal*, 4 (December 1971), 38-43.

Sarma, M.N. "Nayantara Sahgal's Novels," *Journal of Indian Writing in English*, 4 (January 1976), 35-45.

Shirwadkar, Meena. "Indian English Women Novelists," *Perspectives on Indian Fiction in English*, ed. M.K. Naik. New Delhi : Abhinav Publications, 1985.

Thomas, T.K. "The Hindu Ethos — A Novelist's Perspective," *Religion and Society*, 20 (December 1973), 54-71.

Zuckerman, Ruth Von Horn. "*This Time of Morning* and *Storm in Chandigarh*," *Mahfil*, 6 (Winter 1970).

IV. NOVELS BY OTHER WRITERS

Abbas, K.A. *Defeat for Death*. Bombay : Padmaja Publications, 1944.

——. *Inquilab*. Bombay : Jaico, 1955.

——. *Tomorrow is Ours*. Bombay : Popular Book Depot, 1943.

Ali, Aamir. *Conflict*. Bombay : National Information and Publication Ltd., 1947.

Ali, Ahmed. *Twilight in Delhi*. London : Hogarth Press, 1940.

Anand, Mulk Raj. *Death of a Hero : Epitaph for Maqbool Sherwani*. Bombay : Kutab-Popular, 1963.

Anand, Mulk Raj. *Gauri*. New Delhi : Arnold-Heinemann, 1976.

——. *Morning Face*. Bombay : Kutab-Popular, 1968.

——. *Private Life of an Indian Prince*. Delhi : Hind Pocket Books, n.d.

——. *The Sword and the Sickle*. Bombay : Kutab-Popular, 1955.

Chatterjee, Bankim Chandra. *Rajmohun's Wife*. Calcutta : Bangiya Sahitya Parishad, 1940.

Day, Lal Behari. *Govinda Samant or History of a Bengal Rayat*. London : Macmillan, 1874.

Dutt, Kylash Chunder. "A Journal of Forty-eight Hours of the Year 1945," *Calcutta Literature Gazette,* June 6, 1835.

Dutt, Sochee Chunder. "The Republic of Orissa : Annals from the Pages of the Twentieth Century," *Saturday Evening Harkaru*, May 25, 1845.

——. "Shunkur : A Tale of the Indian Mutiny of 1857," *The Work of Sochee Chunder Dutt*. London : Lovell Reeve & Co., 1885.

——. *The Young Zamindar*. London : Remington, 1885.

Gill, Raj. *The Rape*. New Delhi : Sterling Publishers, 1974.

Ghose, A. Sarath Kumar. *The Prince of Destiny*. London : Rebman, 1909.

Hosain, Attia. *Sunlight on a Broken Column*. New Delhi : Arnold Heinemann, 1979.

Karaka, D.F. *We Never Die*. Bombay : Thacker & Co., 1944.

Mitra, S.K. *Hindupore*. London : Luzac & Co., 1909.

Nahal, Chaman. *Azadi*. Delhi : Orient Paperbacks, 1979.

Narayan, R.K. *The Painter of Signs*. Mysore : Indian Thought Publications, 1977.

——. *Waiting for the Mahatma*. Mysore : Indian Thought Publications, 1964.

Rao, Raja. *Comrade Kirillov*. New Delhi : Orient Paperbacks, 1978.

Rao, Raja. *Kanthapura*. Delhi : OUP, 1974.

Singh, Khushwant. *I Shall Not Hear the Nightingale.* London : John Calder, 1959.

——. *Train to Pakistan*. Bombay : Pearl Publications, 1957.

Sheoray, A.G. *Dusk before Dawn : A Novel of Post-Freedom India*. New Delhi : Bell Books, 1978.

Venkataramani, K.S. *Kandan, the Patriot*. Madras : Svetaranya Ashrama, 1932.

——. *Murugan, the Tiller*. Madras : Svetaranya Ashrama, 1929.

□□□

INDEX

D

E

G

H

I

J

K

L

M

N

O

P

R

V

W

Y

Z